STRATHCLYDE UNIVERSITY LIBRARY

30125 00346144 8

D1615088

This book is to be returned on or before
the last date stamped below.

18 NOV 1988

18 MAR 1993

1 5 MAR 2002

4 JAN

13 APR 1993

12 APR 1990

13 JUL 1993

- 2 AUG 1991

07 APR 1994

27 MAY 1994

LIBREX —

Cambridge Studies in Speech Science and Communication

Advisory Editorial Board J. Laver (Executive editor) A. J. Fourcin J. Gilbert
M. Haggard P. Ladefoged B. Lindblom J. C. Marshall

From text to speech

The MITalk system

In this series:

The phonetic bases of speaker recognition Francis Nolan
Patterns of sounds Ian Maddieson
Neurolinguistics and linguistic aphasiology David Caplan

#/26 68869

From text to speech
The MITalk system

Jonathan Allen,
M. Sharon Hunnicutt and
Dennis Klatt

With Robert C. Armstrong and
David Pisoni

ANDERSONIAN LIBRARY
★
WITHDRAWN
FROM
LIBRARY
STOCK
★
UNIVERSITY OF STRATHCLYDE

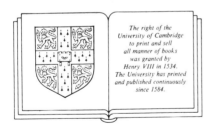

The right of the
University of Cambridge
to print and sell
all manner of books
was granted by
Henry VIII in 1534.
The University has printed
and published continuously
since 1584.

Cambridge University Press

Cambridge
London   New York   New Rochelle
Melbourne   Sydney

Published by the Press Syndicate of the University of Cambridge
The Pitt Building, Trumpington Street, Cambridge CB2 1RP
32 East 57th Street, New York, NY 10022, USA
10 Stamford Road, Oakleigh, Melbourne 3166, Australia

© Cambridge University Press 1987

First published 1987

Printed in Great Britain at the University Press, Cambridge

British Library cataloguing in publication data

From Text to speech : MITalk system. –
(Cambridge studies in speech science and communication)
1. Automatic speech recognition
I. Allen, Jonathan, *1934–*
II. Hunnicutt, M. Sharon.   III. Klatt, Dennis H.
621.3819′598   TK7882.S65

Library of Congress cataloguing in publication data

Allen, Jonathan, 1934–
From text to speech.
(Cambridge studies in speech science and communication)
1. Speech processing systems.   2. Speech synthesis.
I. Hunnicutt, M. Sharon.   II. Klatt, Dennis H.
III. Title.   IV. Series.
TK7882.S65A45   1986   006.5   85–24280

ISBN 0 521 30641 8

D
621.3819′598
ALL

Contents

Contents

Appendixes

List of figures

List of tables

List of contributors

Jonathan Allen.
> Professor of Electrical Engineering and Computer Science, and Director of the Research Laboratory of Electronics, Massachusetts Institute of Technology, Cambridge, Massachusetts.

M. Sharon Hunnicutt.
> Speech Transmission Laboratory, Department of Speech Communication and Music Acoustics, Royal Institute of Technology, Stockholm, Sweden.

Dennis H. Klatt.
> Senior Research Scientist, Department of Electrical Engineering and Computer Science, and Research Laboratory of Electronics, Massachusetts Institute of Technology, Cambridge, Massachusetts.

Robert C. Armstrong.
> Department of Electrical Engineering and Computer Science, and Research Laboratory of Electronics, Massachusetts Institute of Technology, Cambridge, Massachusetts.

David B. Pisoni.
> Professor of Psychology, Speech Research Laboratory, Department of Psychology, Indiana University, Bloomington, Indiana.

Preface

The MITalk system described in this book is the result of a long effort, stretching from the early 1960s to the present. In this preface, a view is given of the work's historical evolution. Within this description, acknowledgements are made of the project's many contributions. In recognizing these contributions, it is best to organize them into four groups. First, there is the development of the MITalk system itself, its evolution, and the many diverse contributions made to its structure and content. Second, there was the 1979 summer course which resulted in a comprehensive summary of the work to that date, and also provided the occasion to write a set of course notes. Next, there have been continuing efforts (since 1980) which included re-writes of the system's software, and the efforts to organize this book which involved substantial new writing and rule formulations, and explicit examples directly keyed to the current working system. Finally, there is the sponsorship of the program's many facets over the years.

In the early 1960s, much interest in speech synthesis emerged within the Cognitive Information Processing Group at MIT's Research Laboratory of Electronics. This group, led by M. Eden and S. J. Mason, focused on the development of sensory aids for the blind. Many approaches were taken, but it was recognized that the development of a reading machine for the blind that could scan printed text and produce spoken output was a major goal. Research efforts in both character recognition and speech synthesis from text were initiated. By 1968, a functional reading machine was demonstrated. Once the characters were recognized (using a contour scanning algorithm), text-to-speech conversion was accomplished in two phases. First, a morph decomposition analysis of all words was performed by using techniques developed by F. F. Lee (in his 1965 doctoral thesis). A morph lexicon sufficient for these demonstrations was developed. It was anticipated that any exceptional words not analyzed into morphs would be pronounced by using spelled speech. As a result, these words were heard as a sequence of individually pronounced letters. The dictionary provided names of the phonetic segments for each morph, and synthesis was performed using the algorithms developed and published by Holmes, Mattingly, and Shearme. An analog synthesizer was used to produce the output speech waveform based on the work of these three researchers, the resonances for the speech being provided by digitally controlled operational amplifiers. The demonstration of this system was impressive, although the

1

vocabulary was restricted, and the output speech quality required extensive learning. At that time, the computer implementation used for research consisted of a Digital Equipment Corporation PDP-1 used for character recognition and morph analysis, which was coupled to MIT Lincoln Laboratory's TX-0 computer (the only one of its kind) for the synthesis algorithms. T. P. Barnwell III and E. R. Jensen were responsible for building much of this computational environment. This required great effort and coordination, since all coding was performed in assembly language.

Following the late 1960s, the character recognition and speech synthesis efforts continued independently of one another with the work of B. Blesser, M. Eden, and D. E. Troxel focused on the character recognition efforts. J. Allen joined the faculty in September, 1968. Goals for a fundamental and comprehensive research program aimed at the computation of high-quality speech using unrestricted English text as input were formulated. In addition, strong coupling continued with the Speech Communication and Linguistics groups within the Research Laboratory of Electronics, led by K. N. Stevens and M. Halle, respectively.

With the desire to convert unrestricted English text to speech, a new scheme was developed for the pronunciation of all possible English words. This required elaborate extensions to the morph decomposition process, as well as the construction of a comprehensive morph lexicon to serve the entire language. Furthermore, spelled speech was rejected as inadequate, and plans for the development of a comprehensive set of letter-to-sound rules that would complement the morph analysis process were established. In order to build a new morph lexicon, a copy of the Brown corpus was obtained and sorted (shortest word first). Initial phonetic segment labels were obtained from a computer-readable copy of the Merriam Pocket Dictionary. Beginning with a nascent lexicon containing all bound morphs and function words, each word from the Brown corpus was successively analyzed. This led to the interactive addition of new morphs and a great deal of experience with morph analysis procedures. This process was accomplished by J. Allen and D. A. Finkel, with algorithmic and programming support from E. R. Jensen and F. X. Carroll. The process spanned many months, and led to the extension of morph analysis routines to include multiple decompositions and attendant selection rules. The computational support for this work was a Digital Equipment Corporation PDP-9 computer with 24K words of memory and DEC tapes for peripheral storage. Readers familiar with this equipment will have some appreciation of the sheer magnitude of the effort required to build the morph lexicon and acquire the necessary data to support the extensions and refinements to the morph analysis routines. Subsequent to the initial construction of the lexicon, an elaborate editing of all entries was made by M. S. Hunnicutt. This led to substantial improvements in the system's overall performance.

When words could not be found in the morph lexicon, or could not be analyzed into morphs from the lexicon, letter-to-sound rules were utilized. Prior to the MITalk research, letter-to-sound rules had been proposed to cover the entire language. But, with MITalk, it was realized that high-frequency function words often violate perspicuous forms of these rules, and that such letter-to-sound rules do not span morph boundaries. Based on these observations, a complementary set of letter-to-sound rules could be introduced into MITalk, but these rules would not be used unless morph analysis failed. Realizing this fact, affix stripping was utilized, and the more reliable consonants were converted first, leaving the vowels for last. This approach was proposed by J. Allen, and extensive sets of these rules were developed by M. S. Hunnicutt working with F. X. Carroll. Several sets of these rules were developed and elaborately tested. In addition, in the late '60s at MIT, there was great interest in lexical stress and phonological rules for this purpose which were initially developed by M. Halle and N. Chomsky. These rules were reformulated and extended to include the effect of affixes. This was the first time that lexical stress rules had been used in a text-to-speech system. The development of rules for this purpose, along with their unification with the letter-to-sound rules, was accomplished by M. S. Hunnicutt. In addition, the text preprocessing rules were also provided by M. S. Hunnicutt, as well as the routines for morphophonemics and stress adjustment used in conjunction with the morph analysis.

In a 1968 doctoral thesis, J. Allen developed a parsing methodology for use in a text-to-speech system, with particular emphasis on the computation of necessary syntactic markers to specify prosodic correlates. This parsing strategy led to the development of a phrase-level parser which avoided the complications of clause-level parsing and the problems of syntactic ambiguity at that level, but also led to the introduction of inaccuracy due to incomplete clause-level analyses. This approach was augmented and extended by P. L. Miller and C. J. Drake, and was tested extensively in the context of the morph lexicon and analysis routines.

In light of the phonetic segment labels, stress marks, and syntactic markers obtained by the previously mentioned programs, it was necessary to develop a prosodic framework for the following phonemic synthesis. A durational framework was developed by D. H. Klatt together with R. Carlson and

B. Granstrom. The latter two researchers devoted a year to this project on leave from the Royal Institute of Technology in Stockholm, Sweden. In addition to the durational framework, a comprehensive investigation of fundamental frequency effects was made by J. Allen, D. O'Shaughnessy, and A. Weibel. O'Shaughnessy's doctoral thesis contains an extensive compendium of these results, and he is responsible for the fundamental frequency generation algorithm currently implemented in MITalk. A. Weibel contributed a characterization of fundamental frequency contours in questions.

Given the prosodic framework mentioned above, phonetic segment labels, stress marks, and junctural marks provided by the syntactic analysis, then phonemic synthesis routines can be utilized to produce the output speech waveform. The MITalk system is based on a phonemic speech synthesis model developed by D. H. Klatt. All of the algorithms for the specification of the control parameters utilized by this model were developed by him. During the stay of R. Carlson and B. Granstrom, further refinements, modifications, and tests were performed in the context of the overall MITalk system. At that time, many issues concerned with consistency and the integration of the entire system were addressed.

In the late 1970s, the computational environment for the research was changed from the PDP-9 computer to a DEC-System 20, with output speech provided by a PDP-11. A special interface was constructed between the DEC-20 and the PDP-11, and an all-digital special purpose speech synthesis processor was constructed by G. S. Miranker. This processor was capable of exercising the phonemic synthesis model in real-time. The DEC-System 20, a large time-shared machine, was ideally suited to the modular nature of the MITalk system. It permitted many researchers individually and interactively to build the system's overall structure. Beginning in the mid '70s, a great deal of attention was focused on the MITalk system's overall organization. The problems of coordinating such a large system with its many contributors cannot be overemphasized. As a result, standard interfaces were established between all modules. Over the years, extremely valuable system programming contributions were provided by E. R. Jensen, F. X. Carroll, R. S. Goldhor, G. E. Kopec, and Y. Willems.

As the entire system was built in a coordinated manner, and as experience with the interaction of all constituent algorithms increased, there was a clear necessity for a comprehensive evaluation of the system. Fortunately, D. Pisoni visited the Research Laboratory of Electronics and was attracted to the problem of perceptual evaluation. He performed a broad review of the testing literature, extended and developed new testing methodologies, and provided a systematic assessment of MITalk's output speech quality.

Throughout all of the research, many important individual projects were completed which focused on issues in speech analysis and processing, and in linguistics. The many participants in these endeavors focused individually on a variety of important research issues, but they also shared in the motivation provided by the goals of the overall system, as well as in the daily interaction with others involved in complementary aspects of the system. This tension between individual research and overall system building evolved with MITalk, and provided each contributor with a strong sense of satisfaction derived not only from individual efforts, but also from the system's overall achievement.

In the summer of 1979, it was felt that the MITalk system was at a sufficiently complete state that a specialized, intensive course devoted to its exposition was appropriate. Accordingly, from June 25th through June 29th, a special short course was offered. Lectures covered all modules of the MITalk system, and laboratory exercises combined with demonstrations provided further contact with the system. The individuals involved with the course included J. Allen, D. H. Klatt, M. S. Hunnicutt, R. Carlson, B. Granstrom, and D. Pisoni. In addition, a set of notes for this course was developed. M. S. Hunnicutt wrote the sections of the notes covering text preprocessing, morphological analysis, phrase-level parsing, morphophonemics and stress adjustment, letter-to-sound and lexical stress, and fundamental frequency contour generation. D. H. Klatt wrote the sections on speech synthesis technology and the Klatt formant synthesizer. D. H. Klatt, R. Carlson, and B. Granstrom wrote the sections on the phonological component, the prosodic component, and the phonetic component. D. Pisoni wrote the section on measurement of intelligibility and comprehension directly reproduced as Chapter 13 of the present volume. J. Allen provided the introduction, a section on implementation, and the summary. These notes have constituted the most comprehensive overview of MITalk until the publication of this book.

Since 1979, the MITalk system has been available for license, and has been acquired by many industrial firms and universities. Bell Northern Research acquired the system for research purposes and recoded it in VAX-VMS PASCAL. They have kindly supplied a copy of their version to us. In turn, this version was converted to run under Berkeley 4.2 BSD UNIX, using the syntax of Berkeley PASCAL, although some routines in the new version are written in C. This latest version was accomplished by R. Armstrong, and it has many new features. The most notable feature is the overall control structure which easily permits assembling subsets of the overall system, and the provision of a variety of displays to view the functions of various modules. This system has been used successfully on several occasions, and is described in Chapter 14.

With this new UNIX version of MITalk, J. Allen and R. Armstrong have undertaken extensive writing and editing which build on the 1979 summer course notes in order to construct the current text. In particular, all examples are a direct result of the current implementation, and new rule formulations have been added to the text by using a generalized notation for phonological rules. These rule improvements have been achieved by R. Armstrong. Several new sections have been added, and extensive editing has been performed along with an expanded and more explicit representation of the actual algorithms and rules used in the system. Thus, the present text is the product of the original authors of the 1979 summer course notes (mentioned above), plus expansion in detail, examples, and both explicit and extensive rule formulations added by J. Allen and R. Armstrong. M. S. Hunnicutt, D. H. Klatt, and D. Pisoni have reviewed these changes for accuracy, and the extensive formatting necessary to produce the camera-ready copy for this book was done by R. Armstrong.

It is a pleasure to acknowledge the several sponsors of this work over the years. In the early stages, research was sponsored by the Joint Services Electronics Program, as well as the National Institutes of Health. For many years, continuing and generous support has been provided by an anonymous individual donor, supplying the flexibility necessary to pursue appropriate research directions. The four years of concentrated effort which led to the system's 1979 version was supported by the National Science Foundation. It is important to note the donation of a hardware pitch detector from MIT's Lincoln Laboratory, designed and built by T. Bially. The detector was instrumental in providing the very large volume of pitch contours used as the database to construct fundamental frequency rules.

The MITalk system is the result of an exciting and satisfying project. Much important research has been performed as a result of its needs, and the overall system is an impressive statement of our knowledge in this field. Certainly, there is still more that needs to be done in order to provide highly natural speech in discourse environments. But, MITalk's contributions are likely to play an essential role in any of these continuing developments.

1

Introduction

In this book, we are concerned with describing a successful approach to the conversion of unrestricted English text to speech. Before taking up the details of this process, however, it is useful to place this task in context. Over the years, there has been an increasing need for speech generated from computers. In part, this has been due to the intrinsic nature of text, speech, and computing. Certainly speech is the fundamental language representation, present in all cultures (whether literate or not), so if there is to be any communication means between the computer and its human users, then speech provides the most broadly useful modality, except for the needs of the deaf. While text (considered as a string of conventional symbols) is often considered to be more durable than speech and more reliably preserved, this is in many ways a manifestation of relatively early progress in printing technology, as opposed to the technology available for storing and manipulating speech. Furthermore, text-based interaction with computers requires typing (and often reading) skills which many potential users do not possess. So if the increasingly ubiquitous computer is to be useful to the largest possible segment of society, interaction with it via natural language, and in particular via speech, is certainly necessary. That is, there is a clear trend over the past 25 years for the computer to bend increasingly to the needs of the user, and this accommodation must continue if computers are to serve society at large. The present search for expressive programming languages which are easy to use and not prone to error can be expected to lead in part to natural language interaction as the means best suited to human users, with speech as the most desirable mode of expression.

1.1 Constraints on speech synthesis

It is clear, then, that speech communication with computers is both needed and desirable. Within the realm of speech output techniques, we can ask what the nature of these techniques is, and how they are realized. In order to get a view of the spectrum of such procedures, it is useful to consider them as the result of four different constraints which determine a design space for all possible speech output schemes. Each technique can then be seen as the result of decisions related to the impact of each of the four constraint areas.

1.1.1 *Task*

The application task determines the nature of the speech capability that must be provided. When only a small number of utterances is required, and these do not have to be varied on line, then recorded speech can be used, but if the task is to simulate the human cognitive process of reading aloud, then an entirely different range of techniques is needed.

1.1.2 *Human vocal apparatus*

All systems must produce as output a speech waveform, but it is not an arbitrary signal. A great deal of effort has gone into the efficient and insightful representation of the speech signal as the result of a signal source in the vocal tract exciting the vocal tract "system function", which acts as a filter to produce the speech waveform. The human vocal tract also constrains the speed with which signal changes can be made, and is also responsible for much of the coarticulatory smoothing or encoding that makes the relation between the underlying phonetic transcription and the speech waveform so difficult to characterize.

1.1.3 *Language structure*

Just as the speech waveform is not arbitrarily derived, the myriad possible speech gestures that could be related to a linguistic message are constrained by the nature of the particular language structure involved. It has been consistently found that those units and structures which linguists use to describe and explain language do in fact provide the appropriate base in terms of which the speech waveform can be characterized and constructed. Thus, basic phonological laws, stress rules, morphological and syntactic structures, and phonotactic constraints all find their use in determining the speech output.

1.1.4 *Technology*

Our ability to model and construct speech output devices is strongly conditioned by the current (and past) technology. Speech science has profited greatly from a variety of technologies, including x-rays, motion pictures, the sonograph, modern filter and sampled-data theory, and most importantly the modern digital computer. While early uses of computers were for off-line speech analysis and simulation, the advent of increasingly capable integrated circuit technology has made it possible to build compact, low-cost, real-time devices of great capability. It is this fact, combined with our substantial knowledge of the algorithms needed to generate speech, that has propelled the field of speech output from computers into the "real world" of practical commercial systems suitable for a wide variety of applications.

1.2 Synthesis techniques

With these constraints in mind, we can examine the various approaches to speech output from computers. A great many techniques have been developed, but they can be naturally grouped in an insightful way. Our purpose here is to create a context in which text-to-speech conversion of unrestricted English text using synthesis-by-rule can be considered. This comparison will permit us to highlight the difference between the various approaches, and to compare system cost and performance.

1.2.1 *Waveform coding*

The simplest strategy would be to merely record (either in digital or analog format) the required speech. Depending on the technology used, this approach may introduce access time delays, and will be limited in capacity by the recording medium available, but the speech will generally be of high quality. No knowledge of the human vocal apparatus or language structure is needed; these systems being a straightforward match of the task requirements to the available storage technology. Since memory size is the major limitation of these schemes, efforts have been made to cut down the number of bits per sample used for digital storage. A variety of techniques has been used, from simple delta modulation, through adaptive delta modulation and adaptive differential PCM, to adaptive predictive coding which can drop the required bit rate from over 50 Kbit/sec to under 10 Kbit/sec while still retaining good quality speech. Simple coder/decoder circuits can be used for recording and playback. When the message vocabulary is small and fixed, these systems are attractive. But if messages must be concatenated, then it is extremely difficult to produce good quality speech because aspects of the speech waveform have been "bound" at recording time to the values appropriate for all message situations which use the smaller constituent messages.

1.2.2 *Parametric representation*

In order to further lower the storage requirements, but also to provide needed flexibility for concatenation of messages, several schemes have been developed which "back up" from the waveform itself to a parametric representation in terms of a model for speech production. These parameters may characterize salient information in either the time or frequency domain. Thus, for example, the speech waveform can be formed by summing up waveforms at several harmonics of the pitch weighted by the spectral prominence at that frequency, a set of resonances can be excited by noise or glottal waveforms, or the vocal tract shape can be simulated along with appropriate acoustic excitation. As compared to waveform coding, more computation is now required at playback time to recreate the speech

9

waveform, but the storage requirements per message are cut down. More importantly, the parametric representation represents an abstraction on the speech waveform to a level of representation where the attributes that contribute to speech quality (e.g. formant frequencies and bandwidths, pitch, excitation amplitudes) can be insightfully manipulated. This allows elementary messages to be concatenated in a way that provides for smooth transitions at the boundaries. It also allows for changes (e.g. in pitch) well within the individual message units, so that substantial changes in prosodic parameters (pitch and timing) can be made. The most popular parametric representations in use today are based on formants or linear predictive coding (LPC), although vocal tract articulatory models are also used. Message units of widely varying sizes are employed, ranging from paragraphs, through sentences, phrases, words, syllables, demisyllables, and diphones. As the size of the message unit goes down, fewer basic messages are needed for a large message set, but more computation is required, and the difficulties of correctly representing the coarticulation across message boundaries go up. Clearly, these schemes aim to preserve as much of the quality of natural speech as possible, but to permit the flexible construction of a large set of messages using elements which require little storage. With the current level of knowledge of digital signal processing techniques, and the accompanying technology, these schemes have become very important for practical applications. It is well to remember, however, that parametric representation systems seek to match the task with the available processing and memory technology by using a knowledge of models for the human production of speech, but little (if any) use is made of the linguistic structure of the language.

1.2.3 *Synthesis-by-rule*

When message units are concatenated using parametric representations, there is a tradeoff between speech quality and the need to vary the parameters to adapt the message to varying environments. Researchers have found that many allophonic variations of a message unit (e.g. diphone) may be needed to achieve good quality speech, and that while the vocabulary of needed units is thus expanding, little basic understanding of the role of structural language constraints in determining aspects of the speech waveform is obtained. For this reason, the synthesis process has been abstracted even further beyond the level of parametric representation to a set of rules which seek to compute the needed parameters for the speech production model from an input phonetic description. This input representation contains, in itself, very little information. Usually the names of the phonetic segments, along with stress marks and pitch and timing, are provided. The latter prosodic correlates are often computed from segmental and syntactic structure and stress marks, plus semantic information if available. In this way, synthesis-by-rule techniques can utilize a very low bit-rate message description (<100 bits/sec) as input, but substantial computation must be used to compute the model parameters and then produce the speech waveform. Clearly there is complete freedom to specify the model parameters, but of course also the need to control these parameters correctly. Since the rules are still imperfect, the resulting speech quality is not as good as recorded human speech, but recent tests have shown that high intelligibility and comprehensibility can be obtained, and when sentence and paragraph-level messages must be synthesized, the rule system provides the necessary degrees of freedom to produce smooth-flowing good quality speech. It is interesting to consider that synthesis-by-rule systems delay the binding of the speech parameter set and waveform to the input message by using very deep language abstractions, and hence provide a maximum of flexibility, and are thus well suited to the needs of converting unrestricted text to speech. The designers of these systems must, however, discover the relationship between the underlying linguistic specification of the message and the resulting speech signal, a topic which has been central to speech science and linguistics for several decades. Thus synthesis-by-rule both benefits from and contributes to our general knowledge of speech and linguistics, and the steady improvement in speech synthesis-by-rule quality reflects this joint progress. While it is believed that current synthetic speech quality is acceptable for many applications, it can certainly be expected to continue to improve with our increasing knowledge.

1.2.4 *Text-to-speech conversion*

The synthesis-by-rule techniques described above require a detailed phonetic transcription as input. While this input requires very little memory for message storage, a frequent requirement is to convert text to speech. When it is desired to convert unrestricted English text to speech, the flexibility of synthesis-by-rule is needed, so that means must be afforded to convert the input text to the phonetic transcription needed by the synthesis-by-rule techniques. It is clear, then, that first the text must be *analyzed* to obtain the phonetic transcription, which is then subjected to a *synthesis* procedure to yield the output speech waveform. The analysis of the text is heavily linguistic in nature, involving a determination of the underlying phonemic, syllabic, morphemic and syntactic form of the message, plus whatever semantic and pragmatic information can be gleaned. Text-to-speech conversion can thus be seen as a collection of techniques requiring the successful integration of the task constraints with other constraints provided by the nature of the human vocal apparatus, the linguistic structure of the language, and the implementation technology. It is thus the most complex form of speech synthesis system, but also the most fundamental in design and useful in application, since it seeks to mirror the human cognitive capability for reading aloud. Other cognitive models attempt to synthesize speech directly from "concept" for those applications where the underlying linguistic structure is already available (Young and Fallside, 1979). These schemes have the advantage of (presumably) more detailed syntactic and semantic structures than can be obtained from text, and are hence of great interest for high-quality synthesis, but the pervading presence of text in our culture makes the text-to-speech capability of great practical importance. It is worth emphasizing that both text and speech are surface manifestations of underlying linguistic form, and hence that text-to-speech conversion consists first of discovering that underlying form, and then utilizing it to form the output speech.

In the chapters that follow, we will discuss the MITalk text-to-speech system in detail. The aim of this system is to provide high-quality speech from unrestricted English text using the fundamental results of speech science, computing, and linguistics. We aim to do it "right", in the belief that adherence to basic principles will provide more insightful methods, avoid *ad hoc* "fixes", and produce the best possible quality of speech. We will also discuss the range of possible applications, and the implementation base for both a research system, and a compact, low-cost module utilizing state-of-the-art integrated circuit technology. First, however, a brief outline of the parts of the system will be presented.

1.3 Functional outline of MITalk

At the highest level, the system consists of an analysis phase, followed by a synthesis phase. Each of these processes is in turn broken down into a cascaded set of modules. In turn, each module has been described functionally as a set of algorithms operating on well-defined input and output data structures, and each module is afforded a chapter in the sequel for its exposition. In this introduction, we summarize briefly the functional content of the modules.

1.3.1 *Analysis of text*

1.3.1.1 *Symbols to standard form* A preprocessor is used to convert symbol strings such as "$3.17", "Mr.", "M.I.T.", and "1979" to text suitable for linguistic analysis by the remainder of the system.

1.3.1.2 *Phonetic transcription* For each word, a phonetic transcription is computed. A dictionary of 12,000 morphs (prefixes, roots, and suffixes) is used, which contains the spelling, pronunciation, and part-of-speech information for each morph. Most words are analyzed into a string of morphs. In this way, more than

95 percent of the input text (consisting of high-frequency, foreign, and polysyllabic words) can be transcribed to phonetic notation. For rare or new words, plus misspellings (e.g. "recieve"), letter-to-phonetic segment rules are used.

1.3.1.3 *Lexical stress* The effects of suffixes, as well as that of compounding, on lexical stress are computed, permitting the use of both stress marks in the transcription and changes in vowel color.

1.3.1.4 *Phonological recoding* Once the initial phonetic transcription is obtained, some recoding is done based on the sentence-level context, including consonant "flapping", insertion of glottal stops, and selection of alternate pronunciations of "the".

1.3.1.5 *Parsing* To aid the selection of prosodic correlates, a phrase-level parsing is performed. Also, a part-of-speech determination for each word is computed to provide input for the parser.

1.3.1.6 *Semantic analysis* Only those semantic effects due to particular lexical items, such as negatives, are found, but these have important effects on pitch.

1.3.2 *Synthesis of speech*

1.3.2.1 *Timing* Prepausal lengthening, pause duration, and polysyllabic shortening are determined, plus the basic duration of each segment and the effect of clusters.

1.3.2.2 *Fundamental frequency* A declination line is found, plus pitch rises on stressed syllables, continuation rises to signal continued throughout, and a number of segmental effects. Contours appropriate to questions are also found.

1.3.2.3 *Phonetic targets* Given the prosodic framework, phonetic target parameters are determined for each phonetic segment, utilizing a "context window" five segments wide. There are twenty such parameters that vary with time.

1.3.2.4 *Continuation smoothing* The target values are smoothed to yield a full set of parameters every 5 msec.

1.3.2.5 *Parameter conversion* The phonetic parameters must be converted to coefficients that can be used by the digital formant synthesizer.

1.3.2.6 *Waveform generation* The terminal synthesizer utilizes the coefficients (updated every 5 msec) to generate the speech waveform. A special purpose hardware synthesizer is used to perform this task in real-time. Speech samples are produced at a 10 kHz rate, and then converted to analog form via a D/A converter and low-pass filter.

It can be seen that there are many steps from input text to output speech, but study of each module can lead to an insightful understanding of the overall process. Because of the modular nature of the overall system, changes to individual algorithms can be readily accommodated as new ideas are developed. Indeed, this has been our habit for quite some time.

In the sequel, we describe the algorithmic base of the system, its implementation and evaluation, together with a view to the future. It is certainly hoped that this work can serve not only as an important contribution to speech output for many computer-based systems, but also as a point of focus for a continuing flow of speech and language research.

I
Analysis

2

Text preprocessing

2.1 Overview

Unrestricted text may contain a wide variety of symbols, abbreviations, and conventions. In order to convert text to speech, it is necessary to find an appropriate expression in words for such symbols as "3", "%", and "&", for abbreviations such as "Mr.", "num.", "Nov.", "M.I.T.", and conventions such as indentation for paragraphs. This text processing must be done before any further analysis to prevent an abbreviation from being treated as a word followed by an "end-of-sentence" marker, and to allow symbols with word equivalents to be replaced by strings analyzable by the lexical analysis modules.

FORMAT is the first module of the MITalk system and performs the conversion of unrestricted text to a sequence of words and punctuation recognizable by the later modules. The following list contains a number of topics and symbol types which need to be considered.

1. Blank space(s)
2. Paragraphs
3. Sentence-initial capitals
4. Other capitals
5. Abbreviations
6. Numbers, including:
       a. Integers
       b. Numbers with a decimal point
       c. Dates
       d. Time
7. Alphanumerics
8. Formulas
9. Punctuation, including:
       a. Period
       b. Comma
       c. Question mark
       d. Exclamation point

     e. Semicolon

     f. Colon

     g. Apostrophe

     h. Single and double quotes

     i. Ellipsis (...)

     j. Percent sign

     k. Ampersand

     l. Parentheses

     m. Brackets

     n. Dashes

     o. Hyphens

10. Symbols not recognizable by computer (and hence not recognized by FORMAT), including:

     a. Italics

     b. Boldface

     c. Underlining

     d. Superscripts and subscripts

     e. Dieresis/umlaut (ö)

     f. Cedilla (ç)

     g. Various forms of special notation

2.2 Input

FORMAT accepts as input the original unrestricted English text to be analyzed. This text is a sequence of *lines* of letters and symbols expressed in a computer-readable form (in all implementations of MITalk, the ASCII character set is used). The actual letters recognized are:

1. Uppercase and lowercase letters

2. Numeric digits

3. Period (or decimal point), question mark, and exclamation point

4. Comma, semicolon, and colon

5. Apostrophe

6. Single and double quote marks

7. Parentheses, brackets, and braces

8. Percent sign, dollar sign, and ampersand

9. Slash

Any character which is not recognized by FORMAT causes a warning message and is treated as a space.

The size of individual words and sentences is limited, but set at a high value to include all reasonable cases. Words are allowed 40 characters each, and the maximum number of words per sentence is 200. If the limit of 40 characters per word is exceeded, the word is truncated and a message indicating the problem and number of allowable characters per word is printed for the user.

2.3 Output

The output of FORMAT is a sequence of words and punctuation marks. FORMAT scans each input line from left to right and converts each recognized construct (word, number, symbol, etc.) into an appropriate word or sequence of words. Since case is not significant in the later modules of MITalk, each word is written in all uppercase letters.

An example of input and output is shown here in Figure 2-1. (Input text is in **boldface**.)

```
Mr. Jones gets 35.3%.
 FORMAT: MISTER
 FORMAT: JONES
 FORMAT: GETS
 FORMAT: THIRTY
 FORMAT: FIVE
 FORMAT: POINT
 FORMAT: THREE
 FORMAT: PERCENT
 FORMAT: .
 FORMAT: .
```

Figure 2-1: Example of FORMAT processing

2.4 Formatting operations

The various translations performed by FORMAT are described in detail below.

2.4.1 *Paragraphs and sentences*

Whitespace (i.e. spaces and/or tabs) at the beginning of a line followed by a capitalized word is taken to denote the beginning of a paragraph. FORMAT translates this whitespace into a period (.) which later gets translated into a pause.

An additional pause is inserted after each sentence longer than five words (also after each group of short sentences longer than five words). As with the paragraph beginning, this pause is effected by adding an extra period after the sentence. This emulates a human speaker pausing for breath every so often.

The end of a sentence is delimited by a period, question mark, or exclamation point. Not all periods denote the end of a sentence, however. If a period ends an abbreviation, then it is only taken as an end-of-sentence marker if it is at the end of a line and if it is followed by whitespace and a capitalized word. A period inside a numeric string is considered to be a decimal point, of course.

2.4.2 *Words, abbreviations, and special symbols*

FORMAT recognizes a word as an alphabetic string delimited by a punctuation or whitespace character (the *newline* character which separates lines is considered to be whitespace). If a word is followed by a period, then FORMAT looks in a table of abbreviations to see if a translation is specified for that word. Table 2-1 shows the abbreviation table currently in use. If a translation is found, then the translated word(s) are output in place of the original abbreviation.

Table 2-1: Abbreviation translations performed by FORMAT

Ms	→	MIZ
Mr	→	MISTER
Mrs	→	MIZZES
Dr	→	DOCTOR
Num	→	NUMBER
Jan	→	JANUARY
Feb	→	FEBRUARY
Mar	→	MARCH
Apr	→	APRIL
Aug	→	AUGUST
Sept	→	SEPTEMBER
Oct	→	OCTOBER
Nov	→	NOVEMBER
Dec	→	DECEMBER
etc	→	ET CETERA
Jr	→	JUNIOR
Prof	→	PROFESSOR

A word that is in capital letters, or which contains digits as well as letters, is considered to be a symbol and is translated by pronouncing each character separately (e.g. for **USA** and **MIT**). When a letter is to be pronounced, it is represented by a special noun morph which has the proper pronunciation for the letter (e.g. **A** →**LETTER-A**). A word that is in lowercase, or which has only the first letter capitalized, is simply converted to uppercase and output.

2.4.3 *Apostrophes and single quotation marks*

If an apostrophe is embedded in a word, then the entire word is output as a unit.

The apostrophe is also included in the word if it appears after the last letter in the word and that last letter is an **s**. An apostrophe in any other position is considered to be a single quotation mark and is output as a punctuation character.

2.4.4 *Hyphens and dashes*

If a dash character is embedded between two words, it is considered to be a hyphen separating compound word elements. In the current implementation, the hyphen is deleted and the compound is treated as two separate words (e.g. **two-layer** → **TWO LAYER**). This solution prevents the correct stress pattern from being placed on a hyphenated compound, but, on the other hand, it prevents incorrect decompositions which might result from simply concatenating the two roots at this point.

If a dash appears at the end of the last word on a line, then the dash is considered to be a word-splitting hyphen. In this case, FORMAT deletes the hyphen from the end of the current word and appends to that word the first word on the next line. This rule reassembles words which are divided at the end of a line on a syllable boundary.

An isolated dash is output as a punctuation character and eventually becomes a pause. A string of dashes (isolated or embedded) is converted to a single dash and output as punctuation.

2.4.5 *Special symbols*

A percent sign (%) is replaced by the words **PER CENT**. An ampersand (&) is replaced by the word **AND**.

2.4.6 *Numerals*

FORMAT recognizes a number as a string of digits with optional commas and/or a period (decimal point). There are two ways of pronouncing numbers: each digit in sequence (e.g. **75** → **SEVEN FIVE**), and in decimal form (e.g. **75** → **SEVENTY FIVE**). FORMAT selects the appropriate type of pronunciation based on the form and context of the number.

2.4.6.1 *Integers, commas, and decimal points*   A complete number consists of a set of comma-separated digit triads (the integer portion), optionally followed by a decimal point and fraction digits. The integer portion is pronounced by pronouncing each triad from left to right and appending the appropriate multiplying word to each triad (e.g. **BILLION, MILLION, THOUSAND,** or nothing for the rightmost triad).

A triad is pronounced as follows:
- If the left digit is nonzero, then it is pronounced followed by the word **HUNDRED**.

- If the middle digit is larger than one, then the appropriate "tens" word is pronounced (e.g. **TWENTY, THIRTY**, etc.). If the middle digit is one, then the appropriate "teens" word is selected based on the rightmost digit (e.g. **TEN, ELEVEN, TWELVE**, etc.).
- If the middle digit is not one and the rightmost digit is not zero, then the rightmost digit is pronounced.

If a period separates two numeric strings, then it is translated into the word **POINT** and the following numeric string is pronounced digit-by-digit (e.g. **.015** → **POINT OH ONE FIVE**). Note that **0** is pronounced **OH** in this case. A **0** is pronounced as **ZERO** only if it is a one-digit number. For example:

- **715** → **SEVEN HUNDRED FIFTEEN**
- **71.50** → **SEVENTY ONE POINT FIVE OH**
- **159,106** → **ONE HUNDRED FIFTY NINE THOUSAND ONE HUNDRED SIX**

2.4.7 *Dollars and cents*

If a dollar sign (\$) precedes a number as described above, then the following modifications to the pronunciation are made:

- The word **DOLLAR** or **DOLLARS** is inserted after the integer part.
- The decimal point is pronounced as **AND** instead of **POINT**.
- The fraction part is pronounced in two-digit decimal form.
- The word **CENT** or **CENTS** is appended after the fraction part.

For example, **\$71.50** → **SEVENTY ONE DOLLARS AND FIFTY CENTS**.

2.4.8 *Years and comma-less numbers*

A string of more than three digits without commas is given special treatment. If the number has four digits, the first of which is **1,** then it is considered to be a year and is pronounced as follows:

- The leftmost two digits are pronounced as "teens".
- If the rightmost two digits are both **0** then they are pronounced as **HUNDRED**. If they are **0** followed by a nonzero digit then they are pronounced individually. Otherwise, the rightmost two digits are pronounced in decimal form.

Digit strings longer than three digits which do not contain commas (and are not candidates for year pronunciation) are pronounced as individual digits. Strings of less than four digits which begin with **0** are also pronounced individually.

Some examples are:

- 0159 → OH ONE FIVE NINE
- 1590 → FIFTEEN NINETY
- 7150 → SEVEN ONE FIVE OH
- 1906 → NINETEEN OH SIX
- 1800 → EIGHTEEN HUNDRED

3

Morphological analysis

3.1 Overview

MITalk is designed to convert unrestricted English text into a synthetic speech waveform. In the initial analysis phase, text character strings are converted to a narrow phonetic transcription consisting of phonetic symbols and prosodic markers. While the output unit types are thus specified, the question remains as to the type of unit to be used with the input character string. Since there is an infinite number of possible English sentences, it is not possible to store all English sentences and their corresponding phonetic transcriptions in a form suitable for the synthesis phase of MITalk. The next smaller unit recognizable from the input string is the word. The number of English words is large, but bounded, so one might consider use of a word lexicon which would contain the spelling and phonetic transcription (together with part-of-speech information) for all English words. Aside from the size of this dictionary, there are several attractive features of this approach. Some form of dictionary must be used to provide pronunciations for *exceptions* to other mechanisms (e.g. rules) used to derive pronunciations. These arise in part from foreign words that have retained the pronunciation of their language of origin (e.g. **parfait** and **tortilla**). Furthermore, all mechanisms derived thus far for the conversion of letter strings to phonetic segment labels provide some errors, and it seems to be inherent in natural languages that no formal means derived for the representation of their structure has covered all observed forms without error. An interesting class of exceptional pronunciation arises for high-frequency words. Initial **th** is pronounced as a voiceless fricative in many words (**thin, thesis, thimble**) but for very frequent words, such as the short function words (**the, this, there, these, those,** etc.), it is pronounced in a voiced manner. Similarly, **f** is always pronounced as an unvoiced fricative, except for the single case **of**. In words such as **shave** and **behave**, the final silent **e** has the effect of lengthening or tensing the preceding vowel, but in the frequent word **have** this is not the case. Finally, the final **s** in **atlas** and **canvas** is unvoiced, but for the function words (**is, was, has**) it is voiced. It thus appears that these high-frequency words should be placed in an exceptions dictionary if a set of rules is to be used for converting letter strings to phonetic segment labels.

23

From the above discussion, it is clear that some form of exceptions dictionary is necessary. Given that all systems will provide such a lexicon, there are two choices that deal with the nonexceptional words. On one extreme, system designers could attempt to provide a "complete" word dictionary. Unfortunately, while the number of words is bounded, new words are constantly invented by productive processes of compounding (e.g. **earthrise** and **cranapple**) and by filling "accidental gaps" (in the phonological sense) as in **brillig**. Furthermore, a comprehensive word lexicon would have to store all regularly inflected forms, which places a large burden on the storage required. So a "complete" word lexicon will not do. This fact has led investigators to consider the other extreme, namely the provision of a set of letter-to-sound rules that would convert input letter strings to phonetic segment labels through some sort of scanning and transformation process. Such rule sets have indeed been constructed (MITalk has an extensive set), and they are very productive. But difficulties remain. It has been difficult to provide a high degree of accuracy from these rule sets, leading to increases in the size of the "exceptions" dictionary. These problems arise in part due to the fact that there is internal structure in words that must be recognized in order to derive the correct pronunciation.

Letter-to-sound rules recognize small structures within words in the form of consonant and vowel clusters. Syllables provide additional structure, but it has not been possible to reliably and consistently find syllable boundaries in the letter string. The minimum syntactic unit of a language, however, is the morpheme, and it has an important role to play in the determination of pronunciations. It will also be seen that when morphemes are represented by letter string segments called "morphs", they can be effectively used as the basis for determining word pronunciation. MITalk uses a morph lexicon that can be viewed as a bridge between the two extreme approaches cited above. Together with an effective analysis procedure, this lexicon provides for accurate pronunciations, including exceptions, and also provides a natural role for letter-to-sound rules which must be present in order to convert unrestricted English text to speech.

Roughly speaking, morphs consist of prefixes, roots, and suffixes. An English word always has at least one root, but may have additional roots as well as prefixes and suffixes. Thus **snow** is a single morph, but **snowplow** is a compound of two morphs, and **snowplows** has two roots and an inflectional suffix providing the plural marker; **relearn** has a prefix as well as a root, and **antidisestablishmentarianism** has no fewer than seven recognizable morphs. These morphs are the atomic constituents of words, and they are relatively stable in a language. They are often the ingredients of newly coined compound words, but new morphs are rarely formed. For this reason, they are good candidates for lexical entries, provided a means can be found to analyze words into their constituent morphs. As will be seen, an effective morph lexicon can have less than 10,000 entries, so that reasonable storage efficiency is provided, particularly in contemporary integrated circuit technology. It is also important to note that with a morph lexicon and associated analysis procedure, there is no need to store all of the regularly inflected forms, as is the case with a whole word lexicon.

Because morphs are the basic constituents of words, it is important to show their utility in determining pronunciations. When morphs are joined together, they often change pronunciation depending on the nature of the morphs involved. Thus, when the plural form of the singular nouns **dog** and **cat** is realized, the final **s** is voiced in **dogs** but unvoiced in **cats**. This is a form of morphophonemic rule having to do with the realization of the plural morpheme in various environments. In order to use these rules, it is necessary to recognize the constituent morphemes of a word, so it is apparent that there is an important class of pronunciation effects facilitated through the detection of morphs and their boundaries. MITalk provides a comprehensive implementation of the morphophonemic rules of English.

In addition to the importance of morphophonemic rules, morphs serve to break up a word for purposes of pronunciation. This observation is important for the proper utilization of letter-to-sound rules. Most sets of letter-to-sound rules treat each word as an unstructured sequence of letters, and use a scanning window to find consonant and vowel letter clusters that can be readily converted to phonetic segment labels. Thus, as we have already seen, **th** is a letter cluster corresponding to a single fricative phonetic segment, as in **thesis**. But in the word **hothouse**, the **th** cluster is broken up by a morph boundary, and no medial fricative is present. Similarly, the letter cluster **sch** has a regular pronunciation in **school** and **scheme**, but in the words **mischance** and **discharge** the cluster is broken up by the internal morph boundary. In English, the vowel digraph **ea** presents many difficulties for a letter-to-sound algorithm, but in the word **changeable** it is clearly broken up. In essence, the morph structure is essential to provide the correct pronunciation. These cases can of course be treated as exceptions, but this will increase the size of the lexicon unnecessarily, and it is also clear that important generalities will be lost. In the MITalk system, morph analysis is always attempted before letter-to-sound rules are used, and care is taken to ensure that letter-to-sound rules are not applied across morph boundaries. Thus, not only does the use of morphs lead to an efficient and productive lexicon, it also naturally provides for important pronunciation effects due to morph structure, and sets an appropriate basis for the formulation of a well-motivated set of letter-to-sound rules devoid of *ad hoc* exceptions.

So far, we have shown how the use of a morph lexicon and accompanying morph analysis procedures provides a sound solution to the accurate translation of English word letter strings to sequences of phonetic segment labels. It is important to realize, however, that morphs are just the surface realization of underlying morphemes, and the distinction between these two units must be maintained. Morphemes are abstract units, and they exist only for purposes of grammatical or distributional equivalence. Their use recognizes that words have internal structure, and that the components of this structure are the constituent morphemes of the word. Historically, morphemes were introduced to define phonological units where *segmentability* was possible, as in the sequence **tall, taller, tallest**. But there is nothing in the definition of a morpheme to imply that it must always be an identifiable segment of the word of which it is a constituent. The morpheme is not a segment of a word, and it has no position in a word. It is an abstract unit arising from linguistic distributional analysis. This can be seen clearly by comparing the words **went** and **walked**. In the latter word, it is easy to see that there are two constituent morphs, **walk** and **ed**, which are in one-to-one correspondence with the underlying abstract morphemes **walk** and PAST. But in the case of **went**, the underlying morphemic analysis provides the two morphemes **go** and PAST, and it is impossible to map these in any nonarbitrary way onto the surface letter string **went**. When segmentation is possible, as is often the case, then morphs can be identified, and MITalk exploits this fact. For the cases where a root is given a grammatical inflection, as in **went**, MITalk provides a special morph type, STRONG, that indicates the presence of the two underlying morphemes. Clearly **went** must go in the *morph* lexicon, as it is an exception to the normal processes of affixation and compounding. Additionally, the morpheme PLURAL provides ample evidence of the many ways in which it may be realized on the surface. We have the pairs **boy/boys**, **thief/thieves**, **child/children**, **tooth/teeth**, and **fish/fish**, as well as many borrowed pairs from other languages such as **concerto/concerti**, **datum/data**, **index/indices**, and **alumnus/alumni**. These irregular plurals must be placed in the lexicon, since MITalk can only deal with morphs that can be found through detection of the regular and productive word formation processes that are susceptible to segmentation. Many of the analysis procedures of MITalk are based on the underlying morphemic constituency of a letter string, although only morphs can be exhibited as letter strings or can occur in the lexicon.

The use of morphs in MITalk is unique, and it is responsible for much of the quality of the phonetic segment label sequences that are used for synthesis. There is no doubt that they introduce several levels of complication. These include the necessity of producing a morph lexicon and the need for a morph segmentation algorithm. The concatenation of morphs to form a word often gives rise to spelling mutations that cause segmentation difficulties, and several "morph coverings" of a word are often found leading to a need for selection criteria. Nevertheless, the gains far outweigh the negative costs, and in the following sections, we elaborate on these robust and effective techniques.

3.2 Input

In MITalk, morphemic analysis is provided in the DECOMP module. DECOMP's input data stream has the same structure as the output stream from FORMAT which precedes DECOMP in the MITalk system. Each record in the data stream contains either a word or a punctuation mark. Words consist of uppercase letters, apostrophes, and/or hyphens. Legal punctuation marks are period, exclamation point, question mark, comma, semicolon, colon, double quotation, single quotation, left and right parentheses, and dash. DECOMP also accesses a compiled binary format morph lexicon.

3.3 Output

The output data stream consists of a sequence of decomposed word records. The following information is contained in each record:

1. Word spelling
2. Word part of speech (possibly more than one)
3. For each part of speech, an optional list of part-of-speech *features*
4. The series of morphs obtained by decomposition
5. For each morph, the following information:
   a. Morph spelling
   b. Morph type
   c. One or two homographs
   d. For each homograph, a pronunciation and part(s) of speech

If no decomposition was found for the word, then the morph list is omitted and the word is assigned a default set of possible parts of speech. Punctuation marks receive a special part-of-speech code (either EndPunctuationMark (EPM) for sentence-ending punctuation or InternalPunctuationMark (IPM) for all others). Part-of-speech processing will be described in detail in the next chapter where the phrase parser is discussed.

3.4 **The algorithm**

The goal of the decomposition process is to obtain a morph *covering* of a word. The word "covering" is used to indicate that a simple concatenation of morph spellings will not, in many cases, provide a correct analysis. It is sometimes the case, particularly when a vocalic suffix is involved, that spelling changes occur at morph boundaries. In addition, there may be several distinct coverings of a given word.

In light of the observations above, the decomposition algorithm consists of three major components:

1. a *recursive morph partitioning algorithm,*
2. a set of *spelling change rules* for use at morph boundaries, and
3. a set of *selectional rules* to distinguish between legal and illegal morph sequences and to choose the best covering when multiple legal coverings exist.

These components are described in detail below.

3.4.1 *Recursive morph decomposition*

The overall control structure of the decomposition procedure is recursive. At each step in the recursion, the right end of the word is matched against the longest lexicon morph possible, then the procedure is recursively invoked on the remaining "uncovered" portion of the word. If this recursive invocation fails to produce a covering, then the original match is discarded and the next longest matching morph is used.

Input to the decomposition procedure consists of:

1. a word or remainder to be covered,
2. a state flag that indicates which morph types are legal in the current context, and
3. a *score value* that is used to rank multiple decompositions according to their likelihood of being correct.

Initially, the entire word is presented as input, the state flag is set to a value indicating that no morphs have been found yet, and the score is set to zero. A concise informal description of the procedure follows:

> find the longest morph which matches the right end of the current string
> WHILE there is a match DO
> > IF the matching morph is compatible with the current context (state)
> > > THEN remove the matched letters from the right side of the string,
> > > > update the current state and score as a function of the type of
> > > > the matched morph.

find a set of possible spelling changes[1] at the right end of the
remainder,

attempt a recursive decomposition for each spelling variation,

save the results of the best-scoring of these variations,

restore the remainder string, state, and score to their original
values.

END IF,

find the next longest morph which matches the right end of the string.

END WHILE.

The decision to search from the right end of the word was made early in the development of the system before the selectional rules were implemented. It was observed that the best decomposition was found first by stripping off suffixes before searching for roots and prefixes. When a later algorithm was developed in which all decompositions were found and a choice made, the strategy was retained. Since only the decomposition with the best score is kept while searching for other possible morph coverings, finding the best decomposition early in the search is still more efficient; potential coverings with worse scores can be discarded as early as possible.

3.4.2 *Morph types*

Not all sequences of morphs are legal in the English language. For this reason (and later, for scoring multiple coverings) each morph in the lexicon has a type code. These morph type codes refine the coarse categories of "prefix", "suffix", and "root" to obtain better performance in finding the correct covering.

The morph type "FREE ROOT" (or simply "ROOT") denotes a word which can appear alone or with suffixes, prefixes, and/or other ROOTs. Typical ROOTs are: **side, cover,** and **spell**. The type "ABSOLUTE" is assigned to words which do not allow most affixes (suffixes or prefixes). These are words such as **the, into, of,** and proper names. (The few affixes permitted are the inflectional suffixes such as plural and possessive forms.) This type is essential in preventing DECOMP from attempting to match the morphs **a** and **I** in many words.

Most prefixes have the type "PREFIX" that denotes a prefix which can combine with roots and other prefixes. Examples are: **pre, dis,** and **mis**. The remaining prefixes can only occur at the beginning of a word and are classified as "INITIAL". Examples are **meta** and **centi**.

Suffixes are classified using two different criteria yielding a total of four

---

[1]Note that unchanged spelling is always one of these possibilities.

morph types. The first criterion is functional and divides suffixes into derivational ("DERIVATIONAL" or "DERIV") and inflectional ("INFLECTIONAL" or "INFL") types. Derivational suffixes have a major effect on the meaning of a root and may change the part of speech (e.g. **ness, ment, y**). Inflectional suffixes merely change the tense, number, or inflection of the root (e.g. **ing, ed, s**). This classification is used primarily by the scoring algorithm.

The other suffix classification is used solely by the spelling change rules. This divides suffixes into vocalic and nonvocalic categories depending on whether the suffix begins with a vowel or consonant, respectively. The type names are "VOCALIC" (or "VOC") and "NONVOCALIC" (or "NONV").

The "STRONG" morph type denotes a root which already contains tense or number information. This type of morph is a combination of root and inflectional *morphemes* which are not reflected directly in the *morph* structure. Examples are **went** (**go+PAST**) and **women** (**woman+PLURAL**).

In addition to free roots, there are two types of *bound* roots. The "LEFT FUNCTIONAL ROOT" (or "LF-ROOT") is a root which must always be followed by a derivational suffix. An example is **absorpt** in **absorptive** and **absorption**. In this case (as with many LF-ROOTs), the morph represents a suffix-caused spelling mutation of a root morpheme which is too complex or idiosyncratic for the spelling change rules to incorporate (e.g. **absorb+ive** → **absorptive**). A "RIGHT FUNC-TIONAL ROOT" (or "RF-ROOT") must always be preceded by a prefix. For example, **mit** in **permit, transmit,** and **submit**. These morphs generally have some etymological basis (and are not simply repeated letter patterns). For example: the root **mit** is derived from the Latin *mittere* -- to send; it is just that the root itself never became part of the English language and its meaning is overlooked by the average speaker.

The hyphen (-) has its own morph type "HYPHEN". This is provided so that hyphenated words which do not appear directly in the lexicon can be properly decomposed.

3.4.3 *Legal morph sequences*
The detection of legal and illegal morph sequences is performed by a finite state machine (FSM).

The grammar recognized by the FSM is summarized in production rules below:[1]

---

[1]These use Wirth's notation: = for production, [ ] for optional factors (zero or one rep.), { } for repeated factors (zero to infinite repetition), ( ) for grouping, and | for alternatives.

effective-root = ROOT | LF-ROOT DERIV | PREFIX RF-ROOT | STRONG

suffix = DERIV | INFL

affixed-word = { PREFIX } effective-root { suffix }

absolute-word = ABSOLUTE | ABSOLUTE INFL { suffix } | INITIAL affixed-word

word = affixed-word | absolute-word

compound-absolute = absolute-word | absolute-word HYPHEN compound | ABSOLUTE INFL { suffix } compound-affixed

compound-affixed = affixed-word | affixed-word HYPHEN compound | affixed-word compound-affixed

compound = compound-affixed | compound-absolute

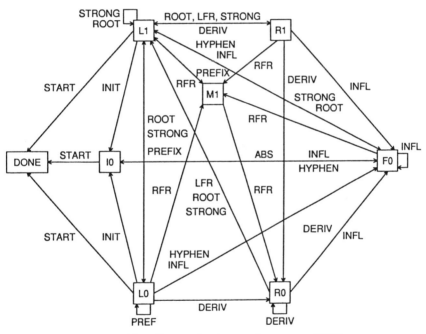

Figure 3-1: State transition diagram for the morph sequence FSM

Figure 3-1 shows the state transition diagram of the FSM. Each state of the FSM represents a summary of the type sequence of the morphs which have been stripped from the word being decomposed. It is this state which is passed as a parameter to the recursive decomposition procedure. The "right context" represented by each state is easily expressed and is summarized below. For each

state, a picture of the input stream is shown using the metalanguage of the grammar above and with "<>" marking the position in the stream represented by the
state. To the right of the marker is context represented by the state. To the left, is
an expression representing the expected structure of the remainder of the word.

F0   word <> {INFL {suffix}}

R0   (affixed-word I LF-ROOT) <> DERIV {suffix}

R1   (affixed-word I LF-ROOT) <> DERIV effective-root

M1   PREFIX <> RF-ROOT {suffix}

L1   {affixed-word I PREFIX I INITIAL} <> effective-root {suffix}

L0   {affixed-word I PREFIX I INITIAL} <> PREFIX effective-root {suffix}

I0   {word HYPHEN} <> (ABSOLUTE I INITIAL affixed-word)

3.4.4 *Selectional rules and scoring*

When multiple morph coverings are found, *selectional rules* are needed to choose
the covering most likely to be correct. For example, a means of favoring
form+al+ly (ROOT + DERIV + DERIV) over **form+ally** (ROOT + ROOT) as the
decomposition of **formally** is needed. A set of derivational rules was devised by
examining all of the multiple coverings produced by DECOMP during the
development of the morph lexicon. The first result of this study was the discovery
of the so-called "standard form" for a (possibly compound) word stated below as
two productions:

std-root = (ROOT I LF-ROOT DERIV)

std-form = {PREFIX} {std-root} (std-root {DERIV} I STRONG) {INFL}
    Coverings which match this form are to be preferred above all others.
    Among coverings that match the standard form, the following partial order-
ings were found (">" means that the pattern on the left is more desirable):

ROOT > anything else

PREFIX+ROOT > ROOT+DERIV > ROOT+INFL > ROOT+ROOT

PREFIX+PREFIX+ROOT > ROOT+ROOT

ROOT+DERIV+DERIV > ROOT+ROOT
    These rules are implemented by associating a cost with each transition of the
FSM and keeping track of the total cost of the decomposition as morphs are
stripped off the word. This cost is the "score value" mentioned above in the algorithm description. The covering with the lowest total cost is the most desirable.

In Figure 3-1 the transition arcs are labeled with the associated incremental cost as well as morph type. The specific cost values are not significant, only their relative values. The values were chosen to cause the FSM to implement the rules above, then fine-tuned to get the best overall performance. The cost of a standard-form covering is easily computed and is the sum of the following:

- 34 units for each PREFIX,
- 101 units for the first effective-root and 133 units for each additional effective-root (if the rightmost effective-root is STRONG, add an extra 64 units to account for the "hidden" inflectional morpheme),
- 35 units for each DERIV, and
- 64 units for each INFL.

The only other notable feature of the scoring is that any transition not part of the standard form incurs a 512-unit penalty. In order to allow a single ABSOLUTE root to match a word, the penalty is suppressed for this case and the cost is taken to be the same as for a single ROOT covering.

The recursive procedure takes advantage of the cost information to reduce the number of matching operations. The cost of the best complete covering found before the current step in the recursion is recorded. As a new morph is matched, the cost of its associated transition in the FSM is added to the running score. In addition, the minimum possible cost for the decomposition of the remainder is also computed. If the sum of this cost and the current cost is not less than the best cost so far, then the new morph is immediately rejected as being too expensive.

3.4.5 *Recognizing morphological mutations*
After a suffix morph has been removed from a word, it is necessary to investigate possible spelling changes which may have taken place during composition. Typical spelling changes (during morph composition) are:

- y → i (embody+ment → embodiment),
- consonant doubling before a vocalic suffix (pad+ing → padding), and
- dropping of "silent e" before a vocalic suffix (fire+ing → firing).

Different morphs have differing behavior in the presence of change-causing suffixes. Three general categories of morph behavior are provided for in DECOMP. In the lexicon, each morph has a *spelling change code* which indicates whether spelling changes are forbidden, required, or optional when the morph is combined with a suffix. The "required" category is currently used exclusively for morphs with consonant endings which are always doubled in the presence of a vocalic suffix. The "optional" category is used for all other morphs which permit spelling changes. Examples are:

- required - **scar+ed →scarred**
- forbidden - **alloy+ing →alloying**
- optional - **change+able →changeable, change+ing →changing**

The spelling changes performed by DECOMP consist of appending a letter, or changing or deleting the last letter. When a morph is matched to the left end of a word, the following procedure is used to determine the set of possible spelling changes: If the matched morph is not a suffix, then no spelling changes are made and recursion proceeds normally. If the matched morph is a nonvocalic suffix and the last remaining letter is an **i**, then the change **i→y** is examined. If the matched morph is a vocalic suffix, then spelling changes are performed by matching a three-character template against the last two remainder letters and the first letter of the matched morph.

If the vocalic suffix is **es**, then a special check is made to determine whether the letter **e** should be considered part of the suffix. If the remainder does not end in **c, ch, g, i, o, s, sh, x,** or **z,** then the **es** match is immediately rejected. This causes the morph **s** to be the next match; the **e** is thus moved from the suffix to the remainder. This rule is motivated by the phonetic properties of the plural suffixes **s** and **es**. The lexicon entry for **s** gives a pronunciation ZZ while the entry for **es** gives IH ZZ. The rule allows DECOMP to make the appropriate decomposition of **tunes→tune+s** rather than **tunes→tune+es** which is found first. The two vowels, **i** and **o,** are permitted to precede **es** to enable correct decomposition of words such as **heroes** and **parties,** even though pronunciation is not correct in such cases; morphophonemic rules are used in a later MITalk module to obtain the proper pronunciation.

Table 3-1 shows the set of template patterns and their resulting spelling change actions. The plus sign (+) in the pattern denotes the boundary between the suffix and the remainder. A dot (.) in the pattern matches any letter. The pattern **xx** matches any doubled letter. The first pattern (from top to bottom of the list) which matches the current remainder/suffix pair controls the set of changes applied.

For each possible spelling of the remainder, the following steps are performed:

1. Make the change.

2. Recursively decompose the remainder.

3. If a morph matches the right end of the remainder, check its spelling

change code to see if it is compatible with the change (or lack of change). If the morph requires a spelling change, then it is rejected if a change was not made. If the morph forbids a change and a change was made, it is also rejected.

Changes which have the notation "(+)" suppress the checking of the spelling change code. This allows the correct decomposition to be found for morphs which normally forbid spelling changes such as **free (free+ing → freeing**, but **free+ed → freed)**. Changes which carry the notation "(*)" are made only for derivational suffixes.

3.5 An example of a decomposition

Figure 3-2 details the process by which DECOMP arrives at the decomposition scarcity → scarce+ity. Lines with the label "Decomp:" are produced during decomposition and document the recursive process. Lines which begin with a quoted string show the parameter states when a new level of recursion is entered. The quoted string itself is the current remainder to be covered and the information in brackets [ ] is the current state of the FSM as described in Section 3.4.3. The number in angle brackets < > is the current score. Lines which begin with "Matched" indicate that a morph match has been found. The morph spelling and type are given followed by the action taken as a result of the match.

Lines labelled with "DECOMP:" show the data on the output stream from DECOMP to the next module. This information is described in Section 3.3 above and the lines are commented in italics.

Initially, the remainder is the entire word **scarcity** and the cost is zero. The longest matching morph is **city**, which is a root and is legal in the rightmost position; hence decomposition proceeds to **scar** which is also a root. This yields the legal double-root covering **scar+city** with a total cost of 234. Next, decomposition backs up to the remainder **scar** to see if there are other possible coverings. Both attempts to cover **scar** fail, however, since the minimum possible cost for each covering would exceed the cost of the one already found.

After the possibilities of **scar** have been exhausted, recursion backs up to **scarcity** to try the next longest morph after **city**. This morph is the derivational suffix **ity** and leaves a remainder **scarce** which is successfully covered by a root. This yields a new low cost; hence **scarce+ity** supersedes **scar+city** as the preferred covering. Spelling changes are attempted on **scarce** but these fail to yield a covering.

Finally, the recursion backs up to **scarcity** to try the shortest match **y**. With the spelling change to **scarcite**, DECOMP is able to match the root **cite** but since

Table 3-1: Morph spelling change rules for vocalic suffixes

Pattern	Change	Example
ck+.	none	packing → pack+ing
	ck → c	picnicking → picnic+ing
xx+i	none	telling → tell+ing
	xx → x	padding → pad+ing
	xx → xxe	silhouetting → silhouette+ing
xx+.	none	yeller → yell+er
	xx → x	reddest → red+est
e+e	e → ee (+)	freed → free+ed
e+i	none	dyeing → dye+ing
e+.	none	changeable → change+able
i+i	none	skiing → ski+ing
i+e	i → y	noisiest → noisy+est
	i → ie (+)	eeriest → eerie+est
	none	efficient → effici+ent
i+.	i → y	variation → vary+ation
	none	deviate → devi+ate
y+i	none (+)	flying → fly+ing
	y → ye (+)	eying → eye+ing
y+.	none	employer → employ+er
.+i	→ e	daring → dare+ing
	none	showing → show+ing
	→ y (*)	harmonize → harmony+ize
.+.	→ e	observance → observe+ance
	none	sender → send+er

the cost of this covering cannot be as low as the one already found, DECOMP does not even bother to match the remaining **scar**. Since no more legal coverings are found, **scarce+ity** becomes the final decomposition.

3.6 The lexicon

3.6.1 *Development and composition*

The present morph lexicon (Hunnicutt, 1976a) contains about 12,000 entries and is sufficient to analyze at least ten times that number of English words, giving the correct morph analysis, pronunciation and part(s) of speech.

```
Decomp: "SCARCITY" [state = word <0> inflectional suffix] =>
Decomp:  Matched "CITY" (root) -- decompose remainder
Decomp:   "SCAR" [state = <101> root] =>
Decomp:    Matched "SCAR" (root) -- decompose remainder
Decomp:     "" [state = <234> root] =>
Decomp:      Matched start of word, final score = 234
Decomp:     Matched "CAR" (root) min. score = 268 -- too expen-
      sive!
Decomp:     Matched "AR" (derivational suffix) min. score = 234
      -- too expensive!
Decomp:  Matched "ITY" (derivational suffix) -- decompose
      remainder
Decomp:   "SCARCE" [state = root <35> derivational suffix] =>
Decomp:    Matched "SCARCE" (root) -- decompose remainder
Decomp:     "" [state = <136> root] =>
Decomp:      Matched start of word, final score = 136
Decomp:   "SCARC" [state = root <35> derivational suffix] =>
Decomp:    Matched "ARC" (root) min. score = 170 -- too expen-
      sive!
Decomp:   "SCARCY" [state = root <35> derivational suffix] =>
Decomp:    Matched "Y" (derivational suffix) min. score = 136 --
      too expensive!
Decomp:  Matched "Y" (derivational suffix) -- decompose
      remainder
Decomp:   "SCARCITE" [state = root <35> derivational suffix] =>
Decomp:    Matched "CITE" (root) min. score = 170 -- too expen-
      sive!
Decomp:   "SCARCIT" [state = root <35> derivational suffix] =>
Decomp:    Matched "IT" (absolute) -- illegal!
 DECOMP: SCARCITY                          word spelling
 DECOMP:   NOUN (NUMBER = SINGULAR)        part of speech and features
 DECOMP:   =>                              decomposition follows
 DECOMP:     SCARCE [ROOT] :               first morph spelling and type
 DECOMP:       1SKE*RS (ADJECTIVE)         pronunciation and part of speech
 DECOMP:       ITY [DERIVATIONAL VOCALIC SUFFIX] : second morph
 DECOMP:         *T-E^ (NOUN)
```

Figure 3-2: Decomposition of "scarcity"

The morph lexicon was obtained by decomposing 50,406 distinct words found in a corpus of 1,014,232 words of running text into constituent morphs (Kucera and Francis, 1967). Beginning with a base of one-, two-, and three-letter words and a decomposition (analysis) algorithm, the lexicon was built up by successively adding to the base all n-letter words (starting with n=4) which either:

1. did not decompose into words of less than n letters,

2. decomposed into incorrect constituent morphs,

3. had a pronunciation other than that obtained by concatenation of the pronunciations of the individual morphs, or

4. had a part of speech which was not derivable from the part-of-speech sets of its constituent morphs.

The first category includes n-letter words consisting of a single morph, words whose constituent morphs did not appear in the lexicon, and words in which an unrecognized spelling change prevented correct analysis.

Although many spelling changes are recognized by the morphological analysis algorithm, some were considered to be either rare or difficult to implement. Spelling changes which are particularly difficult to recognize are those in which a letter is either added or omitted. These changes frequently appear to have been made because of simplified pronunciations. In some cases, a vowel is dropped, as in **administer/administration**. In other cases, repeated consecutive sounds are omitted as in **quietude** (quiet+itude). Words in which letters are inserted may contain an extra sound as in **fixture** (fix+ure) and **armament** (arm+ment), or simply an extra letter as in **picnicked** (picnic+ed) and **stabilize** (stable+ize) in which the spelling change allows retention of the original pronunciation.

There are about 250 words in the morph lexicon which, if they were not lexical entries, would be analyzed by the algorithm into morphs other than those from which they are derived. These are the words mentioned in the second category above. The word **colonize**, for example, is not derived from **colon**; **cobweb** is not derived from **cob**; **bargain** is not derived from **bar** and **gain**.

In some cases of multiple coverings, the selectional rules do not choose the correct analysis. For example, the word **coppery** may be analyzed as either **cop+ery** or as **copper+y**. In both cases, the morph types are the same: **cop** and **copper** are free roots, and **ery** and **y** are vocalic derivational suffixes. That is, the number of morphs and their types are exactly the same in the two possible analyses. When this situation arises, the selectional rules are constrained to choose the first analysis. Because the algorithm first searches for the longest morph from the right end of the word, **cop+ery** is chosen. This analysis is etymologically incorrect, and the polymorphemic word **coppery** is, therefore, a lexical entry.

There are many polymorphemic words in English which differ in pronunciation from that of their constituent morphs. For this reason, the third category above is rather large; it includes about 8 percent of the lexical entries. Some polymorphemic words differ in both pronunciation and stress, the two categories being highly interrelated.

The part of speech of a word is very important in text-to-speech processing. It is used in determining a parse for a sentence which is then used in algorithms determining fundamental frequency and duration. DECOMP includes a part-of-speech processor which determines the part of speech of a word based on information associated with the component morphs in the lexicon. The procedure will be described in detail in the next chapter. If the part of speech of a word is not correctly predicted by its constituent morphs, then the entire word must be placed in the lexicon. For example, the suffix **er** is marked as forming adjectives, adverbs and nouns. There are some words, however, which end in **er** and are both nouns and verbs or are verbs only. Some examples are **batter, checker, chatter,** and **flicker,** which appear in the lexicon.

Although many compounds have the part of speech of their rightmost morph, others do not. Such compounds must be included as lexical entries. A number of the compounds included for this reason are adjectives such as **bygone, borderline, commonplace,** and **freehand.** Others, such as **buttonhole, homestead,** and **bottleneck,** may be used as either nouns or verbs whereas their rightmost morph may be a noun but not a verb.

4

The phrase-level parser

4.1 Overview

The parser for the text-to-speech system is designed to satisfy a unique set of constraints. It must be able to handle arbitrary text quickly, but does not need to derive semantic information. Many parsers attempt to build a deep structure parse from the input sentence so that semantic information may be derived for such uses as question-answering systems. The text-to-speech parser supplies a surface structure parse, providing information for algorithms which produce prosodic effects in the output speech. In addition, some clause boundaries are set according to rules described in Chapter 8. These phrase-level and clause-level structures provide much of the syntactic information needed by the present prosodic algorithms.

It is well known that parsing systems which parse unrestricted text often produce numerous ambiguous or failed parses. Although it is always possible to choose arbitrarily among ambiguous parsings, a failed parse is unacceptable in the text-to-speech system. When one examines ambiguous results from full sentence-level parsers, one finds that the bottom level of nodes (i.e. the phrase nodes) are often invariant among the competing interpretations; the ambiguities arise from possible groupings of these nodes at the clause level, especially for parsers which build binary trees. One also finds that for many failed parses, much of the structure at the phrase level has been correctly determined. The phrase-level parser takes advantage of this reliability, producing as many phrase nodes as possible for use by the MITalk prosodic component.

The phrase-level parser uses comparatively few resources and runs in real-time. This is quite unusual for parsers which handle unrestricted text, but is necessary for a text-to-speech system. It would not be possible in such a practical system to allocate the resources needed for recursion in the grammar and for backtracking control structures. Since extensive backtracking occurs above the phrase level for the most part, the combinatorial explosion associated with this strategy is avoided by restriction to phrase-level parsing.

Phrase recognition is accomplished via an ATN (augmented transition network) interpreter (Woods, 1970) and the grammars for noun groups and verb groups. A "noun group" (NGR), as used in this grammar, means either a pronoun (e.g. **him** or **several**), a pronoun with modification (e.g. **almost anything green**), an integer with or without modification (e.g. **five** or **nearly a hundred thousand**), a noun phrase up to and including the head noun (e.g. **every third car** or **his own red and black car**), or any of the above preceded by a preposition. A "verb group" (VGR) consists of a verb phrase without direct or indirect objects (e.g. **could almost see, might not have been moving, had been very yellow**). Another type of group, the "verbal" (VBL) is also recognized by the verb group network; it is either an infinitive phrase (e.g. **to walk slowly, to be broken**) or a participial phrase (e.g. **walking slowly, have almost given**).

4.2 Input

The input file from DECOMP has been described in Chapter 3. It contains the morph spelling, morph pronunciation, morph type, and parts of speech and features for each homograph of each morph in the analysis of the word. A parts-of-speech set for the entire word is also supplied.

4.3 Output

The output of the parser is a series of *nodes* representing either a parsed constituent (i.e. a phrase), or a word (or punctuation mark) which was not included in a phrase by the parser. Each node representing a phrase contains the words covered by that phrase in the order in which they appear in the text. The output file contains the following information:

1. For each node, the number of words covered by the node, the part of speech (type of constituent) of the node, and a *property list* is given. The property list is a set of attribute-value pairs.
2. Each word is accompanied by its spelling and a part-of-speech set. Only one part of speech is given for those words covered by a node.
3. For each part of speech, a property list is given.

4.4 Parts of speech

4.4.1 *The standard parts of speech in the lexicon*

The following are the parts of speech of open class words and words which do not have any special syntactic or prosodic features. Those names in uppercase are the parts of speech, attributes, and attribute values as they are listed in the source version of the lexicon. A word itself may have any number of parts of speech. The designations TR and FL are abbreviations for "true" and "false", respectively.

NOUN (NUM SING) = singular noun

NOUN (NUM PL) = plural noun

VERB (INF TR) (PL TR) = infinitive form of verb

VERB (SING TR) (PL TR) = past tense verb

ADJ = adjective

ADV (VMOD TR) (ADJMOD TR) =

        adverb which can modify either an adjective or a verb

ADV (ADJMOD TR) = adverb which can modify an adjective

PREP = preposition

CONJ = conjunction

INTG = integer

INTG (NUM SING) = **one**

INTG (DEF FL) = integer which requires **a** (e.g. thousand)

VERBING = present participle

VERBEN = past participle

TO = **to**

SCONJ = sentential conjunction (e.g. **whether**)

CONTR = contraction (e.g. **'re**)

INTERJ = interjection (e.g. **oh**)

4.4.2 *Special parts of speech*

There are three internal parts of speech for punctuation. One is assigned to the single punctuation mark COMMA. The other two include a number of punctuation marks. Punctuation which is internal to a sentence [: ; ( ) ' and "] is assigned the part of speech IPM (internal punctuation mark). Punctuation which can be sentence-final is termed EPM (end punctuation mark).

Some words in the lexicon are recognized as having special syntactic or prosodic features. The syntactic features and the distinctions among the various types of determiners follow from the grammar.

First, consider the adverbs with property (MEAS TR). This indicates that these words can occur in such constructions as **nearly a hundred ladders**. The property (DETMOD TR) marks adverbs which can modify determiners such as **almost any space**. (NEGADV TR) designates an adverb which can appear with an indefinite article and a count noun as in **hardly a salesperson**. The property (NOT TR) on **not** and **never** signals certain prosodic effects.

PDET stands for predeterminer and is the part of speech of a word which can occur before a determiner such as **half his land** or **twice the money**. The property (MEAS TR) applied to PDET indicates that a predeterminer can be present with a measure adverb as in **almost all two hundred divers**. (DEF TR) signifies that the determiner must be definite (**all the pain** is allowable; **all a pain** is incorrect), while (DEF FL) is the opposite (**such the problem** is incorrect, **such a problem** is allowable). (DET TR) marks a predeterminer which must be followed by some determiner. (OF FL) indicates that a predeterminer cannot be followed by **of**, as opposed to **both of the gnomes**. (TYPE A) marks predeterminers which cause certain quantifier-related prosodic effects. (QUANT A) designates the same usage for pronouns.

The CASE and NUM attributes on the pronouns refer to case and number in the usual manner. The TYPE is listed for prosodic reasons. (DETMOD TR) indicates that a pronoun can be modified by a determiner-modifying adverb as in **nearly everyone**.

There are four types of determiners. DETW stands for a wh-word determiner. DETQ signifies a quantified determiner. These are distinguished from the quantifiers (part of speech QUANT) by the fact that they may occur in the same noun group as an ordinal or integer as in **every third Eskimo** or **any six infants**. DETMOD has the same meaning here as for pronouns. TYPE and QUANT again are prosodic indicators. Demonstratives (DEM) and articles (ART) are straightforward.

The ordinals (ORD) include **next** and **last** as well as the ordinal integers. **Quarters, thirds**, etc. are listed as ORD (NUM PL) because they can occur in constructions such as **three quarters the money**, or **two thirds the money**. The feature (DEF TR) on these words indicates that the preceding determiner must be definite. The quantifiers (QUANT) are usually marked for number agreement and for definiteness agreement with the preceding determiner.

The modals (MOD) are marked with the attribute AUX which gives prosodic information. The property (TO TR) indicates that a modal can occur in constructions such as **ought to deliver**, while (TO BE) designates a word which must appear with **be** and **to** as in **was going to abscond**. The rest of the BE and HAVE words have their usual meaning.

4.5 The part-of-speech processor

The part-of-speech processor is part of the DECOMP module in the text-to-speech system. It computes a part-of-speech set for each word in the input, given the morph decomposition and the parts of speech of the morphs. It is based on Allen's

"Preprocessor" (Allen, 1968). The current algorithm goes right-to-left across the morphs and uses the part of speech of the rightmost morph for a compound, as well as for cases where there is a suffix. This is justified by two facts:

1. suffixes (especially the rightmost suffix since it is outermost in the "nesting" of affixes) determine the part of speech of a word with regularity (e.g. **...ness** is a NOUN);
2. the part of speech of compounds is very idiosyncratic (in fact, it is usually determined by semantic rather than syntactic information) and the best heuristic is to use the part-of-speech set of the rightmost root.

A complete description of the part-of-speech processor is given in Appendix A. First, the processor checks to see if there was a decomposition. If there is none, then it calls a routine which assigns the part-of-speech set (NOUN (NUM SING), VERB (PL TR) (INF TR), ADJ) unless the word ends in 'S in which case the part-of-speech set is ((NOUN (POSS TR), NOUN (NUM SING) (CONTR TR)). Next, the program determines whether the last morph in the decomposition is a suffix. If it is not, then the program checks for the part-of-speech determining prefixes. The prefixes **EM**, **EN**, and **BE** indicate that a word is a VERB, while **A** gives the part-of-speech set (ADJ, ADV). (Suffixes have priority over these, as in **befuddlement**.) If none of these are present, then the processor assigns the part-of-speech set of the last morph in the decomposition.

The rest of the processor is essentially a dispatch on the last suffix. In many cases, the next to last morph's part of speech must also be examined. If the last morph is the suffix **ING**, the part of speech is specified as VERBING, while **ED** indicates that the part-of-speech set is (VERBEN, VERB (SING TR) (PL TR)). If the last morph is **S** or **ES**, a number of checks must be made. If the next to last morph is not a suffix and there is a verb-producing prefix, then the part of speech is VERB (SING TR), as in **entitles**. If the penultimate morph has the part of speech VERB, then the same part of speech is assigned. If the previous morph is a NOUN, ADJ, or INTG or is **ER** or **ING**, then the part of speech NOUN (NUM PL) is added to the set. If the next to last morph is an ORD, then the part of speech is also ORD (NUM PL). Finally, if there is still no part of speech, the processor assigns NOUN (NUM PL), as in **the whys and wherefores**.

If the last suffix is **ER**, then three checks are made. If the next to last morph has the part of speech ADV, then the word is a comparative adverb; if it is an ADJ, then the word is a comparative adjective. If it is a NOUN or a VERB, then the word is a singular NOUN, as in **worker**. If the last morph is S', then the word's part of speech is NOUN with the property (POSS TR).

44

For a last suffix of 'S, three checks are performed. If the previous morph is a NOUN, then the part-of-speech set is (NOUN (POSS TR), NOUN .... (CONTR TR)), where "...." are the features that the previous morph had (e.g. (NUM PL)). If the next to last morph is a PRN, then the part of speech is PRN with the previous morph's features and the additional property (CONTR TR). If that morph also has the property (PRNADJ TR), which includes the pronouns ending in **body, one,** and **thing,** then the part-of-speech set also includes PRN with the prior morph's features and the property (CASE POSS), as in **anybody's.**

The last three cases of the dispatch deal with contractions. If the last morph is **N'T,** first the program checks if the previous morph is **NEED.** The part of speech of **needn't** is MOD, and the features are (AUX A) and (NOT TR). If the next to last morph has the part of speech BE, HAVE, or MOD, the processor just adds the property (NOT TR). If the last morph is **'VE** and the previous morph is a modal, then the part of speech is the same as the previous morph with the additional property (CONTR TR), as in **must've.** Finally, if the last morph is one of the verb contractions **'VE, 'D, 'LL,** and **'RE,** the processor checks if the prior morph is the plural morph S. (**The kids've been busy. The boys'll go.**) If so, the word's part of speech is NOUN with the features (NUM PL) and (CONTR TR). Otherwise, if the previous morph is a NOUN or PRN, the property (CONTR TR) is added to the feature set.

If the last suffix is none of the above, then the part-of-speech set of the word is the part-of-speech set of that morph. If a word still has no part of speech (e.g. **only's**), then the routine which assigns "default" parts of speech is called, as in the case of no decomposition.

4.6 The parser algorithm

4.6.1 *Parsing strategy*

The parser reads information from DECOMP on the words in a text one sentence at a time. It then attempts to find phrases in the sentence. The operation of the parsing logic can be thought of as having two levels. The global level reflects the parsing strategy, which has been found to give the best phrases. It is based on three empirical facts:

1. There are many more noun groups (and prepositional phrases) than verb groups in running text.
2. The initial portions of noun groups are easier to detect than verb groups. Verb groups frequently begin with the verb itself which often has both NOUN and VERB in its possible part-of-speech set.

3. Nouns are very often compounded into classifier strings (e.g. **cathode ray tube cleaning fluid**).

The local level merely interprets the ATN grammar.

The global parsing strategy proceeds as follows: it looks for the *longest* noun group (a noun phrase up to the head noun, possibly including an initial preposition) that it can find beginning with the first word in the sentence. If it locates one, then a "node" representing that constituent is constructed, the "current word" pointer is advanced to the word after that constituent and the process begins again at that point. If no noun group is found, the parsing logic attempts to find the longest verb group starting at the word pointer. If it is successful, then a "node" is built, the pointer is incremented, and the process begins again. If neither type of group can be found at a certain point in the sentence, no node is created and the pointer is simply moved to the next word in the sentence and the process begins again.

At the local level, the parser uses the ATN to find a constituent. There are two pointers, one pointing to the word in the sentence currently being examined and one pointing to the current state in the net, which begins at the initial state for noun groups or verb groups. The parser tries each arc leading from the current state *in the order in which they appear in the net*. This net is shown in Tables 4-1 (noun group) and 4-2 (verb group).

Testing an arc is done as follows:

1. If the arc label is JUMP or POP, then the exit routine associated with that arc is tested. If it is successful, then for JUMP the state pointer is advanced to the destination state (the word pointer is not incremented), and the process begins again at that state. For POP, a node is built if the popped constituent is longer than any found so far, and the process continues with the next arc leaving the state. (That is, parsing is exhaustive.) If the tests are unsuccessful, then the parser simply checks the next arc leaving the state.

2. If the arc label is a part of speech and the current word does not have this part of speech, the parser continues with the next arc. If the current word does have this part of speech, the exit routine is tested. If successful, the word pointer is incremented and the state pointer is advanced to the destination state of the arc. If it fails, the next arc is attempted. If the parser is to test the next arc for some state and no arcs remain, then the state pointer is reset to the state from which the arc led which brought the process to the current state, and the process begins again with the next arc in the new state.

NG	VERBING NG-Ving IngVbl
	TO VG-Inf Vbl
	PREP NG-Adv PP
	TO NG-Adv PP
	JUMP NG-Adv NG
NG-Ving	JUMP NG-Adj1 IngAdj
	JUMP NG-N1 IngNoun
	POP NG-Ving Vbl
NG-Adv	ADV NG-Pdet NA
	QUANT NG-Than MorLes
	ADJ NG-Adj Adj
	JUMP NG-Pdet OK
NG-Than	SCONJ NG-ThanA Than
NG-ThanA	ART NG-INtg ThanA
	JUMP NG-Intg OK
NG-Pdet	INTG NG-Times FracNum
	PRN NG-Own Prnps
	PDET NG-Det PD
	DETW NG-Ord DW
	DETQ NG-Ord DQ
	JUMP NG-Det OK
	PRN NG-Prn Pr
NG-Prn	ADV NG-Prn PrnAdv
	ADJ NG-PA PA
	PREP NG-Pdet PrnOf
	POP NG-Prn PrPop
NG-Times	ORD NG-Det FracDen
	NOUN NG-Det Times
NG-Det	NOUN NG-Own Poss
	PRN NG-Own PPoss
	DEM NG-Ord Dem
	ART NG-Ord Art
	PREP NG-Pdet PdetOf
	JUMP NG-Ord NeedDet
NG-Quant	QUANT NG-Adj Quant
	PREP NG-Pdet DetOf
	JUMP NG-Intg OK

NG-PA	POP NG-PA OK
NG-Ord	ORD NG-Quant Ord
	JUMP NG-Quant OfTest
	ADJ NG-Intg IntMod
NG-Own	ADJ NG-Ord Own
	DETQ NG-Adj Every
	JUMP NG-Ord OK
	POP NG-Own PopP
NG-Intg	INTG NG-Intg1 Intg
	JUMP NG-Adj NoMeas
NG-Intg1	INTG NG-Intg1 IntA
	CONJ NG-Frac And
	JUMP NG-IntOrd OK
NG-IntOrd	ORD NG-Adj IntOrd
	JUMP NG-Adj OK
NG-Frac	INTG NG-Denom Numer
	ART NG-Denom A
NG-Denom	ORD NG-Adj Denom
NG-Adj	ADV NG-Adj AdvAdj
	ADJ NG-Adj1 Adj
	VERBEN NG-Adj1 Adj
	VERBING NG-Adj1 VngAdj
	PREP NG-Pdet QuantOf
	JUMP NG-N NeedAdj
	POP NG-Adj IntPop
NG-Adj1	CONJ NG-Adj AConj
	COMMA NG-Adj AComma
	JUMP NG-Adj OK
NG-N	NOUN NG-Own PossN
	NOUN NG-N1 Noun
	VERBING NG-N1 ConjVing
	INTG NG-N1 NIntg
	PREP NG-Adv NounOf
	POP NG-N PopN
NG-N1	CONJ NG-N NConj
	COMMA NG-N NComma
	JUMP NG-N OK

Figure 4-1: Noun group ATN listing

VG	ADV VG Adv		VG-Have	ADV VG-Have Adv
	MOD VG-Inf Mod			MOD VG-To Got
	MOD VG-To ModTo			BEEN VG-Part Been
	HAVE VG-Have Have			JUMP VG-Part NoIng
	MOD VG-Have ModCntr			JUMP VG-To OK
	BE VG-Part Be		VG-Part	MOD VG-To BeMod
	VERB VG-Pop Verb			ADV VG-Part CopAvj
	JUMP VG-Inf Vbl			BEING VG-Part Being
	JUMP VG-Have Vbl			VERBING VG-Pop Ving
VG-Inf	ADV VG-Inf Adv			VERBEN VG-Pop En
	MOD VG-To Get			JUMP VG-Cop Cop
	HAVE VG-Have HavInf		VG-Cop	ADJ VG-Pop OK
	BE VG-Part BInf			JUMP VG-Pop CopNoAj
	VERB VG-Pop VInf		VG-Pop	ADV VG-Pop NoPrep
VG-To	ADV VG-To Adv			POP VG-Pop PopV
	TO VG-Inf OK			

Figure 4-2: Verb group ATN listing

4.6.2 *The verb group grammar*

The verb group grammar appears in Figure 4-3. This is the simpler of the phrase grammars. It has fewer arcs, fewer states and alternate paths, fewer exit routines, and only two POP arcs. Its auxiliary verb structure is very well-defined. Also, there are no multiple parts of speech for one word, causing two paths to be investigated.

Some examples follow of basic verb groups which successfully traverse this net:

sometimes runs **usually would have been jumping**
is being run **have to go**
would have been seen **about to be done**

This basic grammar has been extended to include certain modal arcs used in spoken English. Some examples of these verb groups are:

get to run **does get used**
get to go **can't possibly get to see**

Particles have not as yet been treated. At present, in a simple sentence such as **He picked up the books**, three noun groups are found: **he, picked up,** and **the books**. In the phrase **picked up, picked** is assumed to be a past participle being used as an adjective and **up** is assumed to be the noun, as in the colloquial expression **It's a real up.** In the sentence **He ran out of the room, ran** is considered a verb group, but **out** is considered a noun group (as in **How many outs does the**

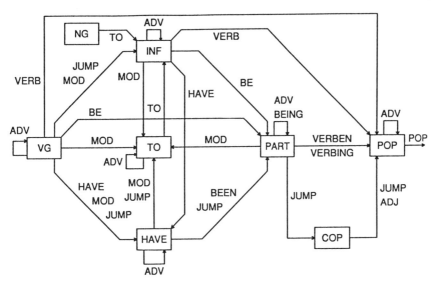

Figure 4-3: ATN diagram for verb groups

team have?), and **of** is included in the prepositional phrase **of the room.** It might be possible to correctly parse some of these particle constructions using a feature on the verb. However, such a feature also allows for incorrect recognition of a preposition as a particle.

4.6.3 *The noun group grammar*

Figure 4-4 contains the noun group grammar. This is the more complex phrase grammar. It has many arcs and branches, and many exit tests. There are many possible sequences to follow in the net; the examples below illustrate some possible paths and some which are correctly blocked (these are starred).

almost any book	*book
about two fifths the book	*almost him
the many books	*a many books
both these women	*both this women
every other book	*every other books
any two books	*some few books
every few books	*a few book
that few books	*that much book
that many books	*his much money
a woman's many books	*a book women

The noun group grammar contains a number of optional arcs or "sidetracks". Examples of cases in which these arcs would be traversed are listed below:

three quarters	his own shoes
more than five shoes	three and a half

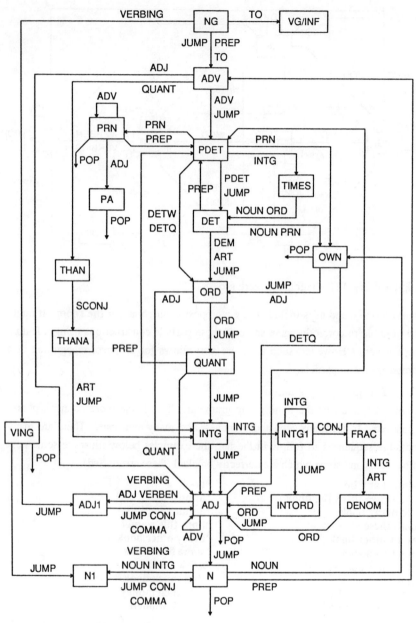

Figure 4-4: ATN diagram for noun groups

red, white and blue   **three and twenty blackbirds**

simple pronoun noun groups, e.g., **he**.

4.7 Some examples

Figure 4-5 shows an example of the phrase-level parse produced by the parser. The text is a portion of a computer-taught course at Stanford. The paragraphs parsed here are taken from the end of a section about predicate calculus.

```
PARSER: NOUN GROUP: MOST OF THE EXERCISES
PARSER: VERB GROUP: ARE
PARSER: NOUN GROUP: TRANSLATIONS
PARSER: UNCLASSIFIED: .
PARSER: VERB GROUP: THERE ARE
PARSER: NOUN GROUP: SEVERAL IMPORTANT CHANGES
PARSER: PREPOSITIONAL PHRASE: IN THE WAY
PARSER: NOUN GROUP: THE QUANTIFIER RULES
PARSER: VERB GROUP: WILL WORK
PARSER: PREPOSITIONAL PHRASE: FOR THE REMAINDER OF THE
    COURSE
PARSER: UNCLASSIFIED: .
PARSER: UNCLASSIFIED: .
PARSER: UNCLASSIFIED: FIRST
PARSER: UNCLASSIFIED: ,
PARSER: NOUN GROUP: THE PROGRAM
PARSER: VERB GROUP: WILL INFORM
PARSER: NOUN GROUP: YOU
PARSER: UNCLASSIFIED: IMMEDIATELY
PARSER: UNCLASSIFIED: IF
PARSER: NOUN GROUP: A QUANTIFIER INFERENCE
PARSER: VERB GROUP: VIOLATES
PARSER: NOUN GROUP: ANY OF THE RESTRICTIONS
PARSER: UNCLASSIFIED: .
PARSER: UNCLASSIFIED: .
PARSER: UNCLASSIFIED: .
PARSER: NOUN GROUP: THAT WAY
PARSER: NOUN GROUP: AN OVERSIGHT
PARSER: VERB GROUP: WON'T COST
PARSER: NOUN GROUP: YOU
PARSER: NOUN GROUP: A LOT OF WORK
PARSER: UNCLASSIFIED: .
PARSER: UNCLASSIFIED: .
PARSER: UNCLASSIFIED: .
PARSER: NOUN GROUP: YOU
PARSER: VERB GROUP: CAN'T USE
PARSER: NOUN GROUP: AMBIGUOUS NAMES
PARSER: PREPOSITIONAL PHRASE: WITH A SHARP
PARSER: PREPOSITIONAL PHRASE: IN THEM
PARSER: UNCLASSIFIED: ANYMORE
PARSER: UNCLASSIFIED: .
PARSER: UNCLASSIFIED: .
PARSER: <EOF>
```

Figure 4-5: Example of PARSER operation

5

Morphophonemics and stress adjustment

5.1 Overview
It is not always possible to simply concatenate the pronunciations of the constituent morphs of a word to get its pronunciation. There are sometimes changes in pronunciation at morph boundaries. Module SOUND1 checks for contexts in which such changes occur, and changes the pronunciation. It also adjusts the lexical stress for compounds and for words having suffixes requiring special stress rules. SOUND1 also performs letter-to-sound conversion for words which were not segmented by DECOMP (this function will be described in the following chapter). It accepts as input all the word and morph information given by DECOMP and the additional phrase part-of-speech information produced by PARSER. Output is a set of phonetic segment labels for each word along with the phrase information from PARSER.

5.2 Input
Input to SOUND1 is the output stream from PARSER. The format of this stream has been described in Chapter 4. It contains morph pronunciation information from DECOMP and phrase and part-of-speech information from PARSER.

5.3 Output
The output stream from SOUND1 consists of a string of phonetic segment labels, stress marks, and syllable and morph boundaries for each word. At the end of each sentence, the phrase information for that sentence is placed in the output stream (this is simply a duplicate of the phrase information from PARSER).

5.4 Morphophonemic rules
The pronunciation for each word which has been segmented by DECOMP is constructed by catenating the pronunciations of its component morphs. The following rules are applied to modify the morph pronunciations when necessary.

5.4.1 *Plurals, possessives, and contractions with "is"*
Words which end in a fricative or affricate close in place of articulation to SS and ZZ, i.e., the set of segments SS, ZZ, SH, ZH, CH, and JJ, form their plurals and possessives by the concatenation of the segment string IH ZZ, or, in its vowel-reduced form, IX ZZ (e.g. **busses, churches, garages, marsh's**). After other

voiced segments, the plural and possessive morphemes are realized as ZZ (e.g. **dogs, potatoes**). After other unvoiced consonants, it is pronounced SS (e.g. **backs, cat's**). Nouns and pronouns contracted with the verb **is** follow the same rules as possessives (e.g. **the dog is**→**the dog's, the cat is**→**the cat's**). It is interesting to note that since the plural or possessive morpheme and the word **is** have the same pronunciation after the set of phonetic segments given special treatment above. No contraction is made with **is**, that is, one would not write

The church's across the street

to mean

The church is across the street.

Presumably, however, someone who does not read or write will not be able to tell which form was being used.

5.4.2 *Past participles*
The analysis for past tense forms is similar. After the segments TT and DD, the extra vowel separation is provided to give the pronunciation IH DD or IX DD (e.g. **mended, minted**). After other voiced segments, the pronunciation DD is chosen (e.g. **whispered, rowed**) and after other unvoiced consonants, the pronunciation TT is chosen (e.g. **hushed**).

5.4.3 *The prefixes* **pre, re,** *and* **de**
Although it is not possible to construct a rule covering the correct pronunciation of these prefixes in all cases, the rule which was chosen is frequently correct. Before free morphs such as **gain**, the **e** is given the long vowel sound of IY (e.g. **regain**). The short vowel sound IH is assigned before bound morphs requiring a prefix (e.g. **prefer**). This rule should only apply if there is no stress on the prefix; any word in which the prefix is stressed should appear in the lexicon as a separate entry (e.g. **preference**).

5.4.4 *Palatalization before suffixes* **ion** *and* **ure**
The suffixes **ion** and **ure** both cue palatalization of alveolar segments preceding them. The affricates they become are dependent upon the segment preceding the alveolar consonant. In addition, a change in the pronunciation of the suffix accompanies this palatalization. In this module, these changes are accomplished by recognition of letter contexts.

Preceding the suffix **ion**, the letter **t** is pronounced CH after **n** or **s** and SH otherwise (e.g. **retention, congestion, completion**). The letter **s** is given the pronunciation SH after l or s (e.g. **emulsion, compression**), the pronunciation ZH after **r** or a vowel (e.g. **subversion, adhesion**), and CH after **n** (e.g. **suspension**).

There are a few words ending in **xion**, such as **complexion**, in which the pronunciation KK SS, as in **complex**, is changed to KK SH.

The suffix **ion** itself, which is pronounced IY - AX NN in some contexts (e.g. **centurion, accordion**), loses the pronunciation of the first vowel, which appears to be absorbed into the palatalized consonant, and is pronounced AX NN after the affricates (all those examples given above). The segment IY becomes more of a glide after **l** and **n**, and is given the pronunciation YY AX NN in such words as **rebellion** and **dominion**.

The palatalization rules for the suffix **ure** are slightly less dependent upon context. The letters **t** and **d** are pronounced CH and JJ, respectively (e.g. **vesture, verdure**). The letter **s** follows the same rules as when it precedes the suffix **ion**, i.e., it is SH after **l** and **s** (e.g. **pressure**), ZH after **r** or a vowel (e.g. **exposure**), and CH after **n**, as in **tonsure**. A rule is also provided for **x** preceding **ure**, changing KK SS to KK SH, as in **flexure**.

5.4.5 *The suffix ic*

Preceding the front vowels represented in the orthography by **e**, **i**, and **y**, the suffix **ic** is changed in pronunciation from IH KK, which contains the velar KK, to the more fronted alveolar-containing IH SS (e.g. **electricity**).

5.5 Stress modification rules

A compound stress rule is applied to words decomposed into more than one root or bound root. The primary stress (or 1-stress) is retained on the leftmost root. Primary stress on other roots is reduced to secondary (or 2-stress) as in **houseboat** (1-stress on **house** and 2-stress on **boat**).

Suffixes which shift the primary stress in a word, such as **ee**, **eer**, **esce**, and **ation** are entered in the morph lexicon with primary stress. The stress on any root to which they attach is reduced to secondary (e.g. **trainee, auctioneer**). This is implemented by checking for primary stress on the leftmost derivational suffix and reducing the root stress when the suffix stress is found.

5.6 An example

The input files from PARSER and the output file resulting from SOUND1's operation for the sentence:

Priscilla noted the houseboat's reflection.

are shown in Figure 5-1. The symbols * and - denote morph and syllable boundaries, respectively.

The word **Priscilla** is not found in the lexicon. This fact is noted in the PARSER output file by the lack of => notation after its spelling. The pronuncia-

```
PARSER: NOUN GROUP (NUMBER = SINGULAR)
PARSER:      PRISCILLA
PARSER:           NOUN (NUMBER = SINGULAR)
PARSER: VERB GROUP (SINGULAR = TRUE) (PLURAL = TRUE)
PARSER:      NOTED
PARSER:           VERB (SINGULAR = TRUE) (PLURAL = TRUE)
PARSER:           =>
PARSER:             NOTE [ROOT] :
PARSER:                1NO^T (VERB, NOUN)
PARSER:             ED [INFLECTIONAL VOCALIC SUFFIX] :
PARSER:                D (VERB, PAST PARTICIPLE)
PARSER: NOUN GROUP (NUMBER = SINGULAR)
PARSER:      THE
PARSER:           ARTICLE (DEFINITE = TRUE)
PARSER:           =>
PARSER:             THE [ABSOLUTE] :
PARSER:                1TH_* (ARTICLE)
PARSER:      HOUSEBOAT'S
PARSER:           NOUN (POSSESSIVE = TRUE)
PARSER:           =>
PARSER:             HOUSE [ROOT] :
PARSER:                1HAU'S (NOUN)
PARSER:                1HAU'Z (VERB)
PARSER:             BOAT [ROOT] :
PARSER:                1BO^T (NOUN)
PARSER:             'S [INFLECTIONAL NONVOCALIC SUFFIX] :
PARSER:                IZ (CONTRACTION, NOUN)
PARSER:      REFLECTION
PARSER:           NOUN (NUMBER = SINGULAR)
PARSER:           =>
PARSER:             REFLECT [ROOT] :
PARSER:                RI-1FLEKT (VERB)
PARSER:             ION [DERIVATIONAL VOCALIC SUFFIX] :
PARSER:                *N (NOUN)
PARSER: UNCLASSIFIED
PARSER:      .
PARSER:           END PUNCTUATION MARK
SOUND1: PP RR "IH - SS 'IH LL - AX
SOUND1: NN 'OW TT * - IH DD
SOUND1: DH 'AH
SOUND1: HH 'AW SS * - BB "OW TT * SS
SOUND1: RR IH - FF LL 'EH KK SH * - AX NN
SOUND1: .
```

Figure 5-1: Input to and output from SOUND1

tion shown in the output is a result of the letter-to-sound and lexical stress application which will be described in the next chapter.

In the lexicon, the pronunciation of the "past" morpheme is given as DD. This is the pronunciation used following all voiced segments except DD. The first morph in **noted** is **note**. Its last segment is TT which is one of the two segments requiring the special pronunciation IH DD or IX DD. In the output of SOUND1, the DD has been converted to IH DD.

Observing the lexical information for the word **house**, we see that there are two homographs. The pronunciation given first, ends in unvoiced SS: this is the nominal pronunciation. The second pronunciation, on the following line, ends in the voiced counterpart, zz. Like any other word containing a morph with more than one homograph, this compound has been inspected in DECOMP to enssure that the homograph listed first in the output file is the homograph having the same part of speech as the word. Thus, SOUND1, choosing the first pronunciation for all morphs, picks the correct nominal pronunciation.

The lexical pronunciation of **'s** is IH zz. In this case, the pronunciation ss must be substituted since the preceding segment is an unvoiced TT.

A third change to **houseboat's** is due to the operation of the compound stress rule. This rule assigns primary stress to the leftmost root in a word containing more than one root, reducing the stress on the rightmost root. Thus, the stress on **boat** is reduced to 2-stress.

Two other changes are demonstrated in the word **reflection**. Lexical pronunciation of the prefix **re** is RR IY. Because **flect** is a bound root and **re** carries no stress, the pronunciation of **re** is changed to RR IH. One of the two suffixes that cues palatalization is also encountered in this word. The segment TT at the end of the pronunciation of **flect** is a member of the set of alveolars that palatalizes in this context. In the output file, TT has been changed to SH. It is unnecessary to change the pronunciation of **ion** since it is entered in the lexicon in its desired form.

6

Letter-to-sound and lexical stress

6.1 Overview

In order to convert unrestricted text to speech, it is necessary to have a scheme which stipulates a pronunciation for words not analyzable by the lexical analysis algorithm. This comprehensiveness is provided by the letter-to-sound section of SOUND1. The letter strings which it receives are converted into stressed phonetic segment label strings (hereafter referred to as segment strings) using two sets of ordered phonological rules (Hunnicutt, 1976b). The first set to be applied converts letters to phonetic segments, first stripping affixes, then converting consonants, and finally converting vowels and affixes. The second set applies an ordered set of rules which determine the stress contour of the segment string.

These rules were developed by a process of extensive statistical analysis of English words. The form of the rules reflects the fact that pronunciation of vowels and vowel digraphs, consonants and consonant clusters, and prefixes and suffixes is highly dependent upon context. The method of ordering rules allows converted strings which are highly dependable to be used as context for those requiring a more complex framework. Detailed studies of allowable suffix combinations, and the effect of suffixation on stress and vowel quality, have also provided for more reliable results.

This component is integral to SOUND1 described in the previous chapter and processes words which were not segmented by DECOMP. Input and output formats are described in that chapter.

6.2 Letter-to-sound

6.2.1 *Operation*

The conversion of a letter string to a phonetic segment string in the letter-to-sound program proceeds in three stages. In the first stage, prefixes and suffixes are detected. Such affixes appear in the list of phonological rules. Each is classified according to:

1. its possible parts of speech,
2. the possible parts of speech of a suffix preceding it,
3. its restriction or lack of restriction to word-final position, and

4. its ability to change a preceding **y** to **i** or to cause the omission of a
preceding **e**.

Prefixes are given no further specification.

Detection of suffixes proceeds in a right-to-left, longest-match-first fashion.
When no additional suffixes can be detected, or when a possible suffix is judged
syntactically incompatible with its right-adjacent suffix by a part-of-speech test
using the first two classifications above, the process is terminated. Finally,
prefixes are detected left-to-right, also by longest match first. If at any time the
removal of an affix would leave no letter in the remainder of the word, the affix is
not removed.

An example of affix detection and analysis is furnished in Figure 6-1 below.
Two possible suffixes, **ish** and **ing**, are detected. The suffix **ing** terminates either a
noun or a verb, and is constrained to follow either a noun-forming or a verb-
forming suffix. The suffix **ish**, however, is adjectival. Therefore, this possible
analysis is rejected, and the correct analysis is chosen. If the string **ish** had been
selected as a suffix, the root to which it attaches would have been assumed to end
in **e**, and would have been pronounced **fine**.

```
finishing
      fin+ish+ing        possible suffix analysis
         ing: (a)    nominal or verbal suffix
              (b)    follows nominal or verbal suffix
         ish: (a)    adjectival suffix
                     parts of speech not compatible
              (b)    follows nominal or adjectival suffix
      finish+ing        correct analysis
```

Figure 6-1: Suffix detection in the word **finishing**

6.2.2 *Domain of application*

The domain of application of the second stage rules excludes any previously
recognized affixes and is assumed to be a single-root morph. This stage is intended primarily for consonant rules and proceeds from the left of the string to the
right. Extending the domain to the whole letter string once again for the third
stage, a phonemic representation is given to affixes, vowels, and vowel digraphs.

Phonemic representations are produced by a set of ordered rules which convert a letter string to a phonetic segment string in a given context. Both left and
right contexts are permitted in the expression of a rule. Any one context may be
composed of either letters or segments. Combination of these possibilities for both
left and right contexts allows for four possible context types.

6.2.3 *Rule ordering*

The method of ordering rules allows converted strings which are highly depend-able to be used as context for those requiring a more complex framework. Because the pronunciation of consonants is least dependent upon context, phonological rules for consonants are applied first, i.e., in the second stage. Rules for vowels and affixes, requiring more specification of environment, are applied in the third and final stage. With the benefit of a previously converted consonant framework and the option of including as context any segment to the left of a string under con-sideration, the task of converting vowels and affixes is simplified.

Within the two sets of rules for conversion of consonants and vowels, order-ing proceeds from longer strings to shorter strings and, for each string, from specific context to general context. The rule for pronunciation of **cch**, then, ap-pears before the rules for **cc** and **ch**, each of which is ordered before rules for **c** and **h**. Procedures for the recognition of prefixes and suffixes also require an ordering: the prefixes **com** and **con** must be ordered before **co**; any suffix ending with the letter **s** must be recognized before the suffix consisting of that letter only.

As an example of ordering rules for a particular string, consider the vowel **a**, and assume that it is followed by the letter **r**. This **a** may be pronounced like the **a** in **warp**, **lariat**, or **carp**, depending upon specification of further context. It is pronounced like the **a** in **carp** if it is followed by **r** and another consonant (other than **r**), and if it is preceded by any consonant segment except ᴡᴡ (note **quarter**, **wharf**). Consequently, a rule for **a** in the context of being preceded by the seg-ment ᴡᴡ and followed by the sequence **r**-*consonant* is placed in the set of rules. Specification of a left context in the rule for the **a** in **carp** is subsequently unneces-sary. If the **a** is preceded by a ᴡᴡ, this rule will already have applied. Using this method, rules may be stated simply and without redundancy.

6.2.4 *Examples of rule application*

In this section, two words will be analyzed according to the phonological rules. Intermediate and final output will be provided for each word. The first stage con-sists of affix detection; the second stage is primarily composed of rules for the pronunciation of consonants in the root; the third stage contains rules for the pronunciation of affixes and of vowels in the root. Generalizations of these rules and related rules will be included in the discussion. The result of application of stress rules (to be discussed later) is given without comment following each derivation.

The first example is shown in Figure 6-2. During Stage 1, no affixes are detected. Converting consonants in Stage 2, **r** is pronounced according to the most

```
Sound1: Stripped   : C  A  R  I  B  O  U        Stage 1
Sound1: Consonants: KK ?? RR ?? BB ?? ??        Stage 2
Sound1: Prefixes   : KK ?? RR ?? BB ?? ??
Sound1: Vowels     : KK AE RR IH BB UW          Stage 3
Sound1: Suffixes   : KK AE RR IH BB UW
 SOUND1:  KK 'AE RR - IX - BB UW
```

Figure 6-2: Application of letter-to-sound rules to **caribou**

general rule in its rule sequence and that **b** has only one given pronunciation. The letter **c**, because it precedes **a**, is pronounced KK.

When **a** precedes **r** which, in turn, precedes either a vowel or another **r** within the same morph, it usually has the pronunciation AE. The letter **i**, following its most general pronunciation, is assigned the segment IH. Morph-final **ou** is given the pronunciation UW.

6.2.4.1 *Generalizations and related rules*   The letter **r** is syllabic if preceded by a consonant other than **r** and followed by a morph-final **e**, e.g., **acre**, or the inflectional suffixes **s** or **ed**.

The letter **c** is palatalized in some cases, as in **special** (preceded by a vowel; followed by the letter **i** and a vowel) and **ancient** (preceded by the letter **n**; followed by **i-vowel**). It is assigned the segment SS later in its rule sequence if it is followed by **e**, **i**, or **y**. It may be noted that this is the same context which assigns the pronunciation IH SS to the suffix **ic**. If **c** is followed by **a**, **o**, or **u**, it is usually pronounced KK, as in this example.

When **a** precedes **r**, and **r** is not followed by either a vowel or another **r** within the same morph, **a** is pronounced AA (e.g. **far**, **cartoon**) unless preceded by the segment WW (e.g. **warble**, **warp**, **war**, **wharf**, **quarter**).

In a word such as **macaroon**, the **a** preceding **r**-*vowel* is assigned pronunciation AE in the phonological rules and is reduced to schwa in the stress rules because it is unstressed.

6.2.4.2 *Second example*

```
Sound1: Stripped   : S  U  B  <  V  E  R  S  >  I  O  N
         Stage 1
Sound1: Consonants: ?? ?? ?? ?? VV ?? RR ZH ?? ?? ?? ??
         Stage 2
Sound1: Prefixes   : SS AX BB < VV ?? RR ZH ?? ?? ?? ??
Sound1: Vowels     : SS AX BB < VV AH RR ZH ?? ?? ?? ??
         Stage 3
Sound1: Suffixes   : SS AX BB < VV AH RR ZH > AX NN
 SOUND1:   SS "AX BB * - VV 'AH RR ZH * - AX NN
```

Figure 6-3: Application of letter-to-sound rules to **subversion**

In Figure 6-3, the affixes **ion** and **sub** are recognized in Stage 1.

There is only one pronunciation provided for the consonant **v**; and **r**, because it does not fit a specified context for syllabic **r**, is given the standard pronunciation. The letter **s** is followed by the sequence **i-vowel**, making it a candidate for palatalization. The palatalization rule which applies, assigns the segment ZH.

In the final stage of letter-to-phonetic segment conversion, the affixes and vowels are considered. The prefix **sub** has only one possible pronunciation. The letter **e**, because it precedes the sequence **r**-*consonant* where the consonant is not an **r**, is given the pronunciation AH. The palatal segment ZH now forms a left context for the suffix **ion**, which, being word-final, is pronounced AH NN.

6.2.4.3 *Generalizations and related rules*   Because the suffix **s** is marked as occurring in word-final position only, the **s** preceding **ion** is not recognized as a suffix. This step also prevents the **er** preceding the **s** from consideration as a possible suffix.

When an **s** preceding the sequence **i**-*vowel* in a root or beginning a suffix is preceded by either a vowel or an **r**, it is usually pronounced ZH. Some examples are **revision, artesian, Persian** and **dispersion**; two exceptions are **controversial** and **torsion**. When **s** is preceded by **l**, and when it occurs as part of the consonant cluster **ss**, the segment preceding the vowel sequence is SH (e.g. **emulsion, Russian**). A third pronunciation is observed when **s** is preceded by **n** (e.g. **transient, comprehension**).

The sequence AH RR is later changed to ER.

The sequence **ion** following a nonpalatalized consonant is pronounced IY AH NN (e.g. **oblivion, criterion, champion**).

The suffix **ion** may be given other pronunciations if not morph-final. For example, it is pronounced IY AA NN in **ganglionic** and **histrionic**.

6.3 Lexical stress placement

The stress rules which have been implemented are a modification of a set of ordered rules developed by Halle and Keyser (1971). Modifications fall into three categories:

1. adjustments due to the condition that input is completely phonemic,
2. reduction of the number of stress levels to 1-stress (primary), 2-stress (stress less than primary) and 0-stress, and
3. addition of special suffix-dependent stress categories.

Additionally, one aspect of the rules has not yet been implemented. Halle's cyclic rules were written to take advantage of known parts of speech. This module was placed after PARSER to utilize this knowledge, but does not utilize it as yet.

Application of the rules proceeds in two phases. The first phase consists of the application of three ordered rules which are applied *cyclically*, first to the root, then to the root and leftmost suffix combined. The process continues with one more suffix adjoined to the string under consideration before each cycle begins, until the end of the word is reached. This *cyclic* phase is devoted solely to the placement of primary stress. Unless otherwise noted, prefixes are considered part of the root.

The second, *noncyclic* phase includes the application to the entire word of ordered rules and reduces all but one of the primary stress marks to secondary or zero stress.

The stress marks used here are ʹ for primary stress and ʺ for secondary stress.

In the following sections, stress placement rules will be given both as formulas and in descriptive (nonsymbolic) form. Each rule which contains more than one case is broken down into cases for which brief descriptions and examples are given. It is important to note that a particular case applies only if the rules for previous cases have not applied, i.e., a maximum of one case per rule is applicable. The subrules in each case are mutually exclusive. The rules are listed in the order in which they apply and are marked either *cyclic* or *noncyclic*.

In this context, *syllable* means a vowel followed by any number of consonants (including none). *Weak syllable* means a short (or nontense) vowel followed by, at most, one consonant before the next vowel. The words *vowel* and *consonant* themselves denote the vocalic and nonvocalic phonetic segment labels output from the letter-to-sound conversion stage, rather than the letters in the original word. In the examples, Klatt symbols are used to represent the segment labels. The short vowels are: AA, EH, IH, AO, UH, AH, AX, AE, and IX. Long vowels are: EY, IY, AY, OW, UW, OY, and AW.

Each formula is a phonetic segment string pattern matching expression. The symbols used in the formulas are defined as follows:

C matches a single consonant. Sub- and superscripts denote lower and upper bounds, respectively, on the number of replications of the preceding term (usually C). For example, C_0 matches any number of consecutive consonants (including none) while C_1^2 matches one or two consonants.

V matches a single vowel.

X and *Y* match segment strings of any length (including null, unless noted otherwise).

Brackets [ ] denote the association of one or more features with a vowel. The features used are long, short, stress, 1-stress, 2-stress, and -stress (lacking stress). The bracket form matches only a vowel with the associated features.

Parentheses ( ) denote an optional term. When a rule with an optional term is tested against a word, matching with the term included is attempted first. Unless otherwise noted, the rule can match the word once at most; if the rule matches with the optional term present, then no match will be attempted with the optional term omitted.

Braces { } denote a list of alternative patterns, separated by tall slashes $/$.

The overall structure of a rule is:

$$V \rightarrow feature \, / \, pattern$$

which translates to:

A vowel receives *feature* in the context of *pattern*

where *pattern* contains the symbol — in the position where the vowel is to appear. The pattern must match the entire word, unless otherwise noted.

A simple example of a rule follows:

$$V \rightarrow [\text{1-stress}] \, / \, X\!-\!C \begin{bmatrix} \text{long} \\ V \end{bmatrix}$$

which means "A vowel receives 1-stress when followed by a consonant and word-final long vowel."

6.3.1 *Main Stress Rule (cyclic)*

1. $V \rightarrow [\text{1-stress}] \, /$

$$X\!-\!C_0 \left\{ \begin{bmatrix} \text{short} \\ V \end{bmatrix} C_0^1 / v \right\} \left\{ \begin{bmatrix} \text{short} \\ V \end{bmatrix} C_0 / v \right\}$$

where X must contain all prefixes (i.e. prefixes are never stressed by this rule).

    a. Assign 1-stress to the vowel in a syllable preceding a weak syllable followed by a morph-final syllable containing a short vowel and zero or more consonants (e.g. **difficult** → DD ′IH FF FF IH KK AH LL TT).

    b. Assign 1-stress to the vowel in a syllable preceding a weak syllable followed by a morph-final vowel (e.g. **oregano** → AO RR ′EH GG AE NN OW).

    c. Assign 1-stress to the vowel in a syllable preceding a vowel followed by a morph-final syllable containing a short vowel and zero or more consonants (e.g. **secretariat**→SS EH KK RR EH TT 'AE RR IY AE TT).

d. Assign 1-stress to the vowel in a syllable preceding a vowel followed by a morph-final vowel (e.g. **oratorio**→AO RR AE TT 'AO RR IY OW).

2. $V \rightarrow [\text{1-stress}] / X\!-\!C_0 \left\{ \left[\begin{matrix} \text{short} \\ V \end{matrix} \right] C_0 / V \right\}$

where X must contain all prefixes.

a. Assign 1-stress to the vowel in a syllable preceding a short vowel and zero or more consonants (e.g. **edit**→'EH DD IH TT, **bitumen**→BB AY TT 'UW MM EH NN).

b. Assign 1-stress to the vowel in a syllable preceding a morph-final vowel (e.g. **agenda**→AE JJ 'EH NN DD AE).

3. $V \rightarrow [\text{1-stress}] / X\!-\!C_0$

where X must contain all prefixes.

a. Assign 1-stress to the vowel in the last syllable (e.g. **stand**→ SS TT 'AE NN DD, **go**→GG 'OW, **parole**→PP AE RR 'OW LL, **hurricane**→HH AH RR IH KK 'AY NN -- reduced to 2-stress by a later rule).

6.3.2 *Exceptions to the Main Stress Rule*

A condition has been placed on the Main Stress Rule relating to assignment of stress, dependent upon four categories of special suffixes. One category is marked to force stress to be placed on either the final or the penultimate syllable of the string under consideration. (It should be noted that later rules may change this assignment.) This stress placement replaces the Main Stress Rule on the cycle in which the special suffix is the rightmost morph. Suffixes in this category include IH FF 'AY (**-ify**), 'AO RR IY (**-ory**), and IH FF IH KK (**-ific**).

The second category of suffixes does not affect stress; the cycle in which such a suffix is rightmost in the domain is skipped. Later cycles, however, do include the suffix as part of their domain of application. Examples are: DD AA MM (**-dom**), MM EH NN TT (**-ment**), and LL EH SS (**-less**).

The third category is a combination of the first two: stress is placed on one of the vowels in the suffix and all three cyclic rules are skipped for the current domain. Examples are: 'IH RR (**-eer**), SS 'EH LL FF (**-self**), and SH 'IH PP (**-ship**).

The last category replaces the Main Stress Rule with the following when the suffix is IH KK (**-ic**): assign 1-stress to the vowel in the first syllable in the word.

6.3.3 *Stressed Syllable Rule (cyclic)*

1. $V \rightarrow$ [1-stress] /

$$X—C_0 \left\{ \left[\begin{array}{c} \text{short} \\ V \end{array} \right] C_0^1 / v \right\} VC_0 \left[\begin{array}{c} \text{1-stress} \\ V \end{array} \right] Y$$

where Y contains no 1-stress and X must contain all prefixes.

   a. Assign 1-stress to the vowel in a syllable preceding a weak syllable followed by a syllable which is followed by the rightmost primary-stressed vowel (e.g. **oxygenate** → ′AA KK SS IH JJ EH NN ′EY TT (stressed on first syllable) -- the stress on the final syllable is later reduced).

   b. Assign 1-stress to the vowel in a syllable preceding a vowel which is followed by a syllable followed, in turn, by the rightmost primary-stressed vowel (e.g. **stereobate** → SS TT ′EH RR IY OW BB ′EY TT (stressed on first syllable) -- the stress on the final syllable is later reduced).

2. $V \rightarrow$ [1-stress] / $X—C_0VC_0 \left[\begin{array}{c} \text{1-stress} \\ V \end{array} \right] Y$

where Y contains no 1-stress and X must contain all prefixes.

   a. Assign 1-stress to the vowel two syllables to the left of the rightmost primary-stressed vowel (e.g. **propaganda** → PP RR ′AA PP AE GG ′AE NN DD AE (stressed on first syllable) -- the stress on this leftmost vowel is later properly reduced).

3. $V \rightarrow$ [1-stress] / $X—C_0 \left[\begin{array}{c} \text{1-stress} \\ V \end{array} \right] Y$

where Y contains no 1-stress and X must contain all prefixes.

   a. Assign 1-stress to the vowel one syllable to the left of the rightmost primary-stressed vowel (e.g. **hormone** → HH ′AO RR MM ′OW NN -- the stress on the final vowel is later reduced).

6.3.4 *Alternating Stress Rule (cyclic)*

1. $V \rightarrow$ [1-stress] / $X—C_0VVC_0 \left[\begin{array}{c} \text{1-stress} \\ V \end{array} \right] C_0$

a. Assign 1-stress to the vowel three syllables to the left of a primary-stressed vowel occurring in the last syllable if the following syllable contains only a vowel (e.g. **heliotrope**→ HH ′IY LL IY OW TT RR ′OW PP -- the stress in the last syllable is later reduced).

$$2. \text{ V} \rightarrow [\text{1-stress}] / X\!\!-\!\!C_0VC_0 \left[\begin{array}{c} \text{1-stress} \\ \text{V} \end{array} \right] C_0$$

a. Assign 1-stress to the vowel two syllables to the left of a primary-stressed vowel occurring in the last syllable (e.g. **gelatinate**→JJ ′EH LL ′AE TT IH NN ′EY TT -- the stress in the first syllable is later deleted; stress in the last syllable is later reduced).

6.3.5 *Destressing Rule (noncyclic)*

This rule is the first destressing phase wherein the selected stressed vowels are reduced in stress and tenseness. The action (→ -stress) in the rules below indicates that the stress marking for the selected vowel is removed. In addition, if the destressed vowel is long, it is shortened as follows: EY → AE, IY → EH, AY → IH, OW → AA, or UW → UH (OY and AW are not modified).

$$1. \text{ V} \rightarrow [\text{-stress}] / C_0VC_0X\!\!-\!\!C \left[\begin{array}{c} \text{stress} \\ \text{V} \end{array} \right] Y$$

where the rule may apply more than once per word.

a. Shorten and destress any vowel not in the first syllable which is followed by a single consonant and a stressed vowel (e.g. **instrumental**→′IH NN SS TT RR (′)UW MM ′EH NN TT AE LL -- the segment UW is reduced to UH, and later to AX).

$$2. \text{ V} \rightarrow [\text{-stress}] / C_0 \left[\begin{array}{c} \text{short} \\ \underline{} \end{array} \right] C \left[\begin{array}{c} \text{stress} \\ \text{V} \end{array} \right] X$$

where the rule may apply in addition to the previous rule.

a. Destress a nonlong vowel in the first syllable which is followed by a single consonant and a stressed vowel (e.g. **gelatinate**→JJ (′)EH LL ′AE TT ′IH NN ′EY TT).

6.3.6 *Compound Stress Rule (noncyclic)*

This rule, as developed by Halle, applies to both compounds and noncompounds. The assumption with letter-to-phonetic segment rules is that words are composed

of affixes and only one root. Therefore, as this rule applies to words converted by letter-to-segment rules in the module, it applies to noncompounds only, and its effect is to locate the primary stress which is to be retained. The action (V →
retain) indicates that 1-stress is to be reduced to 2-stress on all but the matched vowel.

1. $V \rightarrow \text{retain} / X \left[\begin{array}{c} \text{1-stress} \\ \underline{} \end{array} \right] Y \, VC_0 \; \text{IY}$

   where Y does not contain 1-stress.

       a. Retain 1-stress on a vowel if it is followed by at least one syllable and a word-final unstressed IY. Reduce all other 1-stress to 2-stress (e.g. **legendary** → LL ′EH JJ EH NN DD (′ → ″)AE RR IY).

2. $V \rightarrow \text{retain} / X \left[\begin{array}{c} \overline{} \\ \text{1-stress} \end{array} \right] Y \, VC_0$

   where Y does not contain 1-stress.

       a. Retain 1-stress on a vowel if it is followed by a string of one or more syllables without primary stress. Reduce all other 1-stress to 2-stress (e.g. **hurricane** → HH ′AH RR IH KK (′ → ″)EY NN, **gastritis** → GG (′ → ″)AE SS TT RR ′AY TT IH SS, **trinitarian** → TT RR (′ → ″)IH NN IH TT ′AE RR IY AX NN).

3. $V \rightarrow \text{retain} / X \left[\begin{array}{c} \overline{} \\ \text{1-stress} \end{array} \right] Y$

   where Y does not contain 1-stress.

       a. Retain 1-stress on the only vowel to which it has been assigned (e.g. **stand** → SS TT ′AE NN DD, **edit** → ′EH DD IH TT, **difficult** → DD ′IH FF IH KK AH LL TT).

This rule also includes a condition dependent upon two categories of special suffixes. Those suffixes discussed with the Main Stress Rule which do not affect stress placement are excepted from the domain of the Compound Stress Rule if they are either word-final or precede another word-final suffix in the same category. The other category of suffixes is marked for special stress retention (i.e. is allowed to be part of the Y pattern even though stressed). These suffixes are: IH ZZ AX MM (**-ism**), IH VV (**-ive**), and AE TT (vowel-reduced **-ate**).

6.3.7 *Strong First Syllable Rule (noncyclic)*

1. $V \rightarrow$ 2-stress $/ C_0 \left[\begin{array}{c} \text{-stress, long} \\ \underline{} \end{array} \right] X$

   a. Assign 2-stress to the vowel in the first syllable if it is long (e.g. **hydrosanitation** → HH "AY DD RR OW SS 'AE NN IH TT 'EY SH AX NN, **dielectric** → DD "AY 'EH LL 'EH KK TT RR IH KK).

2. $V \rightarrow$ 2-stress $/ C_0 \left[\begin{array}{c} \text{-stress} \\ \underline{} \end{array} \right] C_2 X$

   a. Assign 2-stress to the vowel in the first syllable if it is followed by at least two consonants (e.g. **circumnavigation** → SS "AH RR KK AH MM NN 'AE VV IH GG 'EY SH AX NN).

6.3.8 *Cursory Rule*

1. $V \rightarrow$ 2-stress $/ Y \left[\begin{array}{c} \text{1-stress} \\ \text{V} \end{array} \right] C_0 \text{—CV} X$

   where Y contains no 1-stress.

   a. The vowel following the primary-stressed vowel, if it is not the last vowel in the word, is shortened and its stress removed (e.g. **infirmary** → "IH NN FF 'AH RR MM (")AE RR IY, **cursory** → KK 'AH RR SS (")AO RR IY, **curative** → KK YY 'UH RR (")AE TT IH VV).

This has provision for one class of exceptional suffixes. If the pattern CV*X* in the rule above matches a string of suffixes from the "ignored" category of the Main Stress Rule, then the Cursory Rule is suppressed for this case.

6.3.9 *Vowel Reduction Rule*

This rule reduces unstressed short vowels to the appropriate schwa. The action (V → reduce) indicates that EH and IH are changed to IX while all other short vowels are changed to AX.

1. $V \rightarrow$ reduce $/ X \left[\begin{array}{c} \text{-stress, short} \\ \underline{} \end{array} \right] Y$

   where the rule may match more than once per word.

   a. Reduce EH and IH to IX if not stressed (e.g. **ptolemaic** → TT 'AO LL IX MM 'EY IX KK).

   b. Reduce other short unstressed vowels to AX (e.g. **curator** → KK 'UH RR AX TT AX RR).

It should be noted that stress may be further reduced in PHONO1 (see Chapter 8) according to parts of speech and phrasing.

6.4 An example

Figure 6-4 is an example of the application of both the letter-to-sound and the stress rules. The results after each of the stages of the letter-to-sound rules, and after each of the stress rules, are given. There are two complete cycles of the cyclic stress rules, followed by the noncyclic rules. The rules are followed by application of syllabification rules.

```
Sound1: Stripped  : M  U  L  T  I  <  P  A  G  I  N  >  A
     T  E  >  E  D
Sound1: Consonants: ?? ?? ?? ?? ?? ?? PP ?? JJ ?? NN ??
     ?? ?? ?? ?? ?? ??
Sound1: Prefixes  : MM AX LL TT IH < PP ?? JJ ?? NN ?? ??
     ?? ?? ?? ?? ??
Sound1: Vowels    : MM AX LL TT IH < PP AE JJ IH NN ?? ??
     ?? ?? ?? ?? ??
Sound1: Suffixes  : MM AX LL TT IH < PP AE JJ IH NN > EY
     TT > IH DD
Sound1: Apply MSR : MM AX LL TT IH < PP 'AE JJ IH NN
Sound1: Apply SSR : MM AX LL TT IH < PP 'AE JJ IH NN
Sound1: Apply ASR : MM AX LL TT IH < PP 'AE JJ IH NN
Sound1: Apply MSR : MM AX LL TT IH < PP 'AE JJ IH NN >
     'EY TT
Sound1: Apply SSR : MM AX LL TT IH < PP 'AE JJ IH NN >
     'EY TT
Sound1: Apply ASR : MM AX LL TT IH < PP 'AE JJ IH NN >
     'EY TT
Sound1: Skipping  : MM AX LL TT IH < PP 'AE JJ IH NN >
     'EY TT > IH DD
Sound1: Destress  : MM AX LL TT IH < PP 'AE JJ IH NN >
     'EY TT > IH DD
Sound1: Compound  : MM AX LL TT IH < PP 'AE JJ IH NN >
     "EY TT > IH DD
Sound1: Strong 1st: MM "AX LL TT IH < PP 'AE JJ IH NN >
     "EY TT > IH DD
Sound1: Cursory   : MM "AX LL TT IH < PP 'AE JJ IH NN >
     "EY TT > IH DD
Sound1: Reduce    : MM "AX LL TT IX < PP 'AE JJ IX NN >
     "EY TT > IX DD
 SOUND1:  MM "AX LL - TT IX * - PP 'AE - JJ IX NN * - "EY
     TT * - IX DD
```

Figure 6-4: Example of letter-to-sound and stress rule operation

69

II

Synthesis

7

Survey of speech synthesis technology

7.1 Overview

This brief review of speech synthesis technology is concerned primarily with practical methods of generating spoken messages by computers or special-purpose devices. Basic research directed at modeling articulatory-to-acoustic transformations (Flanagan *et al.*, 1975; Flanagan and Ishizaka, 1976) will not be reviewed.

7.1.1 *Applications*

Applications for synthetic speech output fall into four broad categories:

1. Single word responses (e.g. Speak-'N-Spell)
2. A limited set of messages within a rigid syntactic framework (e.g. telephone number information)
3. Large, fixed vocabulary with general English syntax (e.g. teaching machine lessons)
4. Unrestricted text to speech (e.g. a reading machine for the blind)

The degree of generality and difficulty increases considerably from 1 to 4. Prerecorded messages work well for single-word response applications, whereas an increasing knowledge of the acoustic-phonetic characteristics of speech, phonology, and syntax is required for satisfactory synthesis of general English.

7.1.2 *Three methods of employing MITalk modules*

The entire MITalk text-to-speech system can be used in applications falling in category 4 above, or pieces of the MITalk synthesis routines might be used in other applications. For example, if an abstract phonemic and syntactic representation for an utterance can be stored in the computer or derived by linguistic rules, only modules beginning with PHONO2 in Figure 7-1 are needed. Speech represented in this way requires storage of only about 100 bits per second.

Another way to use the synthesis routines to produce even more natural sounding speech (at a cost in bits and human intervention) is to begin by specifying the input to the phonetic component PHONET in Figure 7-1. If durations and fundamental frequency values are taken from a natural recording rather than being computed by rule, a remarkably human voice quality is achieved. Storage of about 250 bits per second of speech is required, and of course, considerable effort is required to prepare the input representation.

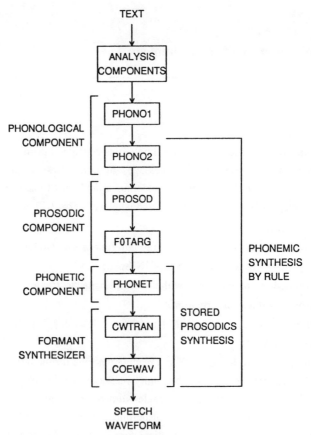

Figure 7-1: Synthesis blocks of the MITalk system

7.2 Background

Automatic voice response machines, based on the principle of concatenating prerecorded speech waveforms, have been used to provide such information as time of day and weather reports by telephone since the early 1930s. More recently, voice response systems have been used to provide rapid telephone access to information stored in computers in such diverse areas as inventory control, credit inquiries, bank balance information, and shipping status inquiries. In most cases, the request can be keyed in by touch-tone telephone.

The earliest voice response units were analog systems in which the vocabulary elements (words and short phrases) were stored as analog recordings of speech waveforms. Many currently available audio response units still operate on this principle (Homsby, 1972). Systems of this type have served very well in a variety of applications where the vocabulary consists of a small number of words and where the messages are simple and follow a rather rigid format. However, there are a number of limitations of such systems which make them unsatisfactory for more general applications, such as automatic conversion of English text to speech.

Figure WORD-BLEND illustrates some of the differences between words spoken in isolation and the same words put together in a fluently spoken sentence. Not only are most words considerably shorter, but there are acoustic changes at the boundaries between words due to coarticulation, and due to phonological rules that change the pronunciation of words in certain sentence contexts. Furthermore, the intonation, rhythm, and stress pattern appropriate to the sentence cannot be synthesized if one simply concatenates prerecorded words. These prosodic qualities turn out to be extremely important. Words that are perfectly intelligible in isolation seem to come too fast and in a disconnected manner when the words are concatenated in such a way that the prosody is wrong.

Thus simple word concatenation schemes have severe limitations as audio response units. In contrast, there are several newer techniques under development that do not have these limitations. These techniques range from complex systems for speech synthesis-by-rule (where a synthetic waveform is computed from a knowledge of linguistic and acoustic rules), to relatively simple systems for creating speech utterances by concatenating prerecorded speech waveform chunks smaller than a word (using vocoder analysis-synthesis technology to gain flexibility in reassembly).

Speech synthesis techniques have been reviewed in Flanagan and Rabiner (1973), Klatt (1974), and Rabiner and Schafer (1976). We describe here some of the current techniques that have been employed. Of particular interest are criteria by which one selects an inventory of basic speech units to be used in utterance assembly, how one selects a method of unit concatenation, and how to specify sentence-level prosodic variables.

7.3 Synthesis techniques

The techniques to be covered in this section include systems for forming messages out of words as the basic units, out of syllables and diphones as the basic units, and out of phonemes as the basic units.

7.3.1 *Word assembly*

7.3.1.1 *Prerecorded words and phrases*   Early methods of spoken message assembly used prerecorded words (or whole phrases) that were concatenated into sentences (Homsby, 1972; Chapman, 1971; Buron, 1968). Brief pauses were in-

73

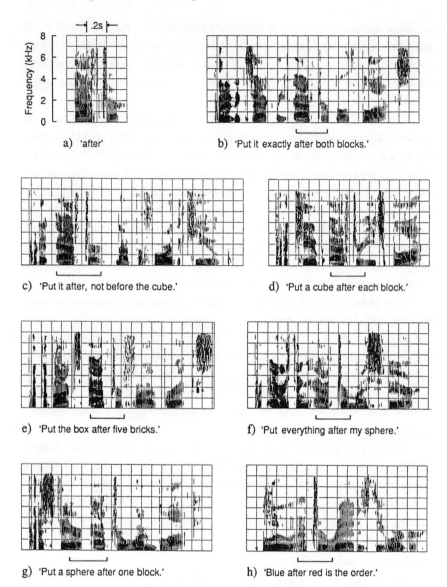

Figure 7-2: An example of the differences between words spoken in isolation and words spoken as a continuous utterance

serted between words, and a reasonable sentence intonation contour was realized by restricting a given prerecorded element to only certain utterance positions. A great deal of care was taken in speaking, recording, and editing the basic vocabulary items.

Word storage has involved various analog and digital techniques that range from recording each word into a half-second slot on a rotating drum, to sophisticated digital techniques for reducing the number of bits that must be stored. Digital methods for representing speech waveforms are reviewed by Rabiner and Schafer (1976) and by Jayant (1974). One remarkable technique developed at Texas Instruments (Wiggins, 1979) involves storing a 1000 bit-per-second linear-prediction representation for each word on integrated circuit chips having a capacity of 200 seconds of speech, and using an IC linear-prediction synthesizer to play selected words (all of this circuitry being offered at $50 in the Speak-'N-Spell children's toy).

7.3.1.2 Formant vocoding of words Rabiner *et al.* (1971a) suggested that one could get rid of the choppiness of waveform concatenation by extracting formant trajectories for each prerecorded word and smoothing formant parameter tracks across word boundaries before formant vocoder resynthesis. A second advantage of formant analysis-synthesis of the words that make up a synthetic utterance is that the duration pattern and fundamental frequency contour can be adjusted to match the accent pattern, rhythm, and intonation requirements of the sentence to be produced. The technique has been used successfully in telephone number synthesis where a known prosodic contour could be superimposed (for example, a pause and a "continuation rise" intonation can be placed just before the fourth digit of a seven digit telephone number). However, the authors did not offer general prosodic rules for sentence synthesis.

7.3.1.3 Linear-prediction coded words Olive (1974) later showed that a similar system could be based on linear prediction encoding. Furthermore, it was determined that a correct fundamental frequency contour for a sentence was perceptually more important than the exact duplication of the durational pattern or careful smoothing of the formant transitions between words.

The advantage of the prerecorded word as a unit is ease of bringing up a limited audio response unit. The disadvantages are that: 1) large vocabularies are impractical, and 2) general timing and fundamental frequency rules that adjust the prosodic characteristics of a word as a function of sentence structure are more easily defined at a segmental level. For example, only the final vowel and postvocalic consonants of a word are lengthened at phrase and clause boundaries (Klatt, 1976b).

75

7.3.2 *Syllables and diphones*

Instead of using words as the basic building blocks for sentence production, a smaller inventory of basic units is required if arbitrary English sentences are to be synthesized. The inventory of basic speech units must satisfy several requirements, including: 1) the ability to construct any English word by concatenating the units one after another, and 2) the ability to change duration, intensity and fundamental frequency according to the demands of the sentence syntax and stress pattern in such a way as to produce speech that is both intelligible and natural.

7.3.2.1 *Syllables*   The intuitive notion of the syllable as the basic unit has considerable theoretical appeal. Any English word can be broken into syllables consisting of a vowel nucleus and adjacent consonants. Linguists have been unable to agree on objective criteria for assigning consonants to a particular vowel nucleus in certain ambiguous cases such as "butter", but an arbitrary decision can be made for synthesis purposes.

The greatest theoretical advantage of the syllable concerns the way that acoustic characteristics of most consonant-vowel transitions are preserved. Context-conditioned acoustic changes to consonants are automatically present to a great extent when the syllable is chosen as the basic unit, but not when smaller units such as the phoneme are concatenated.

The disadvantages of the syllable are: 1) coarticulation across syllable boundaries is not treated, and this coarticulation can be just as important as within-syllable coarticulation, 2) if prerecorded syllables are stored in the form of waveforms, there is no way to mimic the prosodic contour of the intended message, and 3) the syllable inventory for general English is very large. There are currently no syllable-based systems for speech generation.

7.3.2.2 *Demisyllables*   The last two disadvantages of a syllable-based scheme might be overcome by replacing syllables by demisyllables. The demisyllable is defined as half of a syllable, either the set of initial consonants plus half of the vowel, or the second half of the vowel plus any postvocalic consonants (Fujimura and Lovins, 1978; Lovins and Fujimura, 1976). For example, the word "construct" would be divided into **co-, -on, stru-,** and **-uct.** It is claimed that there are less than 1000 demisyllables needed to synthesize any English utterance. Each demisyllable can be represented in terms of a set of linear prediction frames. Concatenation rules include some smoothing across demisyllable boundaries. The problems with demisyllable-based approaches are: 1) how to smooth across demisyllable boundaries to simulate natural coarticulation, and 2) how to adjust durations to match the desired pattern for a sentence. The latter problem is serious because lengthening and shortening of speech tends to take place during the steady-state portions of sustainable phonetic segments, whereas the demisyllable is a mixture of portions of steady states and transitions.

7.3.2.3 *Diphones* The diphone is defined as half of one phone followed by half of the next phone. Peterson *et al.* (1958), and Wang and Peterson (1958) were the first to propose speech synthesis by diphone concatenation. They argued that the diphone is a natural unit for synthesis because the coarticulatory influence of one phoneme does not usually extend much further than halfway into the next phoneme. Since diphone junctures are usually at articulatory steady states, minimal smoothing should be required between adjacent diphones. They speculated that several thousand diphones would be required if real speech waveform segments were used, because each of the diphones would have to be recorded at several different durations and with several different pitch contours.

Dixon and Maxey (1968) later showed that highly intelligible synthetic speech could be fashioned from diphones defined in terms of sets of control parameter time functions to control a formant synthesizer. Only about 1500 diphone elements were required (40 phonemes followed by almost any of 40 phonemes) because duration, intensity, and fundamental frequency could be adjusted independently (by hand, in their case) to take into account effects of stress, intonation, and rhythm. Unfortunately, their diphone definitions were never published.

Olive (1977) proposed that diphones could be defined in terms of two linear-prediction pseudo-area-function targets and a linear transition between them. If durations and fundamental frequency were specified by hand, Olive and Spickenagle (1976) showed that quite natural intelligible speech could be produced by this method of linear-prediction diphone synthesis. The specification of durational rules is a problem, just as in the case of demisyllables, because the most natural framework for stating rules is in terms of phonetic segments.

7.3.2.4 *Prosodic rules* Relatively little work on general prosodic rules has been published within the context of syllable, demisyllable, and diphone concatenation systems. Olive (1974) proposed an unusual set of word-based fundamental frequency rules that depend on syntactic structure, but are not influenced by the stress pattern within a word. Recent work at Bell Laboratories by Liberman and Pierrehumbert on rules for the specification of durations and fundamental frequency contours in a diphone-based system shows considerable promise (Pierrehumbert, 1979).

7.3.3 *Phonemic synthesis-by-rule*

7.3.3.1 Phoneme synthesis from natural speech   Phonemes have been considered as basic speech units because there are only about 40 of them in English, and there are good linguistic reasons for representing speech by phonemes. Unfortunately, there is no possibility of extracting phonemic-sized chunks from natural speech in such a way that they can be reassembled into new utterances because of the large acoustic changes to a phoneme that occur in different phonetic environments. Phonemes are a good starting point for terminal-analog speech synthesis-by-rule programs (discussed below) because the rule programs can utilize a complex set of rules to predict acoustic changes in different phonetic environments, but some other unit is needed for a concatenation scheme.

7.3.3.2 Formant-based synthesis strategies   Synthesis-by-rule schemes employing a formant-resonator speech synthesizer range from the excellent early work of Holmes *et al.* (1964) to the synthesis of intelligible speech from an input representation consisting of an abstract linguistic description (Mattingly, 1968b; Coker, 1967; Coker *et al.*, 1973; Klatt, 1976a). The formant synthesizer accepts input time functions that determine formant frequencies, voicing, friction, and aspiration source amplitudes, fundamental frequency, and individual formant amplitudes for fricatives. The synthesizer produces an output waveform that is intended to approximate the perceptually most relevant acoustic characteristics of speech.

Formant synthesizers come in many different configurations (Dudley *et al.*, 1939; Cooper *et al.*, 1951; Lawrence, 1953; Stevens *et al.*, 1953; Rosen, 1958; Tomlinson, 1966; Liljencrants, 1968; Gold and Rabiner, 1968; Klatt, 1972; Flanagan *et al.*, 1975). Holmes (1961, 1973) has shown that terminal-analog methods of speech synthesis are capable of generating synthetic speech that is indistinguishable from the original recording of a talker if the parameter values are properly chosen.

7.3.3.3 Control strategy   Control parameter values such as formant frequency motions are determined from a phonetic transcription of the intended sentence using a set of heuristic rules. In one case (Coker, 1967), the rules manipulate a simplified articulatory model of the vocal tract. Other rule programs manipulate formant values directly, using heuristics such as the locus theory (Holmes *et al.*, 1964), or a modified locus theory (Klatt, 1979b).

In a fully automatic system, the phonetic transcription, durations, stress, and fundamental frequency targets are derived from an abstract syntactic and phonemic representation for a sentence by a set of rules that approximate a phonological description of English (Klatt, 1976a, 1979a; O'Shaughnessy, 1977; Umeda, 1977).

The input to the rules includes phonemes, stress, word and morpheme boundaries, and syntactic structure.

In time, these methods ought to be able to produce highly intelligible natural speech, but present results are frequently perceived to be somewhat unnatural and machine-like. This appears to be due mainly to the intricate complexity of the speech code and the fact that not all of the rules are known at this time. There is a particular need to improve on the specification of fundamental frequency and duration algorithms, perhaps by making incremental improvements to current algorithms (Umeda, 1976; Klatt, 1979a; Maeda, 1974; O'Shaughnessy, 1977; Pierre-humbert, 1979).

7.4 Applications

7.4.1 *Synthesis of arbitrary English sentences*

From the above discussion, it should be clear that there are a number of promising methods for synthesizing general English. To generate a particular utterance, one must know 1) the phonemic (or phonetic) representation for each word, 2) the stress pattern for each word, 3) aspects of the syntactic structure of the sentence, and 4) the locations of any words that are to receive semantic focus. This information would have to be stored in the computer for each utterance to be synthesized, or it might be generated from a deep-structure representation of the concept to be expressed (Woods *et al.*, 1976; Young and Fallside, 1979).

7.4.2 *Synthesis of arbitrary English names*

Research at Bell Laboratories (Denes, 1979; Liberman, 1979; Olive, 1979) is directed at the ability to synthesize any name from a telephone directory for application in automated directory assistance. The linguistic problems associated with converting spelling to a phonetic representation and stress pattern are severe since it is sometimes necessary to guess the native language of the individual before a good rendering of the pronunciation is possible (Liberman, 1979). Once a phonetic representation has been derived, this experimental system uses diphone synthesis (Olive, 1979) to generate a waveform.

7.4.3 *Text-to-speech conversion*

The transformation of English text to speech is a much more formidable problem than the synthesis of an arbitrary sentence from a knowledge of its underlying linguistic representation. The text does not indicate everything that one would like to know (unless one builds a machine that can recognize the meaning of the text, and thereby disambiguate (frequently occurring) syntactic ambiguities, and determine semantic focus relations).

We have argued in Chapters 2-6 that in order to transform English text to speech, one must first try to derive an underlying abstract linguistic representation for the text. There are at least two reasons why a direct approach is suboptimal: 1) rules for pronouncing words must take into consideration morphemic structure (e.g. consider the pronunciation of the **th** of **outhouse**) and syntactic structure (e.g. there exist many noun-verb ambiguities in English such as **perm'it - p'ermit**), and 2) sentence duration pattern, and fundamental frequency contour depend, to a major extent, on the syntactic structure of the sentence.

There are currently several text-to-speech systems under development in the United States (Nye *et al.*, 1973; Kurzweil, 1976; Caldwell, 1979; Morris, 1979) and elsewhere (Carlson and Granstrom, 1976). The simplest approach is to devise a set of heuristic letter-to-sound rules and then create an exceptions dictionary for frequently occurring words that are processed incorrectly by the letter-to-sound rules (Kurzweil, 1976). The exceptions dictionary is then augmented by function words that are useful for parsing strategies. The phonetic representation for a sentence that is derived in this way serves as the input to a synthesis-by-rule device such as Votrax (Gagnon, 1978) or a software synthesis-by-rule program.

The MITalk system represents a more ambitious approach of generalized morphemic analysis, so as to do a better job of figuring out the pronunciation of words and to better assign parts of speech to each word, and thereby compute phrase and clause boundaries with greater accuracy. The real question is whether current algorithms are good enough to make automatic text-to-speech output acceptable to the user. There is clear indication that motivated users (such as the blind) benefit from these devices after a period of acclimation, but considerable concentration is required.

8

The phonological component

8.1 Overview

The phonological component PHONOL accepts input from the text analysis routines (described in Chapters 2-6) and produces an output that is sent to the prosodic component PROSOD (to be described in Chapter 9). PHONOL is divided into two modules PHONO1 and PHONO2. PHONO1 uses information from the PARSER to specify the syntactic markers that influence the spoken output. PHONO2 contains a set of segmental recoding rules that are activated to select an appropriate allophone for each phoneme, and to simplify certain unstressed phonetic sequences. Rules for pausing are included in both PHONO1 and PHONO2. Pauses of various durations are inserted at sentence boundaries, clause boundaries, and locations in the text of certain punctuation marks such as commas. Some additional pauses are introduced in longer phrases and slow speaking rate so that the talker does not seem to have an inhuman supply of breath.

8.1.1 *Synthesis-by-rule*

If a subset of the MITalk system is to be used as a speech-synthesis-by-rule program by deleting the analysis modules, the preferred first module would be PHONO2 or PROSOD. The input to the system would then be an abstract representation containing phonemes, lexical stress symbols, and syntactic structure symbols for each sentence to be synthesized. Applications for this mode of speech generation by computer include cases where an abstract syntactic and phonemic representation for each sentence is known or can be computed. Speech quality will be better than in the text-to-speech case because analysis errors can be avoided, but considerable linguistic sophistication is required of users. Storage requirements for sentences are minimal -- on the order of 100 bits per sentence.

8.2 Input representation for a sentence

The input to PHONO1 consists of a phonemic pronunciation for each word (i.e. as spoken in isolation), lexical stress pattern, and syntactic information concerning part of speech and phrasal structure. The output from PHONO1 consists of a single string of symbols for each sentence.

The symbol inventory used in PHONO1 and PHONO2 is shown in Table 8-1, and includes 55 phonetic segments, three stress markers, four types of boundary indicators, and five syntactic structure indicators. It will be necessary to augment the inventory of syntactic and semantic symbols in the future, but those listed in the table are all that seem to be needed for a first-order approximation to an acceptable prosodic pattern. An example of the use of some of these symbols to specify the utterance "The old man sat in a rocker" is provided in Figure 8-1.

```
The old man sat in a rocker.
  SOUND1:   DH 'AH
  SOUND1:   'OW LL DD
  SOUND1:   MM 'AE NN
  SOUND1:   SS 'AE TT
  SOUND1:   'IH NN
  SOUND1:   AX
  SOUND1:   RR 'AA KK * - ER
  SOUND1:   .
  SOUND1: <EOF>
  PHONO1: Function word: DH AH
  PHONO1: Content word:  'OW LL DD
  PHONO1: Content word:  MM 'AE NN [End NOUN phrase]
  PHONO1: Content word:  SS 'AE TT
  PHONO1: Function word: IH NN
  PHONO1: Function word: AX
  PHONO1: Content word:  RR 'AA KK * - ER
  PHONO1: Punctuation:   .
  PHONO1: <EOF>
   PHONO2: Function word: DH IY
   PHONO2: Content word:  'OW LX DD
   PHONO2: Content word:  MM 'AE NN [End NOUN phrase]
   PHONO2: Content word:  SS 'AE DX
   PHONO2: Function word: IH NN
   PHONO2: Function word: AX
   PHONO2: Content word:  RR 'AA KK * - ER
   PHONO2: Punctuation:   .
   PHONO2: <EOF>
```

Figure 8-1: Example of PHONO1 and PHONO2 processing

8.2.1 *Phonemic inventory*

A traditional phonemic analysis of English is assumed, except for the special cases listed below:

1. The diphthongs AY, AW, OW, YU are considered to be single phonemes rather than, e.g., AY = AA+YY or AA+IY or AA+IH because none of the two-phoneme alternatives result in particularly simple rules to describe durational behavior and formant trajectories.

2. The affricates CH and JJ are considered to be single phonemes rather than, e.g., CH = TT+SH for the same reasons.

3. Vowel+RR syllabic nuclei are treated internally as the special vowel nuclei IXR ("beer"), EXR ("bear"), AXR ("bar"), OXR ("boar"), and UXR ("pure").

4. Words like "player" and "buyer" should be transcribed with two syllables, i.e., EY+ER and AY+ER.

5. Syllabic consonants appear in words like "butter" BB ′AH TT ER (phonetically BB AH DX ER), "button" BB ′AH TT EN, "bottle" BB ′AA TT EL, and "pop'em" PP ′AA PP EM.

6. The dental flap (DX), glottalized TT (TQ), and velarized LL (LX) are not really phonemes, but are allophones inserted in lexical forms by rules to be described.

7. The pseudo-vowel AXP is inserted between a plosive and a following pause in order to cause the plosive to be released.

8.2.2 *Lexical stress*

Each stressed vowel in the input to PHONO1 is preceded by a stress symbol (′ or ″), where ′ is primary lexical stress (reserved for vowels in open-class content words, only one 1-stress per word). The secondary lexical stress, ″, is used in some content words (e.g. the first syllable of "demonstration"), in compounds (e.g. the second syllable of "baseball"), in the strongest syllable of polysyllabic function words (e.g. "until"), and for pronouns (excluding personal pronouns like "his").

8.2.3 *Stress reduction in function words*

Content words such as nouns, adjectives, adverbs, and main verbs are expected to have one primary lexical stress in the input to PHONO1. Many (but not all) closed-class function words are reduced in stress in PHONO1 so that they do not receive a pitch gesture associated with primary stress. For example, determiners, conjunctions, auxiliary verbs, and personal pronouns are reduced in stress.

Each word of an utterance to be synthesized must be immediately preceded by a word boundary symbol. The distinction between content and function words is indicated by using C: and F:. Open-class words (nouns, verbs, adjectives, and adverbs) are content words; all others are function words. Later modules use this information to select plausible pause locations (between a content word and a function word) in long phrases.

8.2.4 *Syntactic structure*

Syntactic structure symbols are important determiners of sentence stress, rhythm, and intonation. Syntactic structure symbols appear just before the word boundary symbol. Only one syntactic marker can appear at a given sentence position. The strongest syntactic boundary symbol is always used.

An utterance must end with either a period "." signaling a final fall in intonation, or a question mark ")?" signaling the intonation pattern appropriate for yes-no

Table 8-1: Klatt symbols used in the synthesis modules

Vowels

AA B*o*b	AE b*a*t	AH b*u*t	AO b*ough*t	AW b*ou*t
AX *a*bout	AXR b*a*r	AY b*i*te	EH b*e*t	ER b*ir*d
EXR b*ear*	EY b*ai*t	IH b*i*t	IX imp*u*nity	IXR b*ee*r
IY b*ee*t	OW b*oa*t	OXR b*oar*	OY b*o*y	UH b*oo*k
UW b*oo*t	UXR p*oor*	YU b*eau*ty		

Sonorant Consonants

EL bott*le*	HH *h*at	HX the *h*urrah	LL *l*et	LX bi*ll*
RR *r*ent	RX fi*r*e	WW *w*et	WH *wh*ich	YY *y*et

Nasals

EM keep'*em*	EN butt*on*	MM *m*et	NN *n*et	NG si*ng*

Fricatives

DH *th*at	FF *f*in	SS *s*at	SH *sh*in	TH *th*in
VV *v*at	ZZ *z*oo	ZH a*z*ure		

Plosives

BB *b*et	DD *d*ebt	DX bu*tt*er	GG *g*ore	GP *g*ive
KK *c*ore	KP *k*een	PP *p*et	TT *t*en	TQ a*t* Alan

Affricates

CH *ch*in	JJ *g*in

Pseudo-vowel

AXP Plosive release

Stress Symbols

' or 1	primary lexical stress	" or 2	secondary lexical stress

Word and Morpheme Boundaries

–	syllable boundary (ignored)	*	morpheme boundary
C:	begin content word	F:	begin function word

Syntactic Structure

.	end of declarative utterance	)?	end of yes/no question
,	orthographic comma	)N	end of noun phrase
)P	potential breath pause	)C	end of clause

---

questions. If clauses are conjoined, a syntactic symbol is placed just before the conjunction. If a comma could be placed in the orthographic rendition of the desired utterance, then the syntactic comma symbol "," should be inserted. Syntactic commas are treated as full clause boundaries in the rules; they are used to list a series of items and to otherwise break up larger units into chunks in order to facilitate perceptual processing.

The end of a noun phrase is indicated by)N. Segments in the syllable prior to a syntactic boundary are lengthened. Based on the results of Carlson *et al.* (1979), an exception is suggested in that any)N following a noun phrase that contains only one primary-stressed content word should be erased. The NP + VP is then spoken as a single phonological phrase with no internal phrase-final lengthening and no fall-rise F0 contour to set off the noun phrase from the verb phrase.

8.3 Comparison between ideal synthesis input and system performance

An example of the output of the analysis routines of MITalk is presented in Section 8.7 at the end of this chapter. Examples where the analysis routines made an "error" are underlined in Section 8.7, and the seriousness of the error is indicated by a footnote for those errors deemed detrimental to perception. The word "error" is put in quotation marks to emphasize that an error made by an analysis routine need not be an error in some abstract linguistic sense, but only an error in the sense that the symbol is not the one that is desired by the synthesis routines.

There are over 200 words in the sample text of Section 8.7 and over 1000 phonetic segments.

8.3.1 *Phonetic transcription "errors"*

There are 25 phonetic transcription errors, all minor, most of which concern the difference between "I" and schwa. There do not seem to be serious problems with the letter-to-sound rules, in part because they are rarely activated, i.e., about five percent of the time. The rate at which phonetic errors are produced during MITalk analysis, about one percent (i.e. about one word in twenty is in error in running text), is quite good in comparison with text-to-speech systems that rely more heavily on letter-to-sound rules. Sentence intelligibility and comprehension scores are very high given the current analysis abilities.

8.3.2 *Stress "errors"*

There are 12 errors involving lexical stress assignment. Certain common words such as "might" and "each" should be marked with primary lexical stress in the lexicon because they almost always attract a certain amount of semantic focus, but they are not currently assigned stress. Other words, such as "prerecorded", are not handled correctly by the morphological stress reassignment rules.

8.3.3 *Morpheme boundary problems*

The morpheme boundary symbol * is used in the synthesis rules to prevent words like **back*ache** from having a strongly aspirated medial KK. However, in a word such as **applic*ation**, a restructuring of syllable boundaries is desirable so that the medial KK is strongly aspirated. In the present rule system it is not, since the * is in the way. Perhaps the morpheme boundary symbol should be deleted between a root and bound suffix (but not between two root morphemes). In other related cases, the boundary prevents desired resyllabification processes so that **automatic*al*ly** comes out as a six-syllable word, rather than the more normal AO DX - AX - MM 'AE DX - IH - KK LL IY.

8.3.4 *Syntactic "errors"*

There are a rather large number of syntactic "errors" involving the incorrect assignment of phrase and clause boundary locations. There are seven examples of a missing end-of-phrase)N symbol, one missing end-of-clause)C symbol, and 17 cases where an end-of-clause symbol was incorrectly inserted between words with the intent to break up longer phrasal units. This had undesirable perceptual implications. The current algorithm intentionally adds extra clause boundary symbols in order to break up the synthesis into smaller groups of words set off by pauses and intonation breaks. These extra pauses were added because the computer seemed to be able to go for long stretches without "pausing for breath". The trade-off between adding breath pauses to break the speech up into fewer processing chunks versus insertion of a break at a syntactically unacceptable place has yet to be optimized.

8.3.5 *Summary*

Of the analysis errors that were encountered in this admittedly difficult passage, most of the phonetic, stress, and phonological rule errors are easily correctable. However, only a few of the syntax errors can be fixed by straightforward debugging techniques. The most serious limitation of text-to-speech analysis routines seems to be in the area of automatic syntactic analysis. Still, the intelligibility and comprehension results to be presented in Chapter 13 indicate very encouraging overall system performance.

8.4 **Stress rules**

The phonological component assigns a feature *Stress* (value = 0 or 1) to each phonetic segment in the output string. The default value is 0 (unstressed). Vowels preceded by a stress symbol (', ", or !) in the input are assigned a value of 1. Consonants preceding a stressed vowel are also assigned a value of 1 if they are in the same morpheme and if they form an acceptable word-initial consonant cluster.

The stress feature is one way of defining a syllable structure for each word. Stressed consonants are defined to be affiliated with the following vowel, while unstressed consonants are affiliated with a preceding vowel (or their affiliation does not matter to subsequent rules). Segmental stress is used in rules that determine whether TT and DD are flapped, whether consonants and vowels are lengthened, whether voiceless plosives are strongly aspirated, and the degree of formant target undershoot.

For example, consider the consonants preceding the stressed vowel in the words "Atlantic" and "atrocious". In the first word, the TT is realized as a glottal stop (or glottalized alveolar stop). In the second word, the TT is a strongly aspirated full-alveolar stop. The distinction is maintained in the program by assigning segmental stress to both the TT and the RR in "atrocious" (because "tr" is a legal word-initial cluster), while assigning the segmental stress feature only to "l" in "Atlantic" (because "tl" is not a legal word-initial cluster). Given a proper formulation of the flapping rule and glottalized-t rule described below, this stress assignment ensures the selection of the appropriate allophone of TT.

8.5 Rules of segmental phonology

There are currently very few phonological rules of a segmental nature in the program. A number of rules that are sometimes attributed by linguists to the phonological component (e.g. palatalization) are realized in the phonetic component described in Chapter 11 because they involve graded phenomena (e.g. the SS of "fish soup" is partially palatalized, but not identical to SH). The segmental phonological rules that are described below are extremely important. They are not "sloppy speech" rules, but rather rules that aid the listener in hypothesizing the locations of word and phrase boundaries. For example, the second rule listed below ensures that a word-final TT is not perceived as a part of the next word by inserting simultaneous glottalization to inhibit oral pressure buildup during closure, and thus attenuate any release burst.

1. Substitute a postvocalic velarized allophone LX for LL if the LL is preceded by a vowel and followed by anything except a stressed vowel in the same word.

2. Replace TT or DD by the alveolar flap DX within words and across word boundaries (but not across phrase and clause boundaries) if the plosive is followed by a non-primary-stressed vowel and preceded by a nonnasal sonorant. Examples: "butter", "ladder", "sat about".

3. A word-final TT preceded by a sonorant is replaced by the glottal-

ized dental stop TQ (i.e. has a glottal release rather than a t-burst) if the next word starts with a stressed sonorant (unless there is a clause boundary between the words, in which case the TT is released into a pause). Examples: "that one", "Mat ran".

4. A voiceless plosive is not released if the next phonetic segment is another voiceless plosive within the same clause.

5. A glottal stop is inserted before a word-initial stressed vowel if the preceding segment is syllabic (and not a determiner), or if the preceding segment is a voiced nonplosive and there is an intervening phrase boundary. Example: "Liz eats".

6. The word "the" is pronounced DH IY if the next word starts with a vowel.

8.5.1 *An example*

If the six rules of segmental phonology are applied to the sentence shown in Figure 8-1, three allophonic changes are made. The sixth rule replaces the schwa by IY in the word "the". The first rule replaces the phoneme LL by a postvocalic allophone in the word "old". Finally, the second rule replaces the TT in "sat" by an alveolar flap DX. The string of symbols in the lower portion of Figure 8-1 is thus a broad phonetic transcription of the utterance to be synthesized. As the output of the phonological component, it serves as the input to the prosodic component PROSOD that is described in Chapter 9.

8.6 Pauses

Pauses are often used in speech production to mark major syntactic boundaries. Both pauses and prepausal lengthening are important to guide the listener's perception of the underlying syntactic structure of a sentence (Klatt, 1976b). A system of rules has been worked out for determining the locations of pauses in the synthesis, and the duration of each kind of pause.

Pauses of 800 msec, sufficient for a real speaker to take a breath, are introduced after any sentence of more than five words. A longer pause of 1200 msec appears at the end of paragraphs. Brief sentence-internal pauses (400 msec) are triggered by punctuation marks contained in the text, or are inserted by PHONO1 at detectable clause boundaries.

It is desirable to insert another kind of pause in certain sentence-internal positions of very long sentences because of the talker's limited lung volume. An algorithm has been developed for locating such pauses that is based on the number of syllables on either side of the potential sentence-internal breath pause, and the strength of various boundaries in the vicinity of a desired break. If necessary, such pauses may be inserted between a content and function word, even if no phrase boundary has been detected by syntactic analysis routines.

8.7 Evaluation of the analysis modules

The following text was input to the analysis modules of MITalk:

> "This recording is a demonstration of speech synthesis by rule and automatic text-to-speech conversion.
>
> Applications for synthetic speech output fall into four broad categories: those applications that require (1) a single word response (e.g. Speak and Spell), (2) a limited set of messages with a rigid syntactic framework (e.g. telephone number information), (3) a large vocabulary with general English syntax (e.g. teaching machine lessons), and (4) fully general English text to speech (e.g. for a reading machine for the blind).
>
> Prerecorded messages work well for single word response applications, but an increasing knowledge of the acoustic-phonetic characteristics of speech, of phonology, and of syntax is required for satisfactory synthesis of general English. In order to generate a particular utterance, one must specify a phonemic representation for each word, a stress pattern for each word, certain aspects of the syntactic structure of the sentence, such as the locations of phrase and clause boundaries, and the locations of any words that are to receive semantic focus.
>
> This information could be typed into a computer terminal, as was done in this case, or the information might be generated automatically from a deep-structure representation of the concept to be expressed. The speech that you have just heard was produced in June 1979 by the synthesis-by-rule portions of the MITalk text-to-speech system that is being developed at MIT".

The output from PHONO2 is given below. Erroneous segments are underlined and the corrections are given as subscripts. A null subscript ($\varnothing$) means that the segment should be deleted.

```
F: DH "IH SS C: RR IH_AX KK 'OXR DD * IH NG )C)N [1] F: IH ZZ F:
AX C: DD "EH MM AX NN * SS TT RR 'EY SH AX NN F: AX VV C:
SS PP 'IY CH SH C: SS 'IH NN TH AX SS AX SS F: BB AY C: RR 'UW LX
)C F: AE NN C: "AO DX AX MM 'AE DX IH KK C: TT 'EH KK SS TT F:
TT AX C: SS PP 'IY CH SH C: KK AX NN VV 'ER ZH AX NN .   C:
"AE PP LL IH_AX KK *_∅ [2] 'EY SH AX NN * ZZ F: FF OXR C:
SS IH NN TH 'EH DX IH KK AXP_∅ )C_∅ C: SS PP 'IY CH SH C:
```

---

[1] Too many extra ") c" pauses added.

[2] Morph boundary between root and bound morph has detrimental effect.

'AW TT PP "UH TT)N C: FF 'AO LX F: "IH NN TT UW C: FF 'OXR C:

BB RR 'AO DD C: KP 'AE DX IH_{AX} GG "AO RR"_{OXR} IY * ZZ , F:

DH "OW ZZ C: "AE PP LL IH_{AX} KK *_{∅} 'EY SH AX NN * ZZ)N F:

DH "AE TT C: RR IH_{AX} KK WW 'AY ER , C: WW 'AH NN , F: AX C:

SS 'IH NG GG AX LX C: WW 'ER DD C: RR IH SS PP 'AA NN SS , C: 'IY

C: JJ ZH 'IY ⌣)N C: SS PP 'IY KK AXP_{∅})C_{∅} F: AE NN C:

SS PP 'EH LX , , , C: TT 'UW , F: AX C: LL 'IH MM AX TT_{DX} * IH DD

C: SS 'EH DX F: AX VV C: MM 'EH SS IH_{AX} JJ ZH * IH_{IX} ZZ)C)N F:

WW IH TH F: AX C: RR 'IH JJ ZH IH DD C:

SS IH NN TT 'AE KK TT IH KK C: FF RR 'EY MM * WW "ER KK AXP , C:

'IY C: JJ ZH 'IY)N C: TT 'EH LX AX * FF 'OW"_{OW} NN[1] C:

NN 'AH MM BB ER C: "IH NN FF ER MM 'EY SH AX NN , , , C:

TH RR 'IY , F: AX C: LL 'AXR JJ ZH C:

VV OW KP 'AE BB YY AX LL "EH RR"_{EXR} IY)N F: WW IH TH C:

JJ ZH 'EH NN RR AX LX C: 'IH NG GG LL IH_{IX} SH C:

SS 'IH NN TT "AE KK SS , C: 'IY C: JJ ZH 'IY)N C:

TT 'IY CH SH * IH NG C: MM AX SH 'IY NN C: LL 'EH SS EN_{AX NN} * ZZ

, , F: AE NN DD AXP , C: FF 'OXR , C: FF 'UH LX IY C:

JJ ZH 'EH NN RR AX LX C: 'IH NG GG LL IH SH C: TT 'EH KK SS TT F:

TT AX_{UW} C: SS PP 'IY CH SH , C: 'IY C: JJ ZH 'IY)N F: FF OXR F:

AX C: RR 'IY DD * IH NG C: MM AX SH 'IY NN F: FF OXR F: DH AX C:

BB LL 'AY NN DD AXP ⌣∅[2] . C:

PP RR IY,_{IY} * RR IH_{AX} KK 'OXR"_{OXR} DD * IH_{IX} DD C:

MM 'EH SS IH_{AX} JJ ZH * IH_{IX} ZZ)N C: WW 'ER KK C: WW 'EH LX)C_{∅} F:

FF OXR C: SS 'IH NG GG AX LX_{EL} C: WW 'ER DD C:

RR IH SS PP 'AA NN SS C: "AE PP LL IH_{AX} KK *_{∅} 'EY SH AX NN * ZZ ,

F: BB AH DX F: AE NN C: IH NN KK RR 'IY SS * IH NG C:

NN 'AA LX IH JJ ZH)C_{∅} F: AX VV F: DH IY C: AX KK 'UW SS TT IH KK

C: FF AX NN 'EH DX IH KK C:

KP "AE RR"_{EXR} IH_{AX} KK TT AX RR 'IH SS TT IH KK * SS F: AX VV C:

SS PP 'IY CH SH , F: AX VV C: FF "OW_{AX} NN * 'AA LX AX JJ ZH IY ,

F: AE NN F: AX VV C: SS 'IH NN TT "AE KK SS)C F: IH ZZ C:

RR IH KK WW 'AY ER * DD F: FF OXR C:

---

[1]Two primary stresses in one word.

[2]The extra comma at sentence end results in no terminal fall.

SS "AE DX AX SS FF 'AE KK TT $\underset{\varnothing}{\star}$ ER $\star$ IY C:

SS 'IH NN TH AX SS AX SS)C F: AX VV C: JJ ZH 'EH NN RR AX LX C:

'IH NG GG LL $\underline{IH}_{IX}$ SH . F: IH NN C: 'OXR DX ER $\underset{\varnothing}{)C}$ F: TT $\underline{AX}_{UW}$ C:

JJ ZH 'EH NN ER $\star$ "EY DX F: AX C: PP AXR TT 'IH KK YY AX LX ER C:

'AH DX ER $\star$ AX NN SS , C: WW 'AH NN F: MM AH SS TT C:

SS PP 'EH SS AX FF "AY F: AX C: FF $\underline{OW}_{AX}$ NN 'IY MM IH KK C:

RR "EH PP RR $\underline{IH}_{AX}$ ZZ "EH NN TT $\underset{\varnothing}{\star}$ 'EY SH AX NN $\underset{\varnothing}{)C}$ F: FF OXR F:

$\underline{"IY}_{,IY}$ CH SH[1] C: WW 'ER DD AXP , F: AX C: SS TT RR 'EH SS C:

PP 'AE DX ER NN F: FF OXR F: $\underline{"IY}_{,IY}$ CH SH C: WW 'ER DD AXP , C:

SS 'ER $\underline{DX}_{TQ}$ EN C: 'AE SS PP "EH KK TT $\star$ SS F: AX VV F: DH AX C:

SS IH NN TT 'AE KK TT IH KK C: SS TT RR 'AH KK CH SH ER $\underset{\varnothing}{)C}$ F:

AX VV F: DH AX C: SS 'EH NN TT $\underline{EN}_{AX\ NN}$ SS , F: SS "AH CH SH F:

AE ZZ F: DH AX C: LL "OW KK $\underset{\varnothing}{\star}$ 'EY SH AX NN $\star$ ZZ F: AX VV C:

FF RR 'EY ZZ $\underset{\varnothing}{)C}$ F: AE NN C: KK LL 'AO ZZ C:

BB 'AW NN DD RR IY $\star$ ZZ , F: AE NN F: DH AX C:

LL "OW KK $\underset{\varnothing}{\star}$ 'EY SH AX NN $\star$ ZZ F: AX VV F: "EH NN IY C:

WW 'ER DD $\star$ ZZ $)C_{)N}$ F: DH "AE DX F: AXR F: TT $\underline{AX}_{UW}$ C:

RR AX SS 'IY VV C: SS IH MM 'AE NN TT IH KK C: FF 'OW KK AX SS .

F: DH "IH SS C: "IH NN FF ER MM 'EY SH AX NN $)C_{)N}$ F: KK UH DD F:

BB IY C: TT 'AY PP $\star$ TQ F: "IH NN TT UW F: AX C:

KK AX MM PP 'YU TT $\underset{\varnothing}{\star}$ ER C: TT 'ER MM AX NN $\underset{\varnothing}{\star}$ AX LX , F: AE ZZ

F: WW AH ZZ C: DD 'AH NN F: IH NN F: DH "IH SS C: KP 'EY SS , F:

OXR F: DH IY C: "IH NN FF ER MM 'EY SH AX NN $)C_{)N}$ F: MM $\underline{AY}_{,AY}$ TT[2]

F: BB IY C: JJ ZH 'EH NN ER $\star$ "EY TT $\star$ IH TQ C:

"AO DX AX MM 'AE DX $\underline{IH}_{AX}$ KK $\underset{\varnothing}{\star}$ $\underline{AX}_{\varnothing}$ $\underline{LX}_{\varnothing}$ $\underset{\varnothing}{\star}$ LL IY[3])C F:

FF RR AX MM F: AX C: DD 'IY PP C: SS TT RR 'AH KK CH SH ER C:

RR "EH PP RR IH ZZ "EH NN TT $\underset{\varnothing}{\star}$ 'EY SH AX NN $\underset{\varnothing}{)C}$ F: AX VV F:

DH AX C: KK 'AA NN SS "EH PP TT)N F: TT $\underline{AX}_{UW}$ F: BB IY C:

IH KK SS PP RR 'EH SS $\star$ TT AXP . F: DH AX C: SS PP 'IY CH SH)N

F: DH "AE DX F: YU F: HX AE VV C: JJ ZH 'AH SS TQ C:

HH 'ER DD AXP $)C_{)N}$ F: WW AH ZZ C: PP RR AX DD 'UW SS $\star$ TT F: IH NN

C: JJ ZH 'UW NN $)_c$ C: NN 'AY NN TT $\underline{'IY}_{,IY}$ NN

---

[1] "Each" should be intrinsically stressed.

[2] "Might" should be intrinsically stressed.

[3] DECOMP yields poor suffix expansion.

C: SS <u>'EH</u>_{EH} VV AX NN TT IY[1] C: NN 'AY NN)C F: BB AY F: DH AX C:
SS 'IH NN TH AX SS AX SS F: BB AY C: RR 'UW LX C:
PP 'OXR SH AX NN * ZZ <u>)C</u>_{)N} F: AX VV F: DH AX C: MM 'AY TT "AO KK
C: TT 'EH KK SS TT F: TT <u>AX</u>_{UW} C: SS PP 'IY CH SH C:
SS 'IH SS TT AX MM <u>)C</u>_{)N} F: DH "AE DX F: IH ZZ F: BB "IY IH NG C:
DD <u>IH</u>_{AX} VV 'EH LX AX PP * TT F: AE TQ C: 'EH MM C: 'AY C: TT 'IY .

---

[1]It is hard to get stress right in number sequences.

9

The prosodic component

9.1 Overview

The sentence representation produced by the phonological component PHONO2 serves as input to the prosodic component PROSOD that is to be described in this chapter. An example of the input to the prosodic component and the output generated by the prosodic rules is shown in Figure 9-1. The output consists of a string of phonetic segments, with each segment assigned a stress feature and a duration in msec. The fundamental frequency targets which appear in the PROSOD output listing are generated by an obsolete algorithm and are discarded by F0TARG which then generates the proper F0 targets.

9.2 Segmental durations

In a review of the factors that influence segmental durations in spoken English sentences (Klatt, 1976b and references cited therein), it was concluded that only a few of the many rule-governed durational changes are large enough to be perceptually discriminable. The goal of the rule system described below and in Klatt (1979b) is to characterize these perceptually important first-order effects.

The durational definitions that have been adopted include the closure for a stop (any burst and aspiration at release are assumed to be a part of the following segment). For fricatives, the duration corresponds to the interval of visible frication noise (or to changes in the voicing source if no frication is visible). For sonorant sequences, the segmental boundary is defined to be the half-way point in the formant transition for that formant having the greatest extent of transition. These definitions lead to a convenient and largely reproducible measurement procedure, but the physiological and perceptual validity of these boundaries have not been established.

Each segment is assigned a duration by a set of rules presented in detail below. The rules are intended to match observed durations for a single speaker (DHK) reading paragraph-length materials. The rules operate within the framework of a model of durational behavior which states that: 1) each rule tries to effect a percentage increase or decrease in the duration of the segment, but 2) segments cannot be compressed shorter than a certain minimum duration (Klatt, 1973). The model is summarized by the formula:

```
The old man sat in a rocker.
PHONO2: Function word: DH IY
PHONO2: Content word:  'OW LX DD
PHONO2: Content word:  MM 'AE NN [End NOUN phrase]
PHONO2: Content word:  SS 'AE DX
PHONO2: Function word: IH NN
PHONO2: Function word: AX
PHONO2: Content word:  RR 'AA KK * - ER
PHONO2: Punctuation:   .
PHONO2: <EOF>
 PROSOD: [Silence]  30ms. 133.4Hz.
 PROSOD: Function word:
 PROSOD:      DH     50ms. 123.4Hz.
 PROSOD:      IY    105ms. 131.4Hz.
 PROSOD: Content word:
 PROSOD:     'OW    170ms. 174.5Hz. Stressed
 PROSOD:      LX     75ms. 151.0Hz.
 PROSOD:      DD     50ms. 146.0Hz.
 PROSOD: Content word:
 PROSOD:      MM     70ms. 151.0Hz. Stressed
 PROSOD:     'AE    210ms. 157.0Hz. Stressed
 PROSOD:      NN     55ms. 117.9Hz.
 PROSOD:      [End NOUN phrase]
 PROSOD: Content word:
 PROSOD:      SS    100ms. 122.9Hz. Stressed
 PROSOD:     'AE    175ms. 153.9Hz. Stressed
 PROSOD:      DX     20ms. 140.1Hz.
 PROSOD: Function word:
 PROSOD:      IH     55ms. 148.1Hz.
 PROSOD:      NN     50ms. 142.5Hz.
 PROSOD: Function word:
 PROSOD:      AX     60ms. 142.5Hz.
 PROSOD: Content word:
 PROSOD:      RR     80ms. 140.2Hz. Stressed
 PROSOD:     'AA    160ms. 146.2Hz. Stressed
 PROSOD:      KK     65ms. 113.1Hz.
 PROSOD:       *
 PROSOD:       -
 PROSOD:      ER    170ms. 108.1Hz.
 PROSOD: Punctuation:   .
 PROSOD: [Silence] 400ms. 111.2Hz.
 PROSOD: [End sentence]
 PROSOD: <EOF>
```

Figure 9-1: Example of the processing performed by PROSOD

$$DUR=((INHDUR-MINDUR)\times PRCNT)/100+MINDUR \qquad (1)$$

where INHDUR is the inherent duration of a segment in msec, MINDUR is the minimum duration of a segment in msec, and PRCNT is the percentage shortening determined by applying rules 1 to 10 below. The program begins by obtaining values for INHDUR and MINDUR for the current segment from Table 9-1, and by setting PRCNT to 100. The inherent duration has no special status other than a starting point for rule application; it is roughly the duration to be expected in non-sense CVCs spoken in the carrier phrase "Say bVb again" or "Say Cab again". The following ten rules are then applied, where each rule modifies the PRCNT value obtained from the previous applicable rules by an amount PRCNT1, according to the equation:

$$PRCNT=(PRCNT\times PRCNT1)/100 \tag{2}$$

The duration of the segment is then computed by inserting the final value for PRCNT into Equation 1; and, finally, Rule 11 is applied. Justification for the presence of each rule is given in the references cited below, but the detailed formulation of a rule involved considerable trial-and-error effort to match the rule output against a large body of hand-segmented and labeled spectrograms of paragraphs read by speaker DHK.

1.   Pause insertion rule:

    Insert a 200-msec pause before each sentence-internal main clause and at boundaries delimited by a syntactic comma, but not before relative clauses (Goldman-Eisler, 1968; Cooper *et al.*, 1978). The "(R" symbol functions like a ")N" in the duration rules.

2.   Clause-final lengthening:

    The vowel or syllabic consonant in the syllable just before a pause is lengthened by PRCNT1=140 (Gaitenby, 1965; Lindblom and Rapp, 1973). Any consonants between this vowel and the pause are also lengthened by PRCNT1=140 (Oller, 1973; Klatt, 1975).

3.   Non-phrase-final shortening:

    Syllabic segments (vowels and syllabic consonants) are shortened by PRCNT1=60 if not in a phrase-final syllable (Lindblom and Rapp, 1973; Klatt, 1975). A phrase-final postvocalic liquid or nasal is lengthened by PRCNT1=140.

4.   Non-word-final shortening:

    Syllabic segments are shortened by PRCNT1=85 if not in a word-final syllable (Lindblom and Rapp, 1973; Oller, 1973).

5.   Polysyllabic shortening:

    Syllabic segments in a polysyllabic word are shortened by PRCNT1=80 (Lindblom and Rapp, 1973; Lehiste, 1975a).

6.   Non-initial-consonant shortening:

    Consonants in non-word-initial position are shortened by PRCNT1=85 (Klatt, 1974; Umeda, 1977).

Table 9-1: Minimum and inherent durations in msec for each segment type

Vowels

AA	100	240	AE	80	230	AH	60	140
AO	100	240	AW	100	260	AX	60	120
AXR	120	260	AY	150	250	EH	70	150
ER	80	180	EXR	130	270	EY	100	190
IH	40	135	IX	60	110	IXR	100	230
IY	55	155	OW	80	220	OXR	130	240
OY	150	280	UH	60	160	UW	70	210
UXR	110	230	YU	150	230			

Sonorant Consonants

EL	110	260	HH	20	80	HX	25	70
LL	40	80	LX	70	90	RR	30	80
RX	70	80	WW	60	80	WH	60	70
YY	40	80						

Nasals

EM	110	170	EN	100	170	MM	60	70
NN	50	60	NG	60	95			

Fricatives

DH	30	50	FF	80	100	SS	60	105
SH	80	105	TH	60	90	VV	40	60
ZZ	40	75	ZH	40	70			

Plosives

BB	60	85	DD	50	75	DX	20	20
GG	60	80	GP	40	80	KK	60	80
KP	40	80	PP	50	90	TT	50	75
TQ	50	75						

Affricates

CH	50	70	JJ	50	70

Pseudo-vowel

AXP	70	70

7.   Unstressed shortening:

      Unstressed segments are half-again more compressible than stressed seg-
      ments (i.e. set MINDUR=MINDUR/2). Then both unstressed and 2-
      stressed segments are shortened by a factor PRCNT1 that is tabulated
      below for each type of segment. The result is that segments assigned
      secondary stress are shortened relative to 1-stress, but not as much as un-
      stressed segments (Umeda, 1975, 1977; Lehiste, 1975a).

Context	PRCNT1 for -stress and 2-stress
syllabic (word-medial syllable)	50
syllabic (others)	70
prevocalic liquid or glide	10
all others	70

8.   Lengthening for emphasis:

      An emphasized vowel is lengthened by PRCNT1=140 percent (Bolinger,
      1972; Carlson and Granstrom, 1973; Umeda, 1975).

9.   Postvocalic context of vowels:

      a) The influence of a postvocalic consonant (in the same
         word) on the duration of a vowel is given below (House
         and Fairbanks, 1953; Peterson and Lehiste, 1960). In a
         postvocalic sonorant-obstruent cluster, the obstruent deter-
         mines the effect on the vowel (and on the sonorant
         consonant).

Context	PRCNT1
open syllable, word-final	120
before a voiced fricative	160
before a voiced plosive	120
before a nasal	85
before a voiceless plosive	70
before all others	100

      b) The effects are greatest at phrase and clause boundaries: if
         the vowel is non-phrase-final, change PRCNT1 to be closer
         to 100, according to the formula PRCNT1 = 70 +
         0.3*PRCNT1 (Klatt, 1975).

10.   Shortening in clusters:

      Segments are shortened in consonant-consonant sequences (disregarding word boundaries, but not across phrase boundaries) (Klatt, 1973), and in vowel-vowel sequences.

Context	PRCNT1
vowel followed by a vowel	120
vowel preceded by a vowel	70
consonant surrounded by consonants	50
consonant preceded by a consonant	70
consonant followed by a consonant	70

11.   Lengthening due to plosive aspiration:

A 1-stressed or 2-stressed vowel or sonorant preceded by a voiceless plosive is lengthened by 25 msec (Peterson and Lehiste, 1960).

When the rules are applied to the RR of "rocker" in Figure 9-1, the second rule sets PRCNT to 140, the fifth rule reduces PRCNT to 112, the seventh rule reduces MINDUR to 30 msec and PRCNT to 78.4, and the ninth rule increases PRCNT to 94. Then INHDUR, MINDUR, and PRCNT are inserted in Equation 1, and the resulting duration is rounded up to the nearest 5 msec to obtain the value of 175 msec shown in the lower part of Figure 9-1.

The resulting durations are determined in part by a variable that controls the nominal speaking rate SPRATE which can be set to any number between 60 and 300 words per minute. The default value is 180 words per minute. At rates slower than 150 wpm, a short pause is inserted between a content word and a following function word. (At a normal speaking rate, brief pauses are inserted only at the ends of clauses.) Individual segments are lengthened or shortened slightly depending on speaking rate, but most of the rate change is realized by manipulating pause durations (Goldman-Eisler, 1968).

The present rules are only a crude approximation to many of the durational phenomena seen in sentences (e.g. consonant interactions in clusters) and the rules completely ignore other factors. Nevertheless, to a first approximation, the rules capture a great deal of the systematic variation in segmental durations for speaker DHK. When compared with spectrograms of new paragraphs read by this speaker, the rule system produces segmental durations that differ from measured durations by a standard deviation of 17 msec (excluding the prediction of pause durations). The rules account for 84 percent of the observed total variance in segmental durations. Seventeen msec is generally less than the just noticeable difference for a single change to segmental duration in sentence materials (Klatt, 1976a).

A perceptual evaluation of the performance of the rule system is discussed by Carlson *et al.* (1979). The perceptual results are encouraging in that both naturalness and intelligibility ratings of sentences synthesized by these rules are very similar to ratings of the same sentences synthesized using durations obtained from a natural recording.

Complete durational rule systems exist for English (Coker *et al.*, 1973) and Swedish (Carlson and Granstrom, 1976). (We have borrowed heavily from the elegant rule system of Lindblom and Rapp that was augmented and implemented by Carlson and Granstrom.) Partial rule systems have also been proposed for vowels (Umeda, 1975; Liberman, 1977) and for consonants (Umeda, 1977). The rules contained in these systems are similar (not surprisingly), but there are many ways to generalize from the available data. For example, Coker *et al.* (1973) rely heavily on multiple stress levels conditioned by syntactic category (verbs have less stress than nouns) and conditioned by word frequency (common words and words that are repeated in a discourse are reduced in stress). Liberman (1977) includes rules related to rhythm and isochronous principles. Neither of these kinds of rules are incorporated explicitly in our system, but we do achieve partial isochrony through rules that shorten unstressed syllables and consonant clusters (see Carlson *et al.*, 1979). For quantification, we capture durational differences between nouns and verbs by phrase-final lengthening, and we permit the use of the emphasis symbol "!" in the input to capture word frequency and discourse expectancy effects in a binary fashion.

Therefore, it may never be possible to make absolute judgements concerning which rule system is theoretically correct. Effort should rather be directed at systematic optimization of a particular rule system, e.g., one that starts with a linguistically motivated framework for how to represent an input sentence and draws on both speech production data and perceptual constraints to formulate a simple set of rules as a starting point.

10

The fundamental frequency generator

10.1 Overview

An important component in the generation of natural-sounding speech is the fundamental frequency of the voicing source. Such attributes as syntactic structure, emphasis, and sentence type can be partially signaled by the fundamental frequency (F0) contour as well as by duration and amplitude information. In the F0 algorithm used with the text-to-speech system, information from both syntactic and phonologic components is used. It utilizes the phrase structure of each sentence as analyzed by the parser to determine declination lines, to calculate the amount of excursion from the declination line through each phrase, and to insert continuation rises. Lexical stress marks and syllable division are used to determine the location of F0 peaks, and parts of speech provide information needed to determine the relative height of the peaks. Phonemic data provide the information needed to determine segmental influences on fundamental frequency. These influences produce an active variation in peaks and valleys, thus yielding a lively contour (O'Shaughnessy, 1976).

The algorithm currently in use produces two F0 "target values" for each phonetic segment, one to be used at onset and one as a mid-value. This is an adaptation of the original O'Shaughnessy algorithm which produces a value every 5 msec. The production of target values allows a more uniform treatment of parameters, since interpolation for F0 hereafter may be handled in the same way as for most of the other parameters. It is also possible to take advantage of a lower data rate since one or two values per segment replace the previous necessity for one value every 5 msec. The rises and falls which are calculated for each segment are used to specify the target values, the peak point at either the left or right boundary of stressed vowels in content words, and the midpoint target value for other segments. Other midpoint values are determined by interpolation.

The fundamental frequency generation program accepts syntactic information from PARSER (discussed in Chapter 4) and phonemic information from PROSOD (discussed in Chapter 9) in the form of a PROSOD output file. Its output is an augmented PROSOD file containing the two target values for each segment.

10.2 Input

The output file from the PARSER provides phrase group information and the part of speech of individual words to the F0 algorithm. The phrase groups which are recognized are noun phrases, prepositional phrases, verb phrases, and verbal groups. The parts of speech are grouped so as to be more useful in determining how they affect the F0 contour. The word classes listed in Table 10-1 below are given in order of their potential to affect the contour. Those parts of speech in parentheses are provided by the F0 algorithm, but are not used directly in the lexicon. A reflexive pronoun, for example, is listed in the lexicon as having the part of speech PRONOUN and the feature REFLEXIVE. It is passed to the F0 algorithm simply as a PRONOUN.

Table 10-1: Relative peak levels of words according to their parts of speech

Level	Part of speech
0	article
1	conjunction, relative pronoun
2	preposition, auxiliary verb, (unstressable modal, vocative)
3	personal pronoun
6	verb, demonstrative pronoun
7	noun, adjective, adverb, contraction
8	(reflexive pronoun)
9	stressable modal
10	quantifier
11	interrogative adjectives
12	(negative element)
14	(sentential adverb)

There are nine levels which are actually distinguished from one another. Those listed beginning with VERB, i.e., Level 6, are considered important enough to produce a peak in the contour. Words with these "important" parts of speech are referred to as "content" words. The relative height of the peak depends upon the order relation. The features "content" and "function" are also used in another module, PHONO1, to label types of words. All "content" words in PHONO1 are also "content" words in this algorithm. However, certain parts of speech which were given the label "function" are elevated to "content" importance in the F0 algorithm. These are:

- Demonstrative pronouns (this, those)
- Contractions (we'll, boys'll)
- Modals (should, might, will, can)
- Quantifiers (several, many)
- Interrogative adjectives (which, whose)

The F0 algorithm requires a specification of the number of syllables in each word, the location of the stressed syllable within the word, and information concerning syllable boundaries. This information is found in the PROSOD output file. The phonemic information in this file is also used to specify a structure for each syllable. This structure is an allowable ordering of voiced or unvoiced obstruents, sonorants, and a single vowel.

10.3 Output

There are two possible output files. One file is a stream of fundamental frequency values, one value for each 5 msec of the utterance. This file can be merged with the output of PHONET (discussed in Chapter 11) which gives values of the 20 variable parameters each 5 msec. These values are calculated by determining the changes in F0 during a syllable and using the duration of the segments within the syllable to describe a contour with constant slope (absolute value).

A second method, the one currently in use, is to calculate rises and falls on each segment (an intermediate stage in the former method) and to use this information to specify F0 target values for the midpoint of each segment and for the peak point at either the left or right boundary of stressed vowels in content words. Unspecified onset values for segments are determined by linear interpolation between their midpoint target value and the midpoint target value of the preceding segment. This method allows F0 values to be calculated every 5 msec using the same linear smoothing procedure which is used for some of the other parameters, modified slightly by the addition of the possible extra target value as input.

Most peaks are assigned to the right boundary of the stressed vowel in a content word. A fall (and possible continuation rise) following the rise which forms the peak is then assigned to the midpoint or right boundary of the following segment, absorbing any fall or rise that might previously have been assigned to that segment. A peak is assigned to the left boundary of a "nuclear-stressed" syllable, i.e., the stressed syllable in the final content word of a phrase preceding a silence. Preceding unassigned rises or falls are absorbed in the assignment of the peak.

10.4 The O'Shaughnessy fundamental frequency algorithm

The algorithm may be considered as a cascade of two separate systems. The first, or High Level System, uses syntactic information to sketch the contour. The Low Level System uses information generated by the High Level System and additional phonemic data to detail the contour.

10.4.1 *High Level System*

The High Level System predicts a superposed F0 contour by taking into consideration the sentence type, clause contour, phrase contour, and individual word contour. This contour is further augmented in the Low Level System by considering the effect of individual segments.

10.4.2 *Sentence type*

Two global-level *tunes* are assigned depending upon sentence type. *Tune A* is used primarily for declaratives. It causes a linear falling F0 trend in the clause it is assigned to, and a sharp fall on the last content word in the clause and on those words following it. The other tune, *Tune B,* is used for yes/no questions, that is, questions to which an answer of "yes" or "no" is expected. This tune causes a rise followed by a relatively flat F0 trend and a sharp terminal rise.

10.4.3 *Clause contour*

The next factor affecting the contour is set by the syntactic boundaries. A sharp rise is stipulated at the beginning of a syntactic unit, and a sharp fall at the end. In practice, there is only one such contour for each sentence because clauses are not identified by the parser. This contour coincides with the tune contour.

10.4.4 *Phrase contour*

In phrases containing two or more content words, an initial F0 rise is assigned beginning at the first content word and a final F0 fall begins on the last content word. If the phrase is nonfinal, a continuation rise is placed on the last syllable of the last word.

10.4.5 *Word contour*

The individual content words within a phrase are given the most F0 movement. In addition to the sharp rise and fall on the first and last content words in a phrase, a rise-fall contour is described on the stressed syllable of each content word. These excursions reflect the desire of a speaker to have listeners understand the less predictable words in a sentence which are also those words which carry the most information. Function words are very common and describe a syntactic structure which is easily recognized. Content words, on the other hand, must be emphasized somewhat for the utterance to be comprehended, since their occurrence is much less predictable. The amount of F0 movement on each word depends upon its rank in the order of parts of speech of content words (see Table 10-1) and also upon the number of syllables in the word. Words of higher rank contain larger F0 excursion. Function words and unstressed syllables of content words are given a slight (5 Hz) excursion to produce a more natural-sounding contour.

10.4.6 *Prosodic indicators*

A set of "prosodic indicators" is passed from the High Level System to the Low Level System. An *accent* number gives the relative importance of a word. This number ranges from "0" for one-syllable articles to "11+n" for a sentential adverb containing n syllables. An integer representing the *position* of a word in a phrase and the importance of that phrase is also assigned. Higher absolute values are given to words at boundaries marked by punctuation and to words at the boundaries of large or major phrases. Another value assigned to each word is a number indicating the *amount of continuation rise*. Most words are assigned the value "0", but those words ending a nonfinal phrase are usually given a value which reflects the importance of the syntactic boundary which the word immediately precedes. A *level* number applies to words in noun phrases not containing conjunctions. This number either signifies that the F0 level is to rise, or that the F0 level should drop on that word. Other words are given level "0". This indicates a mid-phrase word. Additionally, the *tune* value is defined on each word, and is nonzero on the word ending a clause. The number of phrases is also a necessary input value to the next level.

10.4.7 *The Low Level System*

This level reflects the effects of phonemics, lexical stress, and the number of syllables of the words in the utterance. The number of syllables is used in determining the height of the peak on lexically stressed syllables. Although the first and highest peak in a sentence is constrained to a maximum of about 190 Hz, longer sentences, i.e., sentences with more syllables, begin with higher peaks. This initial height allows more freedom of excursion for following peaks. Higher peaks are also placed on two lexically stressed syllables if they are separated by unstressed syllables, the height of the peaks being dependent upon the number of intervening unstressed syllables.

The F0 pattern is also affected by the phonemics. For example, unvoiced consonants at the beginning of a stressed syllable also cause the contour to fall, rather than rise, into the contour of the stressed vowel. (The rise is added to the peak of the vowel.) See Figure 10-1 for an example of this contour.

The algorithm first sets the peaks on the lexically stressed syllables. Falls and

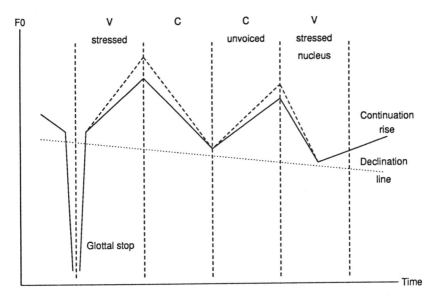

Figure 10-1: Example of F0 contours

rises are then assigned around these peaks. Continuation rises are added to the last syllable of most non-sentence-final phrases (Figure 10-1), and sentence-final words are given rises or falls depending upon their tune. Finally, the F0 contour is completed by specifying the amount of fall on other nonstressed syllables.

The peak on a stressed syllable is proportional to the accent number, but is also decreased through the sentence. The peaks are arrayed along a falling declination line so that peaks of equal height have lower values moving from peaks which are sentence-initial to those which are sentence-final. The rate of declination is steeper for sentences with Tune A, and less steep for sentences with Tune B.

Each content word is given a rise and fall around the peak of its primary-stressed syllable. The basic rise is 40 percent of the distance from the initial value of the lower declination line (110 Hz for Tune A, 125 Hz for Tune B) to the peak value. This basic value is altered for peaks in boundary position. More rise, and thus a lower valley, is assigned to a phrase-initial peak and less rise (i.e. a higher valley) to phrase-final peaks. In addition, intervening unaccented syllables require more rise on the peaks surrounding them. The basic fall value is 20 percent of the distance from the lower declination line to the peak value. This value is increased for a phrase-final fall. Rises and falls within a phrase are further reduced (by 30 percent).

The normal pattern is considered to be one of alternating accented and unaccented syllables. An accented syllable is a stressed syllable of a content word; unaccented syllables are all others. If two accented syllables are adjacent, their rise values are reduced by 40 percent. Two accented syllables separated by two, three, or four unaccented syllables have their rise values increased by 15 percent, 20 percent, and 30 percent, respectively. Additional unaccented syllables cause no further effect. The peak height on an accented syllable preceded by two or three unaccented syllables is decreased by 15 percent and 25 percent, respectively. However, an accented syllable followed by two or three unaccented syllables is increased by 10 percent and 15 percent, respectively. If three accented syllables appear in succession, the fundamental frequency of the second is allowed to fall from the peak of the first, and rise into the peak of the third, i.e., its fall and rise are interchanged in time. A word not covered by a node, and preceded by three or more unaccented syllables, is assigned a rise value equal to the difference between its peak value and 95 Hz.

Words in terminal positions are given special rise and fall values. In a statement (Tune A), the last syllable is given a fall value such that F0 reaches 75 Hz. In a yes/no question (Tune B), a rise is assigned after the last accented syllable's fall (none if it is the last syllable), which gives a final F0 value 20 percent higher than any previous peak.

The highest continuation rise (16 Hz) is assigned to the last syllable of a word, if it is followed by a nonterminal punctuation mark or a conjunction, and if there has been no punctuation or conjunction since the last content word. A continuation rise of 8 Hz is assigned to the last syllable of the last word in a nonfinal phrase, if there have been more than five words since the last word to which a continuation rise was assigned.

If two accented syllables are separated by unaccented syllables, the F0 contour connecting them is either straight or falling. If the difference between the endpoints of the two accented syllables is positive, the previous fall and next rise are adjusted by the same amount (half the difference), so that the F0 contour does not change on intermediate unaccented syllables.

In the case in which the difference in endpoints is negative, that fall is spread over the intermediate unaccented syllables in two ways. If the unaccented syllables occur within a phrase, the falling rate is linear. Each successive unaccented syllable gets an equal share of the fall. For unaccented syllables which are not in the same phrase, a more exponential falling pattern is assigned with the earlier unaccented syllables receiving more of the fall. Unaccented syllables terminating either a Tune A or Tune B clause, fall or rise in equal amounts to the final value.

10.5 Adjustments to the O'Shaughnessy algorithm

Several additions and adjustments have been made to the original algorithm. A third tune has been stipulated for wh-questions, that is, questions which include a question word such as "how" or "who" and to which an answer other than "yes" or "no" is expected. It will produce a high peak on the question word, a steeper falling F0 than in declaratives, and a higher peak on the last accented syllable than is produced for declaratives.

The additional 20 percent rise assigned to an initial unvoiced consonant is added to the left boundary of the following vowel rather than to its peak, so that the contour falls from the initial portion of the vowel if the peak is at the left boundary. Another adjustment is the insertion of a local 5 Hz perturbation on both flat and falling unstressed syllables about their midpoint. A third adjustment is the addition of a dip in the contour at points of glottalization (see Figure 10-1). In addition, the final F0 value in statements has been lowered by 10 Hz, and the range has been narrowed so that an excursion above 190 Hz is rare.

10.6 Potential improvements from additional syntactic information

A number of additional provisions in the O'Shaughnessy algorithm could be used if a more complete parser were available. Identification of dependent and independent clauses, and of matrix and embedded clauses would provide more information for resetting declination lines and calculating continuation rises. Boundaries created by a number of syntactic transformations are also considered in the algorithm. These are clefting, there-insertion, preposing, topicalization, left and right dislocation, extraposition, and ellipsis. Special contours are provided for both appositives and vocatives as well as tag questions and yes/no questions offering alternatives.

11

The phonetic component

11.1 Overview

The phonetic component, PHONET, accepts input from the fundamental frequency component F0TARG (in the form of an array of phonetic segment names, and a segmental stress feature, segmental duration, and two fundamental frequency targets for each phone), and produces output values for 20 synthesizer control parameters every 5 msec. This chapter concerns the strategy for phonetic-to-parametric rule development and a summary of the form and content of individual rules for control parameter specification.

11.1.1 *"Stored prosodics" synthesis*

The phonetic component PHONET and synthesizer components can be operated in stand-alone mode in which the phonetic segment string, durations, and fundamental frequency contour specification that form the input to PHONET are hand-tuned to be as accurate as possible. For example, one might record a natural version of a sentence, extract fundamental frequency, measure segmental durations, select phonetic segments according to the pronunciation used by the real speaker, and format this information in a way that is compatible with PHONET input. The advantage of this approach is the naturalness of the speech that can be produced with an input representation consisting of about 250 bits per second of speech.

This method of generating speech might be compared with the Texas Instruments' Speak-'N-Spell vocoder synthesizer. We suspect that the overall intelligibility and naturalness of the MITalk "stored-prosodics" synthesis is slightly better at 250 bits/second than Speak-'N-Spell at 1200 bits/second. However, the significant disadvantage of MITalk is that there is no automatic procedure for determination of input parameter data for PHONET, whereas Speak-'N-Spell synthesis can be prepared automatically from a linear-prediction vocoder analyzer with only minimal selection and hand tuning.

11.1.2 *Structure of PHONET*

The phonetic component includes a large array of target values for various control parameters for each of about 60 phonetic segment types. Smoothing between target values depends on time constants computed by rule, as well as depending on

108

the parameter value assigned to the time of the segment boundary. These constants are determined by rules that involve features of the current phonetic segment PHOCUR, the previous phonetic segment PHOLAS, and the next phonetic segment PHONEX. In some cases, the rules have to examine features of segments further from the current segment, but this is rare. For example, in **pin**, the time of voicing onset in the vowel preceded by the voiceless plosive PP is delayed by about 50 msec, unless the segment preceding the voiceless plosive is an SS, as in **spin**. The variable control parameters are listed later in Table 11-3.

11.1.3 *History of formant synthesis-by-rule*

As originally demonstrated by John Holmes, successful imitation of a natural utterance depends primarily on matching observed short-term spectra. This technique succeeds, in part, because it reproduces all of the potential cues present in the spectrum, even though we may not know which cues are most important. The speech perception apparatus appears to be aware of any and all (perceptually discriminable) regularities present in the acoustic signal generated by the speech production apparatus, and these regularities should be included in synthetic stimuli if possible.

There have been a number of previous efforts to specify general strategies for formant synthesis-by-rule (see, e.g., Holmes *et al.*, 1964; Mattingly, 1968a; Rabiner, 1968a; Coker *et al.*, 1973; Klatt, 1972, 1976a). However, examination of these publications suggests that consonant-vowel intelligibility is nowhere near as high as in listening to natural speech. For example, Rabiner (1968a) estimated that consonants in his synthetic consonant-vowel nonsense stimuli were 85 percent intelligible to phonetically trained listeners, but that natural tokens of the same syllables were about 99 percent intelligible. Other rule programs, apparently, perform no better, although relevant evaluative data are generally not available.

Why isn't intelligibility higher? Each rule system attempts to make appropriate generalizations and simplifications concerning the form and content of rules for consonant-vowel synthesis. Have the wrong generalizations been made? The results described below in Section 11.2 suggest that this conjecture is true.

11.2 "Synthesis-by-analysis" of consonant-vowel syllables

11.2.1 *Analysis of CV syllables*

The data base that was recorded and analyzed in order to develop new consonant-vowel synthesis rules consists of speech samples obtained from six talkers who were native to a single midwestern dialect region -- three males and three females (Klatt, 1979b). The intent was to use the data from all six talkers to establish the *form* of the synthesis rules, but the actual parameter values inserted in the rules came from a more extensive analysis of the speech of one of the male subjects (since data averaged across several male and female talkers would probably not make for a very good synthetic talker). Subjects read a list of 336 different CVC nonsense syllables once, except for the designated talker (DHK) who read the list twice on three separate occasions.

The kind of analysis that was performed on the data base is illustrated in Figure 11-1. The speech was low-pass filtered at 4.9 kHz and digitized at 10k samples per second. Linear prediction spectra were computed at a number of (hand-selected) locations in a syllable. The waveform segment, such as the one shown at the top in Figure 11-1, was first differenced (to attenuate very low frequency background noise) and multiplied by a Kaiser window (Beta=7.0) prior to 11-pole linear prediction analysis. The linear prediction spectrum is shown at the bottom of the figure along with the discrete Fourier transform. The 25.6 msec time-weighting window has an effective averaging duration of about 10 msec. The same window was used at all analysis points, except during the sustained frication noise of fricatives, where the window duration was increased so as to better estimate the spectral characteristics of the noise.

Spectral samples were obtained: 1) during the consonantal steady state (or at burst onset for a plosive), 2) at voicing onset (or early in the consonant-vowel transition for voiced consonants), and 3) shortly after the end of the consonant-vowel transition. Formant frequencies were also estimated by locating the peaks in a linear prediction spectrum. Formant motions were plotted every 10 msec during voiced portions of syllables. Intensity and fundamental frequency were also estimated and plotted as a function of time.

In this chapter, it is only possible to present some of the highlights of the analyses. For example, Figure 11-2 presents first and second formant frequency trajectories of sixteen vowel nuclei, as averaged across all consonantal environments for the designated talker. Most of the vowels appear to be diphthongized to some extent. (The true diphthongs are shown with dashed vectors.) In particular, it is a characteristic of this common midwestern dialect to terminate the short vowels IH, EH, AE, and UH in a schwa-like offglide. These average data for vowels are used as a starting point for consonant-vowel synthesis.

Analysis of consonants revealed two major conclusions concerning the form of rules appropriate for synthesis of a consonant before any vowel:

1. Some consonants, particularly obstruents, take on significantly different characteristics depending on whether the following vowel is a front vowel, a back unrounded vowel, or a back rounded vowel.

110

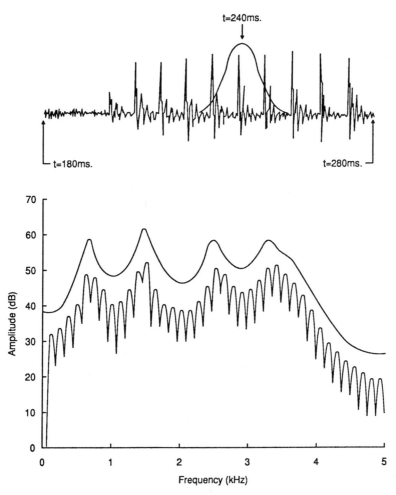

Figure 11-1: Spectrum analysis of a speech waveform

2. Within each set of vowels, spectra associated with each consonant are surprisingly invariant, and formant transitions into the vowel obey a modified "locus" equation.

These conclusions are illustrated in the next two figures. Figure 11-3 displays average spectra of plosive bursts before each vowel. Each curve is the average of six tokens of a syllable obtained from a single talker. Burst spectra are similar before vowels in a particular category, even though these (linear prediction) spectra have not been normalized for speaking level. Burst spectra for GG differ strikingly across vowel sets, and burst spectra for DD are modified before rounded vowels. Similar changes are seen for voiceless plosives and for fricatives.

111

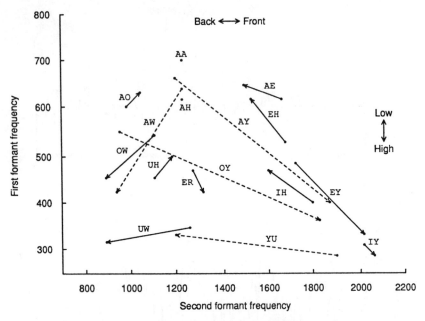

Figure 11-2: First and second formant motions in English vowels

Figure 11-4 contains a plot of average frequencies for the lowest three formants, as measured at voicing onset following plosive release in syllables containing BB, DD, and GG. Values before 16 vowel nuclei are plotted on the vertical axis as a function of the formant frequency seen in the early part of the vowel. Notice that, for the first formant, data can be well approximated by a straight line. However, the value of F1 at voicing onset, i.e., when F1 is first perceptible, is as high as 500 Hz before low vowels because most of the rapid rise in F1 at release takes place prior to voicing onset.

If formant values at voicing onset fall on a straight line in this kind of plot, a "locus theory" description of the data is possible; that is, there exists a locus theory equation with two free parameters that can predict F1 at voicing onset from a knowledge of the vowel target. An example of this synthesis procedure will be presented shortly.

Before describing aspects of the synthesis strategy, it should be noted that there exist articulatory motivations for dividing vowels into these three sets. Anticipatory coarticulation of the vowel features "front-back" and "rounded-unrounded" can explain all of the acoustic observations noted in the figures.

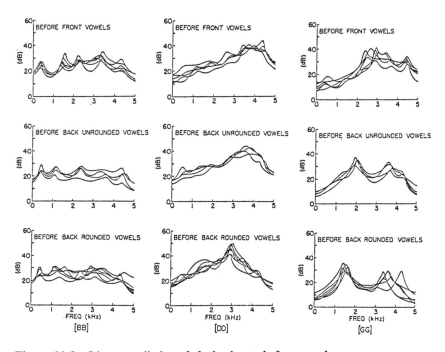

Figure 11-3: Linear prediction of plosive bursts before vowels

11.2.2 *Synthesis strategy*

A possible synthesis strategy for predicting formant frequency motions in CV syllables is illustrated in Figure 11-5 for the syllable **go**. The vowel is first defined in terms of straight-line segments. Then the formant values associated with the consonant and the consonant-vowel transition are imposed, again using straight-line segments and a locus theory equation to determine formant values at the CV boundary. Formant motions associated with the vowel are defined in the upper panel. Perturbations imposed by the initial consonant are indicated in the lower panel.

Many of the remaining synthesis parameters, such as formant bandwidths and formant amplitudes in frication spectra, must be determined by trial-and-error comparisons of synthetic and natural linear prediction spectra. These adjustments took several iterations. Experience showed that small errors in frication spectra, or frication level, or the time course of intensity buildup, would result in an increased identification error rate, so that the tedious trial-and-error optimization of these parameters is important. The resulting control parameter values are tied to a par-

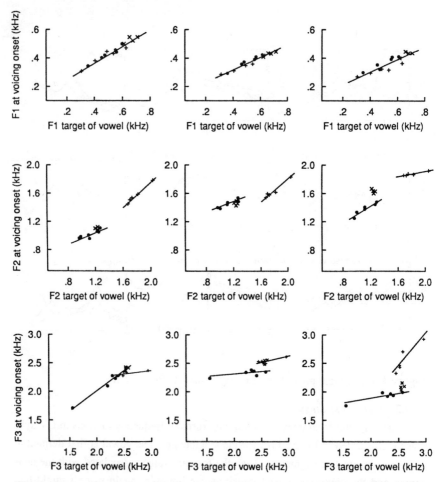

Figure 11-4: Frequency of the lowest three formants measured at voicing onset for syllables involving BB, DD, and GG

ticular software synthesizer (Klatt, 1980; see Chapter 12), but perhaps future publication of the numbers would be of some value to those who wish to implement the synthesizer program.

11.2.3 *Intelligibility evaluation*

The intelligibility of CV syllables produced by the rules was evaluated by synthesizing 336 different CVt syllables in a random order. The tape was played to five phonetically trained listeners who transcribed both the consonants and the vowels. The vowel identification rate was 99 percent and the consonant identification rate was 95 percent. While these results are encouraging, we continue to seek

114

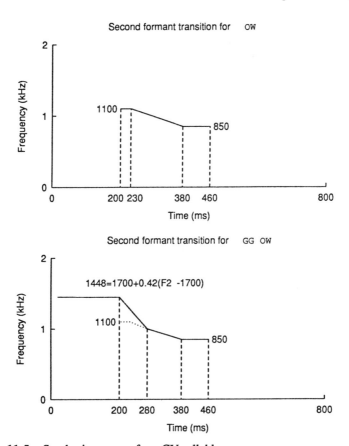

Second formant transition for   OW

Second formant transition for   GG OW

Figure 11-5: Synthesis strategy for a CV syllable

ways to improve the consonants and plan to extend this work to clusters and to postvocalic allophones.

How can the intelligibility of the consonant-vowel syllables be further improved? Of particular interest are two questions: 1) will the generalizations concerning vowel categories and the form of the locus equations have to be modified, or is it only necessary to modify the numbers that go into the equations, and 2) is a spectral-matching procedure of the type outlined above sufficient for the purpose of intelligibility optimization? The generalizations that have been made will probably not have to be modified or abandoned. Each time that the perceptual data have indicated a problem with a particular CV syllable or class of syllables, reinspection of the spectral match between the synthesis and the average spectra for talker DHK has revealed fairly substantial differences, and correction of the

differences has led to clear improvement in intelligibility. At least one more itera-
tion of this procedure is needed. Furthermore, within the constraints imposed by
the synthesizer itself, matching of linear-prediction spectra is adequate to the task.

11.3 General rules for the synthesis of phonetic sequences

The rule program used in MITalk differs from the limited CV synthesis algorithm
described above. The MITalk phonetic component PHONET is patterned after a
Fortran-based synthesis-by-rule program described by Klatt (1976a). Since that
time, both the program structure and the constants contained in target tables for
each phone have been modified. These modifications were made in order to incorporate some of the new consonant-vowel synthesis rules described in the previous
section, and to simplify the rule structure.

The general procedure for drawing control parameter values is:

1. Draw the target value for the first segment.

2. Draw the target value for the next segment.

3. Smooth the boundary between the segments using one of the
   templates shown in Figure 11-6 (note that DISCON does no
   smoothing).

4. Go to step 2 unless there are no more segments.

The transition between target values for each control parameter may either be discontinuous or smooth. The boundary value and transition duration in each direc-
tion from the logical phoneme boundary are computed by rules that take into account manner features of the segments involved.

11.3.1 *Vowels*

The control parameters that are usually varied to generate an isolated vowel are the
amplitude of voicing AV; the fundamental frequency of vocal fold vibrations F0;
the lowest three formant frequencies F1, F2, and F3; and bandwidths B1, B2, and
B3. The fourth and fifth formant frequencies might be varied to simulate spectral
details, but this is not essential for high intelligibility. To create a natural breathy
vowel termination, the amplitude of aspiration AH and the amplitude of quasi-
sinusoidal voicing AVS are activated.

Table 11-1 includes suggested target values for variable control parameters
that are used to differentiate among English vowels. Formant frequency and
bandwidth targets were obtained by trial-and-error spectral matching to a large set
of CV syllables spoken by talker DHK. Bandwidth values are often larger than
closed-glottis values obtained by Fujimura and Lindqvist (1971), because the
bandwidths of Table 11-1 have been adjusted to take into account changes to ob-

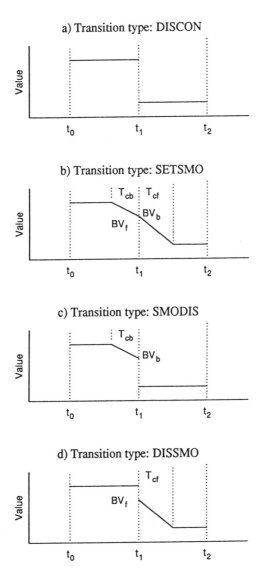

Figure 11-6: Templates for smoothing adjacent phonetic segment targets

served formant amplitudes caused by factors such as glottal losses and irregularities in the voicing source spectrum. Where two values are given, the vowel
is diphthongized or has a schwa-like offglide in the speech of talker DHK. Durations of steady states and transition portions of diphthongized vowels depend on
total vowel duration, and are different for each vowel.

The mechanism for synthesizing a diphthongized vowel is shown in Figure
11-7. Each of the constants shown in the figure is stored in tables for all diphthongized vowels, including those having schwa offglides.

11.3.2 *Consonants*

Additional control parameters must be varied for the synthesis of various classes of
consonants. Table 11-2 includes target values for variable control parameters that
are used to synthesize portions of English consonants (frication spectra of fricatives, burst spectra of plosives, nasal murmurs for nasals, and steady portions of
sonorants).

The sonorant consonants WW, YY, RR, and LL are similar to vowels and require the same set of control parameters to be varied in order to differentiate
among them. Formant values given in Table 11-2 for the prevocalic sonorants RR
and LL depend somewhat on the following vowel. The source amplitude, AV, for
a prevocalic sonorant should be about 10 dB less than in the vowel. The sonorant
HH can be synthesized by taking formant frequency and bandwidth parameters
from the following vowel, increasing the first formant bandwidth to about 300 Hz,
and replacing voicing by aspiration.

The fricatives characterized in Table 11-2 include both voiceless fricatives
(AF=60, AV=0, AVS=0) and voiced fricatives (AF=50, AV=47, AVS=47). Formants to be excited by the frication noise source are determined by the amplitude
controls A2, A3, A4, A5, A6, and AB. The amplitude of the parallel second formant, A2, is zero for all of these consonants before front vowels, but the second
formant is a front cavity resonance for velars before nonfront vowels and A2 is
excited. The values given for F2 and F3 are not only valid during the fricative, but
also can serve as "loci" for the characterization of the consonant-vowel formant
transitions before front vowels. These are virtual loci in that formant frequency
values observed at the onset of glottal excitation are somewhere between the locus
and the vowel target frequency -- the amount of virtual transition being dependent
on formant-cavity affiliations.

The specification of frication spectra in the table is accurate only before front
vowels in the speech of talker DHK. Before back and rounded vowels, systematic
changes are observed to the fricative spectra because of anticipatory coarticulation.

118

Table 11-1: Parameter values for the synthesis of selected vowels

Vowel	F1	F2	F3	B1	B2	B3
IY	310	2020	2960	45	200	400
	290	2070	2960	60	200	400
IH	400	1800	2570	50	100	140
	470	1600	2600	50	100	140
EY	480	1720	2520	70	100	200
	330	2020	2600	55	100	200
EH	530	1680	2500	60	90	200
	620	1530	2530	60	90	200
AE	620	1660	2430	70	150	320
	650	1490	2470	70	100	320
AA	700	1220	2600	130	70	160
AO	600	990	2570	90	100	80
	630	1040	2600	90	100	80
AH	620	1220	2550	80	50	140
OW	540	1100	2300	80	70	70
	450	900	2300	80	70	70
UH	450	1100	2350	80	100	80
	500	1180	2390	80	100	80
UW	350	1250	2200	65	110	140
	320	900	2200	65	110	140
ER	470	1270	1540	100	60	110
	420	1310	1540	100	60	110
AY	660	1200	2550	100	70	200
	400	1880	2500	70	100	200
AW	640	1230	2550	80	70	140
	420	940	2350	80	70	80
OY	550	960	2400	80	50	130
	360	1820	2450	60	50	160

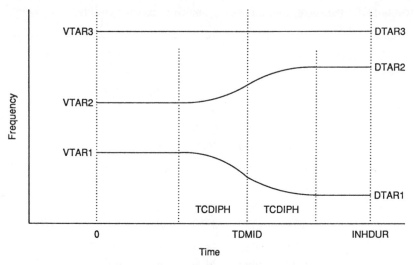

Figure 11-7: Constants used to specify the inherent formant and durational characteristics of a sonorant

In addition to differences in source amplitudes, voiced and voiceless fricatives differ in that F1 is higher and B1 is larger when the glottis is open.

The affricate parameters in Table 11-2 refer to the fricative portion of the affricate. Similarly, the plosive parameters in Table 11-2 refer to the brief burst of frication noise generated at plosive release. Formant frequency values again serve as loci for predicting formant positions at voicing onset.

The parameters that are used to generate a nasal murmur include the nasal pole and zero frequencies FNP and FNZ. The nasal pole and zero are used primarily to approximate vowel nasalization at nasal release by splitting F1 into a pole-zero-pole complex. The details of nasal murmurs that have been described by Fujimura (1962) are approximated by formant bandwidth adjustments rather than by the theoretically correct method of pole-zero insertion. The reason is that it is not possible to simulate both the higher frequency pole-zero details of nasal murmurs and vowel nasalization simultaneously without moving the frequency of the nasal pole and zero very fast at release, which would generate an objectionable click in the output, and vowel nasalization has been found to be perceptually more important. A nasalized vowel is generated by increasing F1 by about 100 Hz, and by setting the frequency of the nasal zero to be the average of this new F1 value and 270 Hz (the frequency of the fixed nasal pole).

Not included in Tables 11-1 and 11-2 are steady-state target values for unstressed allophones, postvocalic allophones, flaps, glottal stops, voicebars, and

Table 11-2: Parameter values for the synthesis of selected components of English consonants before front vowels

Sonorant

	F1	F2	F3	B1	B2	B3
WW	290	610	2150	50	80	60
YY	260	2070	3020	40	250	500
RR	310	1060	1380	70	100	120
LL	310	1050	2880	50	100	280

Fricative

	F1	F2	F3	B1	B2	B3	A2	A3	A4	A5	A6	AB
FF	340	1100	2080	200	120	150	0	0	0	0	0	57
VV	220	1100	2080	60	90	120	0	0	0	0	0	57
TH	320	1290	2540	200	90	200	0	0	0	0	28	48
DH	270	1290	2540	60	80	170	0	0	0	0	28	48
SS	320	1390	2530	200	80	200	0	0	0	0	52	0
ZZ	240	1390	2530	70	60	180	0	0	0	0	52	0
SH	300	1840	2750	200	100	300	57	48	48	46	0	0

Affricate

	F1	F2	F3	B1	B2	B3	A2	A3	A4	A5	A6	AB
CH	350	1800	2820	200	90	300	0	44	60	53	53	0
JH	260	1800	2820	60	80	270	0	44	60	53	53	0

Plosive

	F1	F2	F3	B1	B2	B3	A2	A3	A4	A5	A6	AB
PP	400	1100	2150	300	150	220	0	0	0	0	0	63
BB	200	1100	2150	60	110	130	0	0	0	0	0	63
TT	400	1600	2600	300	120	250	0	30	45	57	63	0
DD	200	1600	2600	60	100	170	0	47	60	62	60	0
KK	300	1990	2850	250	160	330	0	53	43	45	45	0
GG	200	1990	2850	60	150	280	0	53	43	45	45	0

Nasal

	FNP	FNZ	F1	F2	F3	B1	B2	B3
MM	270	450	480	1270	2130	40	200	200
NN	270	450	480	1340	2470	40	300	300

consonant clusters. Characterization of even the static properties of these phonetic segments is beyond the scope of the present chapter.

11.3.3 *Structure of the output parameter file*

The output file consists of one complete set of control parameter values per 5 msec of speech. The control parameters that are varied are identified in Table 11-3.

Table 11-3: Variable control parameters specified in PHÓNET

N	Symbol	Name
1	AV	amplitude of voicing in dB
2	AF	amplitude of frication in dB
3	AH	amplitude of aspiration in dB
4	AVS	amplitude of sinusoidal voicing in dB
5	F0	voicing fundamental frequency in Hz
6	F1	first formant frequency in Hz
7	F2	second formant frequency in Hz
8	F3	third formant frequency in Hz
9	F4	fourth formant frequency in Hz
10	FNZ	nasal zero frequency in Hz
11	B1	first formant bandwidth in Hz
12	B2	second formant bandwidth in Hz
13	B3	third formant bandwidth in Hz
14	A2	second parallel formant amplitude in dB
15	A3	third parallel formant amplitude in dB
16	A4	fourth parallel formant amplitude in dB
17	A5	fifth parallel formant amplitude in dB
18	A6	sixth parallel formant amplitude in dB
19	AB	bypass path amplitude in dB
20		not currently used

11.4 Summary

PHONET differs from a number of other formant-based synthesis-by-rule programs (e.g. Votrax, Kurzweil, Holmes, Mattingly, Rabiner, or Hertz) primarily in terms of the total number of context-dependent rules that have been formulated in order to model details of the spectra of phonetic transitions. A complete description of these rules is given in Appendix C.

12

The Klatt formant synthesizer

12.1 Overview

The final two modules of the MITalk system (CWTRAN and COEWAV) simulate
a formant synthesizer (Klatt, 1980). Figure 12-1 shows the interface between these
modules and the hardware which produces the actual speech. Synthesizer control
parameter data are specified every 5 msec by rules contained in the phonetic component described in Chapter 11. There are 39 control parameters that specify the
actions of the software synthesizer, of which only 20 are varied as a function of
time.

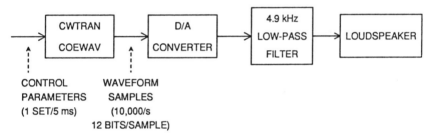

Figure 12-1: Interface between synthesizer software and hardware

The Klatt formant synthesizer consists of two logically distinct modules,
CWTRAN and COEWAV. The first module, CWTRAN, accepts control
parameter data such as formant frequencies, formant bandwidths, and fundamental
frequency (all specified in Hz), as well as source amplitudes and amplitudes of
each parallel formant (specified in dB) and derives a set of difference-equation
coefficients for each digital formant resonator and a set of linear amplitude coefficients. The second synthesizer subroutine, COEWAV, accepts as input this coef-
ficient and amplitude array for a 5 msec frame and computes the next 5 msec
chunk of waveform.

Considerable system speed improvement can be obtained by implementing
the final module, COEWAV, as a hardware digital filter. A TTL implementation
has been constructed (Miranker, 1978). Whether the software subroutine or the
VTM is used, output waveform samples are played through a digital-to-analog
converter, analog low-pass filter, and loudspeaker.

12.1.1 *Software simulation vs. hardware construction*

The advantages of a software implementation over the construction of special-purpose *analog* hardware are substantial. The synthesizer does not need repeated calibration, it is stable, and the signal-to-noise ratio (quantization noise in the case of a digital simulation) can be made as large as desired. The configuration can easily be changed as new ideas are proposed. For example, the voices of women and children can be synthesized with appropriate modifications to the voicing source and cascade vocal tract configuration. Graphic terminals are usually available in a computer facility and can be programmed to view control parameter data or selected portions of the output speech waveform. Short-time spectra can also be computed and displayed in order to make detailed spectral comparisons between natural and synthetic waveforms.

12.1.2 *Formant synthesis vs. articulatory synthesis*

Speech synthesizers fall into two broad categories: 1) articulatory synthesizers that attempt to model faithfully the mechanical motions of the articulators, and the resulting distributions of volume velocity and sound pressure in the lungs, larynx, and vocal and nasal tracts (Flanagan *et al.*, 1975), and 2) formant synthesizers which derive an approximation to a speech waveform by a simpler set of rules formulated in the acoustic domain. The present chapter is concerned only with formant models of speech generation since current articulatory models require several orders of magnitude more computation, and the resultant speech output cannot be specified with sufficient precision for direct optimization of the rules by trial-and-error comparisons with natural speech.

The synthesizer design is based on an acoustic theory of speech production presented in Fant (1960), and is summarized in Figure 12-2. According to this view, one or more sources of sound energy are activated by the build-up of lung pressure. Treating each sound source separately, we may characterize it in the frequency domain by a source spectrum $S(f)$, where f is frequency in Hz. Each sound source excites the vocal tract which acts as a resonating system analogous to an organ pipe.

Since the vocal tract is a linear system, it can be characterized in the frequency domain by a linear transfer function $T(f)$, which is the ratio of lip-plus-nose volume velocity $U(f)$ to source input $S(f)$. Finally, the spectrum of the sound pressure that would be recorded some distance from the lips of the talker $P(f)$ is related to lip-plus-nose volume velocity $U(f)$ by a radiation characteristic $R(f)$ that describes the effects of directional sound propagation from the head.

Each of the above relationships can also be recast in the time (waveform)

124

$$P(f) = S(f)^*T(f)^*F(f)$$

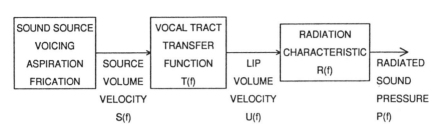

Figure 12-2: Components of the output spectrum of a speech sound

domain. This is actually how a waveform is generated in the computer. The synthesizer includes 'components to simulate the generation of several different kinds of sound sources (described in Section 12.1.10), components to simulate the vocal tract transfer function (Figure 12-3), and a component to simulate sound radiation from the head (Figure 12-14).

12.1.3 *Cascade vs. parallel*

A number of hardware and software speech synthesizers have been described (Dudley *et al.*, 1939; Cooper *et al.*, 1951; Lawrence, 1953; Stevens *et al.*, 1955; Fant, 1959; Fant and Martony, 1962; Flanagan *et al.*, 1962; Holmes *et al.*, 1964; Epstein, 1965; Tomlinson, 1966; Scott *et al.*, 1966; Liljencrants, 1968; Rabiner *et al.*, 1971a; Klatt, 1972; Holmes, 1973). They employ different configurations to achieve what is hopefully the same result: high-quality approximation to human speech. A few of the synthesizers have stability and calibration problems, and a few have design deficiencies that make it impossible to synthesize a good voiced fricative, but many others have an excellent design. Of the best synthesizers that have been proposed, two general configurations are common.

In one type of configuration, called a parallel formant synthesizer (see e.g. Lawrence, 1953; Holmes, 1973), the formant resonators that simulate the transfer function of the vocal tract are connected in parallel, as shown in the lower portion of Figure 12-3. Each formant resonator is preceded by an amplitude control that determines the relative amplitude of a spectral peak (formant) in the output spectrum for both voiced and voiceless speech sounds. In the second type of configuration, called a cascade formant synthesizer (see e.g. Fant, 1959; Klatt, 1972), sonorants are synthesized using a set of formant resonators connected in cascade, as shown in the upper part of Figure 12-3.

The advantage of the cascade connection is that the relative amplitudes of formant peaks for vowels come out just right (Fant, 1956) without the need for in-

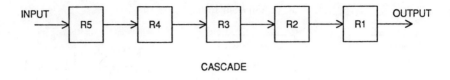

CASCADE

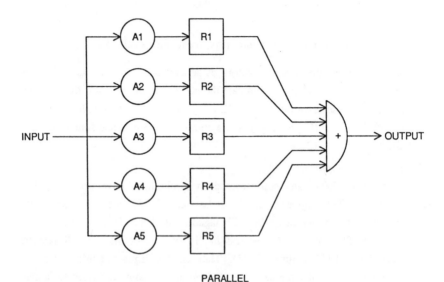

PARALLEL

Figure 12-3: Parallel and cascade simulation of the vocal tract transfer function

dividual amplitude controls for each formant. The disadvantage is that one still needs a parallel formant configuration for the generation of fricatives and plosive bursts -- the vocal tract transfer function cannot be modeled adequately when the sound source is above the larynx, so that cascade synthesizers are generally more complex in overall structure.

A second advantage of the cascade configuration is that it is a more accurate model of the vocal tract transfer function during the production of nonnasal sonorants (Flanagan, 1957). It will be shown that the transfer functions of certain vowels cannot be modeled very well by a parallel formant synthesizer. Although not optimal, a parallel synthesizer is particularly useful for generating stimuli that violate the normal amplitude relationships between formants, or if one wishes to generate, e.g., single-formant patterns.

The software simulation to be described has been programmed for normal use as a hybrid cascade/parallel synthesizer (Figure 12-4a), or alternatively for special-

126

purpose use as a strictly parallel synthesizer (Figure 12-4b). The experimenter must decide beforehand which configuration is to be employed. The change in configuration depends on the state of a single switch, and the program is smart enough to avoid performing unnecessary computations for resonators that are not used. To the extent possible, the synthesizer has been adjusted so as to generate about the same output waveform whether the cascade/parallel configuration or the all-parallel configuration is selected.

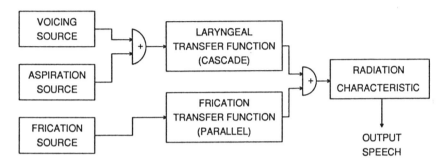

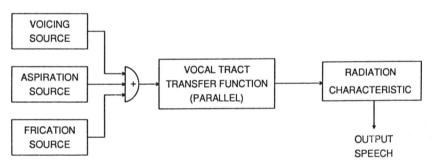

Figure 12-4: Cascade/parallel configurations supported by MITalk

12.1.4 *Waveform sampling rate*

Most of the sound energy of speech is contained in frequencies between about 80 and 8000 Hz (Dunn and White, 1940). However, intelligibility tests of band-pass filtered speech indicate that intelligibility is not measurably changed if the energy in frequencies above about 5000 Hz is removed (French and Steinberg, 1947). Speech low-pass filtered in this way sounds perfectly natural. Thus we have selected 10,000 samples per second as the digital sampling rate of the synthesizer.

127

12.1.5 *Parameter update rate*

Control parameter values are updated every 5 msec. This is frequent enough to mimic even the most rapid formant transitions and brief plosive bursts. If desired, the program can be modified to update parameter values only every 10 msec with relatively little decrease in output quality.

12.1.6 *Digital resonators*

The basic building block of the synthesizer is a digital resonator having the properties illustrated in Figure 12-5. Two parameters are used to specify the input-output characteristics of a resonator, the resonant (formant) frequency F and the resonance bandwidth BW. In Figure 12-5, these values are 1000 Hz and 50 Hz, respectively. Samples of the output of a digital resonator, $y(nT)$, are computed from the input sequence, $x(nT)$, by the equation:

$$y(nT)=Ax(nT)+By(nT{-}T)+Cy(nT{-}2T) \tag{1}$$

where $y(nT{-}T)$ and $y(nT{-}2T)$ are the previous two sample values of the output sequence $y(nT)$. The constants A, B, and C are related to the resonant frequency F and the bandwidth BW of a resonator by the impulse-invariant transformation (Gold and Rabiner, 1968):

$$
\begin{aligned}
C &= -e^{2\pi BWT} \\
B &= 2e^{-\pi BWT}\cos(2\pi fT) \\
A &= 1{-}B{-}C
\end{aligned}
\tag{2}
$$

The constant T is the reciprocal of the sampling rate and equals 0.0001 seconds in the present 5-kHz simulation.

The values of the resonator control parameters F and BW are updated every 5 msec, causing the difference equation constants to change discretely in small steps every 5 msec as an utterance is synthesized. Large, sudden changes to these constants may introduce clicks and burps in the synthesizer output. Fortunately, acoustic theory indicates that formant frequencies must always change slowly and continuously, relative to the 5-msec update interval for control parameters.

A digital resonator is a second-order difference equation. The transfer function of a digital resonator has a sampled frequency response given by:

$$T(f)=\frac{A}{1-Bz^{-1}-Cz^{-2}} \tag{3}$$

where $z=e^{j2\pi fT}$, j is the square root of -1, and f is frequency in Hz which ranges from 0 to 5000 Hz. The transfer function has a (sampled) impulse response identical to a corresponding analog resonator circuit at sample times nT (Gold and Rabiner, 1968). But the frequency responses of an analog and digital resonator are not exactly the same, as seen in Figure 12-5.

DIGITAL RESONATOR

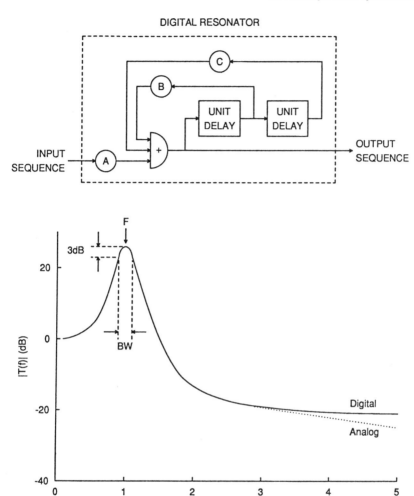

Figure 12-5: Block diagram and frequency response of a digital resonator

12.1.7 *Digital antiresonator*

An antiresonance (also called an antiformant or transfer-function zero pair) can be realized by slight modifications to these equations. The frequency response of an antiresonator is the mirror image of the response plotted in Figure 12-5 (i.e. replace dB by -dB). An antiresonator is used in the synthesizer to shape the spectrum of the voicing source and another is used to simulate the effects of nasalization in the cascade model of the vocal tract transfer function.

The output of an antiformant resonator, $y(nT)$, is related to the input $x(nT)$ by the equation:

$$y(nT)=A'x(nT)+B'x(nT-T)+C'x(nT-2T) \qquad (4)$$

where $x(nT-T)$ and $x(nT-2T)$ are the previous two samples of the input $x(nT)$, the constants A', B' and C' are defined by the equations:

$$A'=1/A$$
$$B'=-B/A \qquad (5)$$
$$C'=-C/A$$

where A, B, and C are obtained by inserting the antiresonance center frequency F and bandwidth BW into Equation 2.

12.1.8 *Low-pass resonator*

As a special case, the frequency F of a digital resonator can be set to zero, producing, in effect, a low-pass filter which has a nominal attenuation skirt of -12 dB per octave of frequency increase and a 3-dB down break frequency equal to $BW/2$. The voicing source contains a digital resonator RGP used as a low-pass filter that transforms a glottal impulse into a pulse having a waveform and spectrum similar to normal voicing. A second digital resonator, RGS, is used to low-pass filter the normal voicing waveform to produce the quasi-sinusoidal glottal waveform seen during the closure interval for an intervocalic voiced plosive.

12.1.9 *Synthesizer block diagram*

A block diagram of the synthesizer is shown in Figure 12-6. There are 39 control parameters that determine the characteristics of the output. The name and range of values for each parameter are given in Table 12-1. As seen from the table, as many as 22 of the 39 parameters are varied to achieve optimum matches to an arbitrary English utterance. The constant parameters in Table 12-1 have been given values appropriate for a particular male voice, and would have to be adjusted slightly to approximate the speech of other male or female talkers. The list of variable control parameters is long, compared with some synthesizers, but the emphasis here is on defining strategies for the synthesis of high-quality speech. We are not concerned with searching for compromises that would minimize the information content in the control parameter specification.

12.1.10 *Sources of sound*

There are two kinds of sound sources that may be activated during speech production (Stevens and Klatt, 1974). One involves quasi-periodic vibrations of some structure, usually the vocal folds. Vibration of the vocal folds is called voicing. (Other structures such as the lips, tongue tip, or uvula may be caused to vibrate in sound types of some languages, but not in English.)

The second kind of sound source involves the generation of turbulence noise

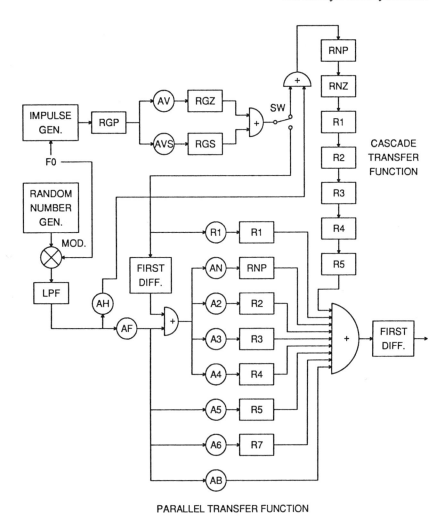

Figure 12-6: Block diagram of the cascade/parallel formant synthesizer

by the rapid flow of air past a narrow constriction. The resulting noise is called aspiration if the constriction is located at the level of the vocal folds as, for example, during the production of the sound HH. If the constriction is located above the larynx as, for example, during the production of sounds such as SS, the resulting noise is called frication noise. The explosion of a plosive release also consists primarily of frication noise.

When voicing and turbulence noise generation co-exist, as in a voiced fricative such as ZZ or a voiced HH, the noise is amplitude modulated periodically by

131

Table 12-1: List of control parameters for the software formant synthesizer

N	Symbol	Name	Min.	Max.	Typ.
1 V	AV	Amplitude of voicing (dB)	0	80	0
2 V	AF	Amplitude of frication (dB)	0	80	0
3 V	AH	Amplitude of aspiration (dB)	0	80	0
4 V	AVS	Amplitude of sinusoidal voicing (dB)	0	80	0
5 V	F0	Fundamental freq. of voicing (Hz)	0	500	0
6 V	F1	First formant frequency (Hz)	150	900	500
7 V	F2	Second formant frequency (Hz)	500	2500	1500
8 V	F3	Third formant frequency (Hz)	1300	3500	2500
9 V	F4	Fourth formant frequency (Hz)	2500	4500	3300
10 V	FNZ	Nasal zero frequency (Hz)	200	700	250
11 V	AN	Nasal formant amplitude (dB)	0	80	0
12 V	A1	First formant amplitude (dB)	0	80	0
13 V	A2	Second formant amplitude (dB)	0	0	0
14 V	A3	Third formant amplitude (dB)	0	80	0
15 V	A4	Fourth formant amplitude (dB)	0	80	0
16 V	A5	Fifth formant amplitude (dB)	0	80	0
17 V	A6	Sixth formant amplitude (dB)	0	80	0
18 V	AB	Bypass path amplitude (dB)	0	80	0
19 V	B1	First formant bandwidth (Hz)	40	500	50
20 V	B2	Second formant bandwidth (Hz)	40	500	70
21 V	B3	Third formant bandwidth (Hz)	40	500	110
22 C	SW	Cascade/parallel switch	0(c)	1(p)	0
23 C	FGP	Glottal resonator 1 frequency (Hz)	0	600	0
24 C	BGP	Glottal resonator 1 bandwidth (Hz)	100	2000	100
25 C	FGZ	Glottal zero frequency (Hz)	0	5000	1500
26 C	BGZ	Glottal zero bandwidth (Hz)	100	9000	6000
27 C	B4	Fourth formant bandwidth (Hz)	100	500	250
28 V	F5	Fifth formant frequency (Hz)	3500	4900	3850
29 C	B5	Fifth formant bandwidth (Hz)	150	700	200
30 C	F6	Sixth formant frequency (Hz)	4000	4999	4900
31 C	B6	Sixth formant bandwidth (Hz)	200	2000	1000
32 C	FNP	Nasal pole frequency (Hz)	200	500	250
33 C	BNP	Nasal pole bandwidth (Hz)	50	500	100
34 C	BNZ	Nasal zero bandwidth (Hz)	50	500	100
35 C	BGS	Glottal resonator 2 bandwidth (Hz)	100	1000	200
36 C	SR	Sampling rate (Hz)	5000	20000	10000
37 C	NWS	Number of waveform samples per chunk	1	200	50
38 C	G0	Overall gain control (dB)	0	80	48
39 C	NFC	Number of cascaded formants	4	6	5

the vibrations of the vocal folds. In addition, the vocal folds may vibrate without meeting in the midline. In this type of voicing, the amplitude of higher frequency harmonics of the voicing source spectrum is significantly reduced and the waveform looks nearly sinusoidal. Therefore, the synthesizer should be capable of generating at least two types of voicing waveforms (normal voicing and quasi-sinusoidal voicing), two types of frication waveforms (normal frication and amplitude-modulated frication), and two types of aspiration (normal aspiration and amplitude-modulated aspiration). These are the only kinds of sound sources required for English, although trills and clicks of other languages may call for the addition of other source controls to the synthesizer in the future.

12.1.11 *Voicing source*

The structure of the voicing source is shown at the top left in Figure 12-6. Variable control parameters are used to specify the fundamental frequency of voicing (F0), the amplitude of normal voicing (AV), and the amplitude of quasi-sinusoidal voicing (AVS).

An impulse train corresponding to normal voicing is generated whenever F0 is greater than zero. The amplitude of each impulse is determined by AV, the amplitude of normal voicing in dB. AV ranges from about 60 dB in a strong vowel to 0 dB when the voicing source is turned off. Fundamental frequency is specified in Hz; a value of F0=100 would produce a 100-Hz impulse train. The number of samples between impulses, T0, is determined by SR/F0, e.g., for a sampling rate of 10,000 and a fundamental frequency of 200 Hz, an impulse is generated every 50th sample. Under some circumstances, the quantization of the fundamental period to be an integral number of samples might be perceived in a slow, prolonged fundamental frequency transition as a sort of staircase of mechanical sounds (similar to the rather unnatural speech one gets by setting F0 to a constant value in a synthetic utterance). But the problem is not sufficiently serious to merit running the source model of the synthesizer at a higher sampling rate. If desired, some aspiration noise can be added to the normal voicing waveform to partially alleviate the problem and create a somewhat breathy voice quality.

12.1.12 *Normal voicing*

Ignoring for the moment the effects of RGZ, we see that the train of impulses is sent through a low-pass filter, RGP, to produce a smooth waveform that resembles a typical glottal volume velocity waveform (Flanagan, 1958). The resonator frequency FGP is set to 0 Hz and BGP to 100 Hz. The filtered impulses thus have a spectrum that falls off smoothly at approximately -12 dB per octave above 50 Hz. The waveform generated does not have the same phase spectrum as a typical glottal pulse, nor does it contain spectral zeros of the kind that often appear in natural voicing, but neither of these differences is judged to be very important perceptually.

The antiresonator RGZ is used to modify the detailed shape of the spectrum of the voicing source for particular individuals with greater precision than would be possible using only a single low-pass filter. The values chosen for FGZ and BGZ in Table 12-1 are such as to tilt the general voicing spectrum up somewhat to match the vocal characteristics of speaker DHK. The waveform and spectral envelope of normal voicing that are produced by sending an impulse train through RGP and RGZ are shown in Figure 12-7.

12.1.13 *Quasi-sinusoidal voicing*

The amplitude control parameter AVS determines the amount of smoothed voicing generated during voiced fricatives, voiced aspirates, and the voicebars present in intervocalic voiced plosives. An appropriate wave shape for quasi-sinusoidal voicing is obtained by low-pass filtering an impulse by low-pass digital resonators RGP and RGS. The frequency control of RGS is set to zero to produce a low-pass filter, and BGS=200 determines the cutoff frequency beyond which harmonics are strongly attenuated.

The waveform and spectral envelope of quasi-sinusoidal voicing are shown in Figure 12-7. After the effects of the vocal tract transfer function and radiation characteristic are imposed on the source spectrum, the output waveform of quasi-sinusoidal voicing contains significant energy only at the first and second harmonics of the fundamental frequency. AVS ranges from about 60 dB in a voicebar or strongly voiced fricative to 0 dB if no quasi-sinusoidal voicing is present. Some degree of quasi-sinusoidal voicing can be added to the normal voicing source (in combination with aspiration noise) to produce a breathy voice quality (e.g. AH=AV-3, AVS=AV-6).

12.1.14 *Frication source*

A turbulent noise source is simulated in the synthesizer by a pseudo-random number generator, a modulator, an amplitude control AF, and a -6 dB/octave low-pass digital filter LPF, as shown in Figure 12-6. Theoretically, the spectrum of the frication source should be approximately flat (Stevens, 1971), and the amplitude distribution should be Gaussian. Signals produced by the random number generator have a flat spectrum, but they have a uniform amplitude distribution between limits determined by the value of the amplitude control parameter AF. A pseudo-Gaussian amplitude distribution is obtained in the synthesizer by summing 16 of the numbers produced by the random number generator.

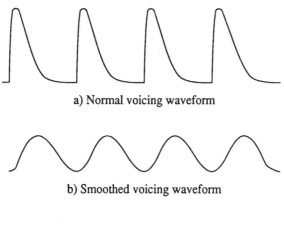

a) Normal voicing waveform

b) Smoothed voicing waveform

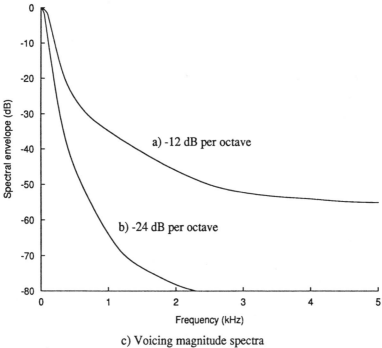

c) Voicing magnitude spectra

Figure 12-7: Four periods from voicing waveforms

In theory, the noise source is an ideal pressure source. The volume velocity of the frication noise depends on the impedance seen by the noise source. Since the vocal tract transfer function $T(f)$ relates source volume velocity to lip volume velocity, one must estimate noise volume velocity to determine lip output. In the general case, this is a complex calculation, but we will assume that source volume velocity is proportional to the integral of source pressure (an excellent approximation for a frication source at the lips because the radiation impedance is largely inductive, but only an approximation for other source locations). The integral is approximated by a first-order low-pass digital filter LPF that is shown in Figure 12-6. Output samples from this filter $y(nT)$ are related to the input sequence $x(nT)$ by the equation:

$$y(nT) = x(nT) + y(nT - T)$$

It will be seen later that, the radiation characteristic is a digital high-pass filter that exactly cancels out the effects of LPF. (For computational efficiency, the radiation characteristic can be moved into the voicing source circuit and the low-pass filter LPF can be removed from the noise source.)

An example of synthetic frication noise volume velocity that was generated in this way is shown in Figure 12-8. The spectrum of this sample of noise fluctuates randomly about the expected long-term average noise spectrum (dashed curve - shifted up by 10 dB for clarity). Short samples of noise vary in their spectral properties due to the nature of random processes.

The output of the random number generator is amplitude modulated by the component labeled "MOD" in Figure 12-6 whenever the fundamental frequency F0 and the amplitude of voicing AV are both greater than zero. Voiceless sounds (AV=0) are not amplitude modulated because the vocal folds are spread and stiffened, and do not vibrate to modulate the airflow. The degree of amplitude modulation is fixed at 50 percent in the synthesizer. The modulation envelope is a square wave with a period equal to the fundamental period. Experience has shown that it is not necessary to vary the degree of amplitude modulation over the course of a sentence, but only to ensure that it is present in voiced fricatives and voiced aspirated sounds.

The amplitude of the frication noise is determined by AF, which is given in dB. A value of 60 will generate a strong frication noise, while a value of zero effectively turns off the frication source.

12.1.15 *Aspiration source*

Aspiration noise is essentially the same as frication noise, except that it is generated in the larynx. In a strictly parallel vocal tract model, AF can be used to

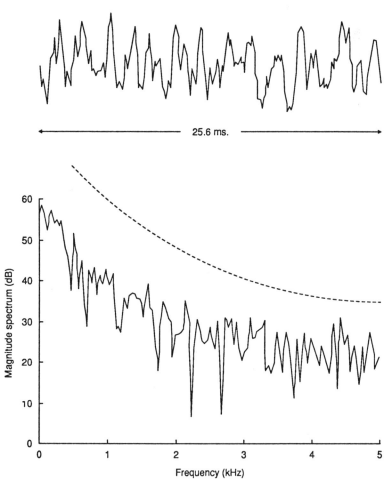

Figure 12-8: Waveform segment and magnitude spectrum of frication noise

generate both frication and aspiration noise. However, in the cascade synthesizer configuration, aspiration noise is sent through the cascade vocal tract model (since the cascade configuration is specially designed to model vocal tract characteristics for laryngeal sound sources), while fricatives require a parallel vocal tract configuration. Therefore separate amplitude controls are needed for frication and aspiration in a cascade/parallel configuration. The amplitude of aspiration noise sent to the cascade vocal tract model is determined by AH, which is given in dB. A value of 60 will generate strong aspiration, while a value of zero effectively turns off the aspiration source. Since frication and aspiration are generated by an identical process in the synthesizer, Figure 12-8 describes the characteristics of the aspiration source as well.

137

12.1.16 *Pitch-synchronous updating of voicing source amplitudes*

The voicing source amplitude controls AV and AVS only have an effect on the synthetic waveform when a glottal impulse is issued. The reason for adjusting voicing amplitudes discontinuously at the onset of each glottal period is to prevent the creation of pops and clicks due to waveform discontinuities introduced by the sudden change in an amplitude control in the middle of a voicing period.

12.1.17 *Generation of plosive bursts with a predictable spectrum*

The noise amplitudes AF and AH are used to interpolate the intensity of the noise sources linearly over the 5 msec (50 sample) interval. (Thus there is a 5 msec delay in the attainment of a new amplitude value for a noise source.) Interpolation permits a more gradual onset for a fricative or HH than would otherwise be possible. There is, however, one exception to this internal control strategy. A plosive burst involves a more rapid source onset than can be achieved by 5 msec linear interpolation. Therefore, if AF increases by more than 50 dB from its value specified in the previous 5 msec segment, AF is (automatically) changed instantaneously to its new target value. The pseudo-random number generator is also reset at the time of plosive burst onset so as to produce exactly the same source waveform for each burst. The value to which it is set was chosen so as to produce as a burst spectrum as flat as possible.

12.1.18 *Control of fundamental frequency*

At times, it is desired to specify precisely the timing of the first glottal pulse (voicing onset) relative to a plosive burst. For example, in the syllable **pa**, it might be desired to produce a 5 msec burst of frication noise, 40 msec of aspiration noise, and voicing onset exactly 45 msec from the onset of the burst. Usually, a glottal pulse is issued in the synthesizer at a time specified by the reciprocal of the value of the fundamental frequency control parameter extant when the last glottal pulse was issued. However, if either AV or F0 is set to zero, no glottal pulse is issued during this 5 msec time interval; in fact, no glottal pulses are issued until precisely the moment that both the AV and F0 control parameters become nonzero. In the case of the **pa** example above, both AV and F0 would normally be set to zero during the closure interval, burst, and aspiration phase; and AV would be set to about 60 dB and F0 to about 130 Hz at exactly 45 msec after the synthetic burst onset.

Since the update interval in the synthesizer is set to 5 msec, voice onset time can be specified exactly in 5 msec steps. If greater precision is needed, it is necessary to change the parameter update interval from 5 msec (NWS=50) to, for example, 2 msec (NWS=20).

138

12.2 Vocal tract transfer functions

The acoustic characteristics of the vocal tract are determined by its cross-sectional area as a function of distance from the larynx to the lips. The vocal tract forms a nonuniform transmission line whose behavior can be determined for frequencies below about 5 kHz by solving a one-dimensional wave equation (Fant, 1960). (Above 5 kHz, three-dimensional resonance modes would have to be considered.) Solutions to the wave equation result in a transfer function that relates samples of the glottal source volume velocity to output volume velocity at the lips.

The synthesizer configuration in Figure 12-6 includes components to realize two different types of vocal tract transfer function. The first, a cascade configuration of digital resonators, models the resonant properties of the vocal tract whenever the source of sound is within the larynx. The second, a parallel configuration of digital resonators and amplitude controls, models the resonant properties of the vocal tract during the production of frication noise. The parallel configuration can also be used to model vocal tract characteristics for laryngeal sound sources, although the approximation is not quite as good as in the cascade model.

12.2.1 *Cascade vocal tract model*

Assuming that the one-dimensional wave equation is a valid approximation below 5 kHz, the vocal tract transfer function can be represented in the frequency domain by a product of poles and zeros. Furthermore, the transfer function contains only about five complex pole pairs and no zeros in the frequency range of interest, as long as the articulation is nonnasalized and the sound source is at the larynx (Fant, 1960). The transfer function conforms to an all-pole model because there are no side-branch resonators or multiple sound paths. (The glottis is partially open during the production of aspiration so that the poles and zeros of the subglottal system are often seen in aspiration spectra; the only way to approximate their effects in the synthesizer is to increase the first formant bandwidth to about 300 Hz. The perceptual importance of the remaining spectral distortions caused by the poles and zeros of the subglottal system is probably minimal.)

Five resonators are appropriate for simulating a vocal tract with a length of about 17 cm, the length of a typical male vocal tract, because the average spacing between formants is equal to the velocity of sound divided by half the wavelength, which works out to be 1000 Hz. A typical female vocal tract is 15 to 20 percent shorter, suggesting that only four formant resonators be used to represent a female voice in a 5 kHz simulation (or that the simulation should be extended to about 6 kHz). It is suggested that the voices of women and children be approximated by setting the control parameter NFC to 4, thus removing the fifth formant from the cascade branch of the block diagram shown in Figure 12-6. For a male talker with a very long vocal tract, it may be necessary to add a sixth resonator to the cascade branch. As currently programmed, NFC can be set to 4, 5, or 6 formants in the cascade branch. (Any change to NFC implies a change in the length of the vocal tract, so such changes must be made with care.)

Ignoring for the moment the nasal pole resonator RNP and the nasal zero antiresonator RNZ, the cascade model of Figure 12-6, consisting of five formant resonators, has a volume velocity transfer function that can be represented in the frequency domain as a product (Gold and Rabiner, 1968):

$$T(f)=\prod_{n=1}^{5}\frac{A(n)}{1-B(n)z^{-1}-C(n)z^{-2}} \tag{6}$$

where the constants $A(n)$, $B(n)$, and $C(n)$ are determined by the values of the nth formant frequency $F(n)$ and nth formant bandwidth $BW(n)$ by the relationships given earlier in Equation 2. The constants $A(n)$ in the numerator of Equation 6 ensure that the transfer function has a value of unity at zero frequency, i.e., the dc airflow is unimpeded. The magnitude of $T(f)$ is plotted in Figure 12-9 for several values of formant frequencies and formant bandwidths.

12.2.2 *Relationship to analog models of the vocal tract*

The transfer function of the vocal tract can also be expressed in the continuous world of differential equations. Equation 6 is then rewritten as an infinite product of poles in the Laplace transform s-plane:

$$T(f)=\prod_{n=1}^{\infty}\frac{s(n)s^*(n)}{[s+s(n)][s+s^*(n)]} \tag{7}$$

where $s=2j\pi f$, and the constants $s(n)$ and $s^*(n)$ are determined by the values of the nth formant frequency $F(n)$ and the nth formant bandwidth $BW(n)$ by the relationships:

$$s(n)=\pi BW(n)+2j\pi F(n)$$

$$s^*(n)=\pi BW(n)-2j\pi F(n)$$

The two formulations 6 and 7 are exactly equivalent representations of the transfer function for an ideal vocal tract configuration corresponding to a uniform tube closed at the glottis and having all formant bandwidths equal to, e.g., 100 Hz. The two formulations are indistinguishable at representing vocal tract transfer functions below 5 kHz. However, in a practical synthesizer, the infinite product of poles can only be approximated (e.g. by building five electronic resonators and a higher-pole correction network (Fant, 1959)).

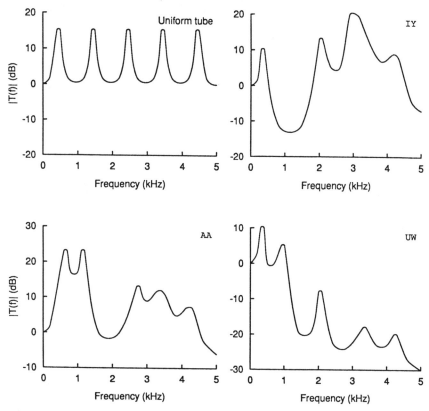

Figure 12-9: Magnitude of the vocal tract transfer function

12.2.3 *Formant frequencies*

Each formant resonator introduces a peak in the magnitude spectra shown in Figure 12-9. The frequency of formant peak "n" is determined by the formant frequency control parameter Fn. (The amplitude of a formant peak depends not only on Fn and the formant bandwidth control parameter BWn, but also on the frequencies of the other formants, which will be discussed below.)

Formant frequency values are determined by the detailed shape of the vocal tract. Formant frequency values associated with different phonetic segments in the speech of speaker DHK are presented in Chapter 11. The frequencies of the lowest three formants vary substantially with changes to articulation (e.g. the observed range of F1 is from about 180 to 750 Hz, of F2 is 600 to 2300 Hz, and of F3 is 1300 to 3100 Hz for a typical male talker). The frequencies and bandwidths of the fourth and fifth formant resonators do not vary as much, and could be held constant with little decrease in output sound quality. These higher frequency resonators help to shape the overall spectrum, but otherwise contribute little to intelligibility. The particular values chosen for the fourth and fifth formant frequencies (Table 12-1) produce an energy concentration around 3 to 3.5 kHz and a rapid falloff in spectral energy above about 4 kHz, which is a pattern typical of many talkers.

12.2.4 *Formant bandwidths*

Formant bandwidths are a function of energy losses due to heat conduction, viscosity, cavity-wall motions, and radiation of sound from the lips and the real part of the glottal source impedance. Bandwidths are difficult to deduce from analyses of natural speech because of irregularities in the glottal source spectrum. Bandwidths have been estimated by other techniques, such as using a sinusoidal swept-tone sound source (Fujimura and Lindqvist, 1971). Results indicate that bandwidths vary by a factor of two or more as a function of the particular phonetic segment being spoken. Typical values for formant bandwidths are also given in Chapter 11. Bandwidth variation is small enough so that all formant bandwidths might be held constant in some applications, in which case only F1, F2, and F3 would be varied to simulate the vocal tract transfer functions for nonnasalized vowels and sonorant consonants.

12.2.5 *Nasals and nasalization of vowels*

It is not possible to approximate nasal murmurs and the nasalization of vowels that are adjacent to nasals with a cascade system of five resonators alone. More that five formants are often present in these sounds and formant amplitudes do not conform to the relationships inherent in a cascade configuration because of the presence of transfer function zeros (Fujimura, 1961, 1962). Typical transfer functions for a nasal murmur and for a nasalized IH are shown in Figure 12-10. These spectra were obtained from the recorded syllable "dim".

Nasalization introduces additional poles and zeros into the transfer function of the vocal-nasal tract due to the presence of a side-branch resonator. In Figure 12-10, the nasal murmur and the nasalized IH have an extra pole pair and zero pair near F1. The oral cavity forms the side-branch resonator in the case of a nasal murmur, while the nose should be considered a side-branch resonator in a nasalized vowel (because the amount of sound radiated through the nostrils is insignificant compared to the effect of the lowered velum on the formant structure of the sound output from the lips).

Nasalization of adjacent vowels is an important element in the synthesis of nasal consonants. Perceptually, the most important change associated with

142

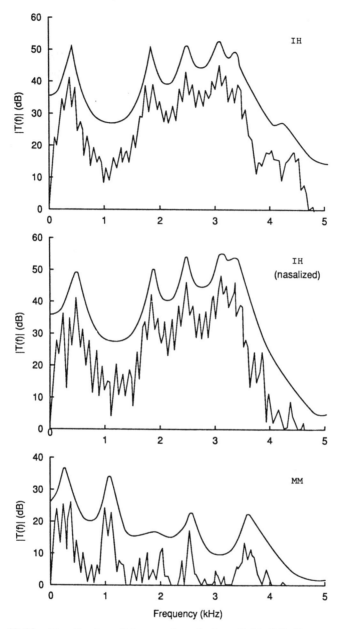

Figure 12-10: Nasalization of the vowel IH in the syllable "dim"

143

nasalization of a vowel is the reduction in amplitude of the first formant, brought on by the presence of a nearby low-frequency pole pair and zero pair. The first formant frequency also tends to shift slightly toward about 500 Hz.

Nasal murmurs and vowel nasalization are approximated by the insertion of an additional resonator RNP and antiresonator RNZ into the cascade vocal tract model. The nasal pole frequency FNP and zero frequency FNZ should be set to a fixed value of about 250 Hz, but the frequency of the nasal zero must be increased during the production of nasals and nasalization. Strategies for controlling FNZ are given in Chapter 11. The RNP-RNZ pair is effectively removed from the cascade circuit during the synthesis of nonnasalized speech sounds if FNP=FNZ.

12.2.6 *Parallel vocal tract model for frication sources*

During frication excitation, the vocal tract transfer function contains both poles and zeros. The pole frequencies are temporally continuous with formant locations of adjacent phonetic segments because, by definition, the poles are the natural resonant frequencies of the entire vocal tract configuration, no matter where the source is located. Thus, the use of vocalic formant frequency parameters to control the locations of frication maxima is theoretically well-motivated (and helpful in preventing the fricative noises from "dissociating" from the rest of the speech signal).

The zeros in the transfer function for fricatives are the frequencies for which the impedance (looking back toward the larynx from the position of the frication source) is infinite, since the series-connected pressure source of turbulence noise cannot produce any output volume velocity under these conditions. The effect of transfer-function zeros is two-fold; they introduce notches in the spectrum and they modify the amplitudes of the formants. The perceptual importance of spectral notches is not great because masking effects of adjacent harmonics limit the detectability of a spectral notch (Gauffin and Sundberg, 1974). We have found that a satisfactory approximation to the vocal tract transfer function for frication excitation can be achieved with a parallel set of digital formant resonators having amplitude controls, and no antiresonators.

Formant amplitudes are set to provide frication excitation for selected formants, usually those associated with the cavity in front of the constriction (Stevens, 1972). The presence of any transfer function zeros is accounted for by appropriate settings of the formant amplitude controls. Relatively simple rules for determination of the formant amplitude settings (and bypass path amplitude values) as a function of place of articulation can be derived from a quantal theory of speech production (Stevens, 1972). The theory states that only formants associated with the cavity in front of the oral constriction are strongly excited. The theory is supported by the formant amplitude specifications for fricatives and plosive bursts presented in Chapter 11. These amplitude control data were derived from attempts to match natural frication spectra.

There are six formant resonators in the parallel configuration of Figure 12-6. A sixth formant has been added to the parallel branch specifically for the synthesis of very-high-frequency noise in SS, ZZ. The main energy concentration in these alveolar fricatives is centered on a frequency of about 6 kHz. This is above the highest frequency (5 kHz) that can be synthesized in a 10,000 sample/second simulation. However, in a SS, there is gradually increasing frication noise in the frequencies immediately below 5 kHz due to the low-frequency skirt of the 6 kHz formant resonance, and this noise spectrum can be approximated quite well by a resonator positioned at about 4900 Hz. We have found it better to include an extra resonator to simulate high-frequency noise than to move F5 up in frequency whenever a sibilant is to be synthesized, because clicks and moving energy concentrations are thereby avoided.

Also included in the parallel vocal tract model is a bypass path. The bypass path with amplitude control AB is present because the transfer function contains no prominent resonant peaks during the production of FF, VV, TH, and DH, and the synthesizer should include a means of bypassing all of the resonators to produce a flat transfer function.

During the production of a voiced fricative, there are two active sources of sound, one located at the glottis (voicing) and one at a constriction in the vocal tract (frication). The output of the quasi-sinusoidal voicing source is sent through the cascade vocal tract model, while the frication source excites the parallel branch to generate a voiced fricative.

12.2.7 *Simulation of the cascade configuration by the parallel configuration*
The transfer function of the laryngeally excited vocal tract can also be approximated by five digital formant resonators connected in parallel. The same resonators that form the parallel branch for frication excitation can be used if suitable values are chosen for the formant amplitude controls.

The following rules summarize what happens to formant amplitudes in the transfer function $T(f)$ of a cascade model as the lowest five formant frequencies and bandwidths are changed. These relationships follow directly from Equation 6, under the assumption that each formant frequency F(n) is at least five to ten times as large as the formant bandwidth BW(n):

1. The formant peaks in the transfer function are equal for the case

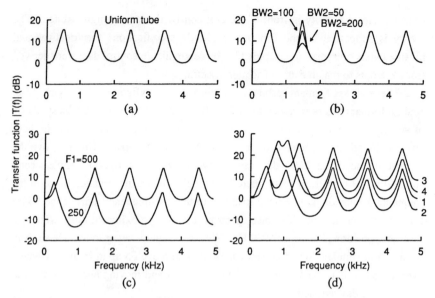

Figure 12-11: Effect of parameter changes on the vocal tract transfer function

where formant frequencies are set to 500, 1500, 2500, 3500, and 4500 Hz and formant bandwidths are set to be equal at 100 Hz. This corresponds to a vocal tract having a uniform cross-sectional area, a closed glottis, open lips (and a nonrealistic set of bandwidth values), as shown in part (a) of Figure 12-11.

2. The amplitude of a formant peak is inversely proportional to its bandwidth. If a formant bandwidth is doubled, that formant peak is reduced in amplitude by 6 dB. If the bandwidth is halved, the peak is increased by 6 dB, as shown in part (b) of Figure 12-11.

3. The amplitude of a formant peak is proportional to formant frequency. If a formant frequency is doubled, that formant peak is increased by 6 dB, as shown in part (c) of Figure 12-11. (This is true of $T(f)$, but not of the resulting speech output spectrum since the glottal source spectrum falls off at about -12 dB/octave of frequency increase, and the radiation characteristic imposes a +6 dB/octave spectral tilt resulting in a net change in formant amplitude of +6 -12 +6 = 0 dB.)

4. Changes to a formant frequency also affect the amplitudes of higher formant peaks by a factor proportional to frequency squared. For ex-

146

ample, if a formant frequency is halved, amplitudes of all higher formants are decreased by 12 dB, i.e. $(.5)^2$, as shown in part (c) of
Figure 12-11.

5. The frequencies of two adjacent formants cannot come any closer
than about 200 Hz because of coupling between the natural modes of
the vocal tract. However, if two formants approach each other by
about this amount, both formant peaks are increased by an additional
3 to 6 dB, as shown in part (d) of Figure 12-11.

The amplitudes of the formant peaks generated by the parallel vocal tract
model have been constrained so that, if A1 to A5 are all set to 60 dB, the transfer
function will approximate that found in the cascade model. This is accomplished
by: 1) adjusting the gain of the higher frequency formants to take into account
frequency changes in lower formants (since a higher formant rides on the skirts of
the transfer function of all lower formants in a cascade model (Fant, 1960)), 2) in-
corporating rules to cause formant amplitudes to increase whenever two formant
frequencies come into proximity, and 3) using a first difference calculation to
remove low-frequency energy from the higher formants; this energy would otherwise distort the spectrum in the region of F1 during the synthesis of some vowels
(Holmes, 1973).

The magnitude of the vocal tract transfer functions of the cascade and parallel
vocal tract models are compared in Figure 12-12 for several vowels. The match is
quite good in the vicinity of formant peaks, but the parallel model introduces transfer function zeros (notches) in the spectrum between formant peaks. The notches
are of relatively little perceptual importance because energy in the formant peak
adjacent to the notch on the low-frequency side tends to mask the detectability of a
spectral notch (Gauffin and Sundberg, 1974).

Many early parallel synthesizers were programmed to add together formant
outputs without filtering out the energy at low frequencies from resonators other
than F1. In other cases, formant outputs were combined in alternating signs. The
deleterious effects of these choices are illustrated in Figure 12-13. Some vowel
spectra are poorly modeled in both of these parallel methods of synthesis. The perceptual degradation is less in the alternating sign case because spectral notches are
less perceptible than energy-fill in a spectral valley between two formants. Comparison of Figure 12-12 and Figure 12-13 indicates that our parallel configuration
is better than either of those shown in Figure 12-13.

A nasal formant resonator RNP appears in the parallel branch to assist in the
approximation of nasal murmurs and vowel nasalization when the cascade branch

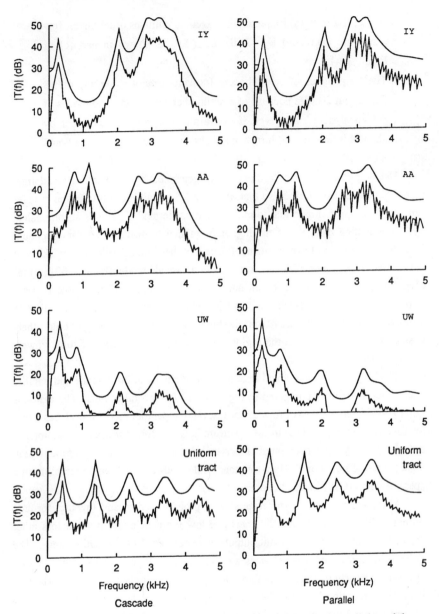

Figure 12-12: Preemphasized output spectra from cascade and parallel models

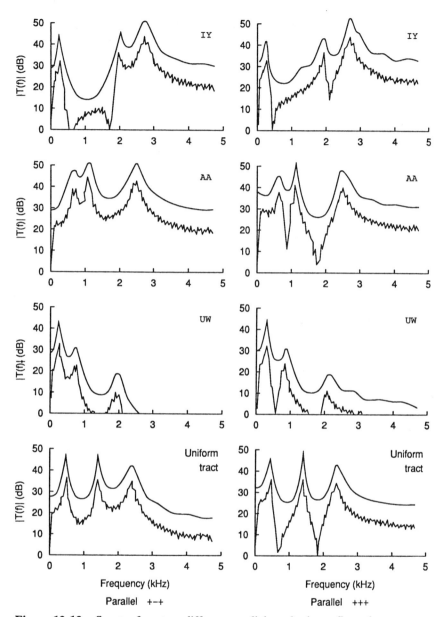

Figure 12-13: Spectra from two different parallel synthesis configurations

149

is not used. Neither the parallel nasal formant nor the parallel first formant resonator is needed in the normal cascade/parallel synthesizer configuration (SW=0), but they are required for the simulation of nasalization in the special-purpose all-parallel configuration (SW=1).

12.3 Radiation characteristic

The box labeled "radiation characteristic" in Figure 12-6 models the effect of directivity patterns of sound radiating from the head as a function of frequency. The sound pressure measured directly in front of and about a meter from the lips is proportional to the temporal derivative of the lip-plus-nose volume velocity, and inversely proportional to r, the distance from the lips (Fant, 1960). The transformation is simulated in the synthesizer by taking the first difference of lip-nose volume velocity:

$$p(nT) = u(nT) - u(nT-T) \tag{8}$$

The radiation characteristic adds a gradual rise in the overall spectrum, as shown in Figure 12-14.

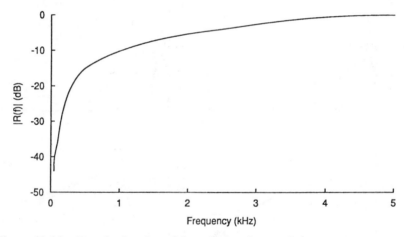

Figure 12-14: Transfer function of the radiation characteristic

13

Some measures of intelligibility and comprehension[1]

13.1 Overview

As the ten year effort to build an unrestricted text-to-speech system at MIT drew to a close, it seemed appropriate to conduct a preliminary evaluation of the quality of the speech output with a relatively large group of naive listeners. The results of such an evaluation would no doubt prove useful in first establishing a benchmark level of performance for comparative purposes, as well as uncovering any problems in the current version of the system that might not have been detected earlier. In addition to obtaining measures of intelligibility of the speech output produced by the text-to-speech system, we were also interested in finding out how well naive listeners could comprehend continuous text produced by the system. This was thought to be an important aspect of the evaluation of the text-to-speech system as a whole, since a version of the current system might eventually be implemented as a device used for computer-aided instruction or as a functional reading machine for the blind (Allen, 1973). Both of these applications are now well within the realm of the available technology (Allen *et al.*, 1979).

In carrying out the evaluation of the system, we patterned several aspects of the testing after earlier work already completed on the evaluation of the Haskins Laboratories reading machine project so that some initial comparisons could be drawn between the two systems (Nye and Gaitenby, 1973, 1974). However, we also added several other tests to the evaluation to gain additional information about word recognition in normal sentential contexts and listening comprehension for a relatively wide range of narrative passages of continuous text. Data were also collected on reading comprehension for the same set of materials to permit direct comparison between the two input modalities. Traditional measures of listening or reading comprehension have not typically been obtained in previous evaluations of the quality of synthetic speech output, and therefore, we felt that some preliminary data would be quite useful before the major components of the present system were implemented as a workable text-to-speech device in an applied context.

---

[1]This chapter was written by D. Pisoni in 1978-9.

In planning the current evaluation project, we also wanted to obtain information about several different aspects of the total system and their contribution to intelligibility and comprehension of speech. To meet this goal, a number of different tests were selected to provide information about: 1) phoneme recognition, 2) word recognition in sentences, and 3) listening comprehension. It was assumed that the results of these three tests together would provide qualitative and quantitative information sufficient to identify any major problems in the operation of the total system at the time of testing in early May of 1979. The results of these three types of tests would also provide much more detailed information about the relative contribution of several of the individual components of the system and their potential interaction.

In carrying out these evaluation tests, we collected a total of 27,128 responses from some 160 naive listeners. A total of 45 minutes of synthetic speech was generated in fully automatic text-to-speech mode. No system errors were corrected at this time and no total system crashes were encountered during the generation of the test materials used in the evaluation.

13.2 Phoneme recognition

After initial discussions, we decided to use the Modified Rhyme Test to measure the intelligibility of the speech produced by the system. This test was originally developed by Fairbanks (1958) and then later modified by House *et al.* (1965). This test was chosen primarily because it is reliable, shows little effect of learning, and is easy to administer to untrained and relatively naive listeners. It also uses standard orthographic responses, thereby eliminating problems associated with phonetic notation. Moreover, extensive data have already been collected with natural speech, as well as synthetic speech produced by the Haskins speech synthesizer (Nye and Gaitenby, 1973), therefore permitting us to make several direct comparisons of the acoustic-phonetic output of the two text-to-speech systems under somewhat comparable testing conditions.

13.2.1 *Method*

13.2.1.1 *Subjects*   Seventy-two naive undergraduate students at Indiana University in Bloomington served as paid listeners in this study. They were all recruited by means of an advertisement in the student newspaper and reported no history of a hearing or speech disorder at the time of testing. The subjects were all right-handed native speakers of English.

13.2.1.2 *Stimuli*   Six lists of 50 monosyllabic words were prepared on the MIT text-to-speech system. The lists were recorded on audio tape via a Revox Model

B77 tape recorder at 7.5 ips with a 3.0 second pause between successive items. Approximately half of the items in a given test list differed in the initial consonant while the remaining half differed in the final consonant.

13.2.1.3 *Procedure*   The seventy-two subjects were divided up into twelve independent groups containing six subjects each for testing. Two groups of subjects were assigned to each of the six original test lists. Subjects were told that this was a test dealing with isolated word recognition and that they were to indicate which word out of six possible alternatives was the one they heard on each trial. Forced-choice response forms were provided to subjects to record their judgements. Subjects were encouraged to guess if they were not sure, but to respond on each trial. No feedback was provided to subjects during the course of testing. Subjects were, however, explicitly informed that the test items were generated on a computer and that the experiment was designed to evaluate the intelligibility of the synthetic speech. An example of the test format is provided in Appendix D.

Testing was carried out in a small experimental room in the Speech Perception Laboratory in the Department of Psychology at Indiana University. This room is equipped with six individual cubicles. The audio tapes were reproduced on an Ampex AG-500 tape recorder and presented to subjects via TDH-39 matched and calibrated headphones at a comfortable listening level of about 80 dB SPL peak reading on a VTVM. A low-level (60 dB), broad-band (0-10 kHz) white noise source (Grason Stadler Model 1724) was also mixed with the speech to mask tape hiss, some nonstationary computer-generated background noise picked up during the recording at MIT, and any ambient noise in the local environment during testing.

13.2.2 *Results and discussion*

Although the Modified Rhyme Test employed real words, our interest was focused on the phoneme errors and resulting perceptual confusions. Overall performance on the test was very good with a total error rate, averaged across both initial- and final-syllable positions, of only 6.9 percent. Performance was somewhat better for consonants in initial position (4.6 percent errors) than final position (9.3 percent errors).

The distribution of all errors across various manner classes is shown graphically in Figure 13-1 for initial- and final-syllable positions separately.

Since the consonants comprising the various manner classes occurred with unequal frequencies in the Modified Rhyme Test, the observed error rates in the data may not be representative estimates of the intelligibility of the same phonemes in continuous speech. Nevertheless, performance is generally excellent

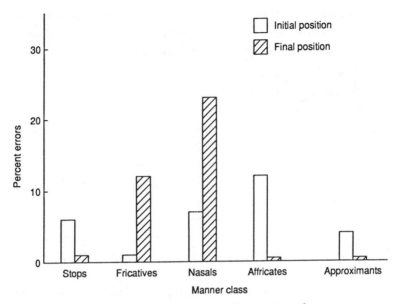

Figure 13-1: Average percent errors across various manner classes

across almost all manner categories, except for the nasals in final position which showed an error rate of 27.6 percent. It should also be noted that while consonants in initial position were identified better than the same ones in final position, the relative distribution of the errors across syllable positions is not comparable, as shown in Figure 13-2 below.

Figure 13-2 provides a detailed breakdown of the errors and the resulting confusions for consonants in initial and final positions. Each bar in the figure shows the total percent errors for a particular phoneme and the rank order of the most frequent confusions.

In examining these data, it should be kept in mind that the error rates which make up the data shown in these two panels are quite low to begin with. The total percent errors were only 4.6 percent in initial position and 9.3 percent in final position. Inspection of this figure shows that, for the most part, the errors are predominantly confusions in place or manner of articulation. Errors in voicing, when they occurred, were substantially lower. The fricatives DH and TH show very high error rates when considered individually, although both of these phonemes occurred with a relatively low frequency in the test when compared with other consonants. The presence of the background masking noise may have contributed to the low performance levels observed with these weak fricatives. As

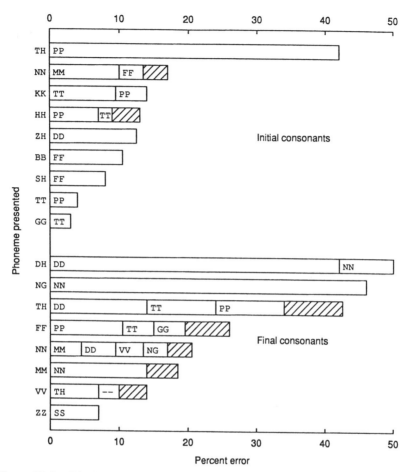

Figure 13-2: Distribution of errors and most frequent perceptual confusions

noted above, the pattern of errors is quite different for consonants in initial and final positions. Such a finding is not unexpected given that different acoustic cues are used to synthesize the same phoneme in different environments.

13.2.3 *Conclusions*

For the most part, the intelligibility of the speech produced by the current version of the text-to-speech system is very high. The overall error rate of 6.9 percent is slightly lower than the error rate of 7.6 percent obtained in the earlier Haskins evaluation using the Modified Rhyme Test. The advantage of initial over final consonants observed in the present study is consistent with data obtained from natural speech by House *et al.* (1965), and Nye and Gaitenby (1973), although it differs slightly from the results found for the synthetic speech in the earlier Haskins evaluation. In the Haskins study, error rates for the synthetic speech in initial and final positions were about the same with a very slight advantage for consonants in final position. The comparable overall error rates obtained for natural speech in the Modified Rhyme Test by House *et al.* and Nye and Gaitenby (1973) were 4 percent and 2.7 percent, respectively.

In the earlier evaluation study, Nye and Gaitenby (1974) checked to ensure that the phonemic input to the Haskins synthesizer was correct. However, no corrections of any kind were made by hand in generating the present materials, either from entries in the morph lexicon or from spelling-to-sound rules. As discussed in the final section of this chapter, several different kinds of errors were uncovered in different modules as a result of generating such a large amount of synthetic speech through the system.

Except for the high error rates observed for the nasals and fricatives in final syllable position, the synthesis of segmental information in the text-to-speech system appears to be excellent, at least as measured in a forced-choice format among minimal pairs of test items. With phoneme recognition performance as high as it is--nearly close to ceiling levels--it is difficult to pick up subtle details of the error patterns that might be useful in improving the quality of the output of the phonetic component of the system at the present time. In addition, the errors that were observed in the present tests might well be reduced substantially if the listeners had more experience with the speech output produced by the system. It is well known among investigators working with synthetic speech that rather substantial improvements in intelligibility can be observed when listeners become familiar with the quality of the synthesizer. Nye and Gaitenby (1974) as well as Carlson *et al.* (1976) have reported very sizeable learning effects in listening to synthetic speech. In the latter study, performance increased from 55 percent to 90 percent correct after the presentation of only 200 synthetic sentences over a two-week period. (See also the discussion of the word recognition and comprehension results below.)

In summary, the results of the Modified Rhyme Test revealed very high levels of intelligibility of the speech output from the system using naive listeners as subjects. While the overall level of performance is somewhat lower than in previous studies employing natural speech, the level of performance for recognition of segmental information appears to be quite satisfactory for a wide range of text-to-speech applications at the present time.

13.3 **Word recognition in sentences**

The results of the Modified Rhyme Test using isolated words indicated very high levels of intelligibility for the segmental output of the text-to-speech system. However, the Modified Rhyme Test employs a closed-response set involving a forced-choice format in what may be considered a relatively low uncertainty testing situation. In the recognition and comprehension of unrestricted text, a substantially broader range of alternatives is available to the listener since the response set is open and potentially infinite in size. Moreover, the sentential context itself provides an important contribution to intelligibility of speech, a fact that has been known for many years (Miller *et al.*, 1951; Miller and Isard, 1963).

To evaluate word recognition in sentence context, we decided to obtain two quite different sets of data. One set was collected using a small number of the Harvard Psychoacoustic Sentences (Egan, 1948). These test sentences are all meaningful and contain a wide range of different syntactic constructions. In addition, the various segmental phonemes of English are represented in these sentences in accordance with their frequency of occurrence in the language. Thus, the results obtained with the Harvard sentences should provide a fairly good estimate of how well we might expect word recognition to proceed in sentences when both semantic and syntactic information is available to a listener. This situation could be considered comparable, in some sense, to normal listening conditions where "top-down" knowledge interacts with sensory input in the recognition and comprehension of speech (see Pisoni, 1978; Marslen-Wilson and Welsh, 1978).

We also collected word recognition data with a set of syntactically normal but semantically anomalous sentences that were developed at Haskins Laboratories by Nye and Gaitenby (1974) for use in evaluating the intelligibility of their text-to-speech system (see also Ingeman, 1978). These test sentences permit a somewhat finer assessment of the availability and quality of "bottom-up" acoustic-phonetic information and its potential contribution to word recognition. Since the materials are all meaningless sentences, the individual words cannot be identified or predicted from knowledge of the sentential context or semantic interpretation. Thus, the results of these tests using the Haskins anomalous sentences should provide an estimate of the upper bound on the contribution of strictly phonetic information to word recognition in sentence contexts. Since the response set is also open and essentially unrestricted, we would anticipate substantially lower levels of word recognition performance on this test than on the Harvard test; in the latter test, syntactic and semantic context is readily available and can be used freely by the listener at all levels of processing the speech input. In addition, the results of the anomalous sentence test can also be compared more or less directly to data collected with these same test sentences by Nye and Gaitenby (1974) and Ingeman (1978). Such comparisons should prove useful in identifying similarities and possible differences in the speech output produced by the two text-to-speech systems.

13.3.1 *Method*

13.3.1.1 *Subjects*   Forty-four additional naive undergraduate students were recruited as paid subjects. They were drawn from the same population as the subjects used in the previous study and met the same requirements. None of these subjects had participated in the earlier study on phoneme recognition.

13.3.1.2 *Stimuli*   Two sets of test sentences were prepared. One set consisted of 100 Harvard Psychoacoustic Sentences. Each sentence contained five key words that were scored as a measure of word recognition. The other set consisted of 100 Haskins anomalous sentences drawn from the original list of materials developed by Nye and Gaitenby (1974). Each of these test sentences contained four key words. Two separate test lists were recorded on audio tape with a 3 second pause between successive sentences. The sentences were output at a speaking rate in excess of 180 words per minute. As before, we did not correct any pronunciation errors. Examples of both types of test sentences are given in Appendixes E and F.

13.3.1.3 *Procedure*   Twenty-one subjects received the Harvard sentences and twenty-three received the Haskins sentences. Testing was carried out in small groups of five or six subjects, each under the same listening conditions described in the previous study.

Subjects in both groups were told that this study was concerned with word recognition in sentences and that their task was to write down each test sentence as they heard it in the appropriate location on their response sheets. They were told to respond on every trial and to guess if they were not sure of a word. For the Harvard sentences, the response forms were simply numbered sequentially with a continuous underlined blank space for each trial. However, since the syntactic structure of all of the Haskins sentences was identical, the response forms differed slightly: blank spaces were provided for the four key words. Determiners were printed in the appropriate locations in standard sentence frames.

The experiment was run in a self-paced format to provide subjects with sufficient time to record their responses in the appropriate space in their booklets. However, subjects were encouraged to work rapidly in writing down their responses. The experimenter operated the tape recorder on playback from within the testing room by remote control. Thus, successive sentences in the test lists were presented only after all of the subjects in a group had finished responding to the previous test sentence, and had indicated this to the experimenter. A short break was taken halfway through a testing session, after completion of the first 50 sentences.

13.3.2 Results and discussion

The responses were scored only for correct word recognition at this time. Phonetic errors, when they occurred, were not considered in the present analyses, although we expect to examine these in some detail at a later time. Each subject receiving the Harvard sentences provided a total of 500 responses, while each subject receiving the Haskins anomalous sentences provided 400 responses to the final analysis.

Performance on the Harvard sentences was quite good with an overall mean of 93.2 percent correct word recognition across all 21 subjects. The scores on this test ranged from a low of 80 percent to a high of 97 percent correct recognition. Of the 6.7 percent errors observed, 30.3 percent were omissions of complete words, while the remainder consisted of segmental errors involving substitutions, deletions, and transpositions. In no case, however, did subjects respond with permissible nonwords that could occur as potential lexical items in English.

As expected, word recognition performance on the Haskins anomalous sentences was substantially worse than the Harvard sentences, with a mean of 78.7 percent correct recognition averaged over all 23 subjects. The scores on this test ranged from a low of 71 percent correct to a high of 85 percent correct. Of the 21.3 percent errors recorded, only 11 percent were omissions of complete words. The difference in error patterns, particularly in terms of the number of omissions, between the two types of sentence contexts suggests a substantial difference in the subjects' perceptual strategies in the two tests. It seems quite likely that subjects used a much looser criterion for word recognition with the Haskins anomalous sentences simply because the number of permissible alternatives was substantially greater than those in the Harvard sentences. Moreover, the presence of one standard syntactic structure probably encouraged subjects to guess more often when the acoustic cues to word identification were minimal. In addition, there seemed to be evidence of semantically based intrusions in the recall data, suggesting that subjects were attempting to assign an interpretation to the input signal even though they knew beforehand that all of the sentences were meaningless.

As noted earlier, substantial learning effects occur with synthetic speech. Even after an initial period of exposure, recognition performance continues to improve. Comparisons of word recognition performance in the first and second half of each of the tests indicated the presence of a reliable learning effect. For both the

Harvard and Haskins sentences, performance improved on the second half of the test relative to the first half. Although the differences were small, amounting to only about 2 percent improvement in each case, the result was very reliable (p < .01) across subjects in both cases.

The performance levels obtained with the Haskins semantically anomalous sentences are very similar to those reported earlier by Nye and Gaitenby (1974), and more recently by Ingeman (1978) using the same sentences with the Haskins synthesizer and text-to-speech system. Nye and Gaitenby (1974) reported an average error rate of 22 percent for synthetic speech and five percent for comparable natural speech. However, Nye and Gaitenby used both naive and experienced listeners as subjects, and found rather large differences in performance between the two groups, as we noted above. This result is presumably due to familiarity and practice listening to the output of the synthesizer. We suspect that if the experienced subjects were eliminated from the Nye and Gaitenby analyses, performance would be lower than the original value reported and would therefore differ somewhat more from the present findings. Nevertheless, the error rate for these anomalous sentences produced with natural speech is still lower than the corresponding synthetic versions, although it is not clear at the present time how much of the difference could be due to listener familiarity with the quality of the synthetic speech.

13.3.3 *Conclusions*

The results of the two word-recognition tests indicate moderate to excellent levels of performance with naive listeners depending on the particular test format used and the type of information available to the subject. In one sense, the results of these two tests can be thought of as approximations to upper and lower bounds on the accuracy of word-recognition performance with the current text-to-speech system. On the one hand, the Harvard test sentences provide some indication of how word recognition might proceed when both semantic and syntactic information is available to a listener under normal conditions. On the other hand, the Haskins anomalous sentences direct the subjects' attention specifically to the perceptual input and therefore provide a rough estimate of the quality of the acoustic-phonetic information and sentence analysis routines available for word recognition in the absence of contextual constraints. Of course, in normal listening situations, and presumably in cases where a text-to-speech system such as the present one might be implemented, the complete neutralization of such contextual effects on intelligibility would be extremely unlikely. Nevertheless, a more detailed analysis of the word-recognition errors in the Haskins anomalous sentence test might provide us with additional information that could be used to modify or improve several of the modules of the system. Whether such additional improvements at these various levels of the system will actually contribute to improved intelligibility and comprehension is difficult to assess at this time, since performance with meaning-ful sentences is already quite high to begin with, as shown by the present results obtained with the Harvard sentences.

In summary, the results of tests designed to measure word recognition in two types of sentential context showed moderate to excellent levels of performance with synthetic speech output from the current version of the text-to-speech system. As in the previous section dealing with the evaluation of the intelligibility of iso-lated words, the present results, particularly with rather diverse meaningful sen-tences, suggest that the quality of the speech output at the present time is probably quite satisfactory for a relatively wide range of applications requiring the process-ing of unrestricted text. While there is room for improvement in the quality of the output from various modules of the system, as suggested by the results of the Has-kins anomalous sentences, it is not apparent whether the allocation of resources to effect such changes in the system would produce any detectable differences. Dif-ferences that might be detected, if any, might well require a very restricted listen-ing environment in which all of the higher-level syntactic and semantic infor-mation is eliminated, a situation that is unlikely to occur when the system is imple-mented in an applied setting. Given these results on word recognition, however, it still remains to be determined how well listeners can understand and comprehend continuous speech produced by the system, a problem we turn to in the next sec-tion of this chapter.

13.4 Comprehension

Research on comprehension and understanding of spoken language has received a great deal of attention by numerous investigators in recent years. It is generally agreed that comprehension is a complex cognitive process, initially involving the input and subsequent encoding of sensory information, the retrieval of previously stored knowledge from long-term memory, and the subsequent interpretation, in-tegration or assimilation of various sources of knowledge that might be available to a listener at the time. Comprehension, therefore, depends on a relatively large number of diverse factors, some of which are still only poorly understood at the present time. Measuring comprehension is difficult because of the interaction of many of these factors and the absence of any coherent model that is broad enough to deal with the diverse nature of language understanding.

One of the factors that obviously plays an important role in listening comprehension is the quality of the input signal expressed in terms of its overall intelligibility. But as we have seen even from the results summarized in the previous sections, additional consideration must also be given to the contribution of higher-level sources of knowledge to recognition and comprehension. In this last section, we wanted to obtain some preliminary estimate of how well listeners could comprehend continuous text produced by the text-to-speech system. Previous evaluations of synthetic speech output have been concerned primarily with measuring intelligibility or listener preferences with little if any concern for assessing comprehension or understanding of the content of the materials (Nye *et al.*, 1975). Indeed, as far as we have been able to determine, no previous formal tests of the comprehension of continuous synthetic speech have ever been carried out with a relatively wide range of textual materials specifically designed to assess understanding of the content rather than form of the speech.

To accomplish this goal, we selected fifteen narrative passages and an appropriate set of test questions from several standardized adult reading comprehension tests. The passages were quite diverse, covering a wide range of topics, writing styles and vocabulary. We thought that a large number of passages would be interesting to listen to in the context of tests designed to assess comprehension and understanding. Since these test passages were selected from several different types of reading tests, they also varied in difficulty and style, permitting us to evaluate the contribution of all of the individual modules of the text-to-speech system in terms of one relatively gross measure.

In addition to securing measures of listening comprehension for these passages, we also collected a parallel set of data on reading comprehension of these materials from a second group of subjects. The subjects in the reading comprehension group answered the same questions after reading each passage silently, as did subjects in the listening comprehension group. This condition was included in order to permit comparison between the two input modalities. It was assumed that the results of these comprehension tests would therefore provide an initial, although preliminary, benchmark against which the entire text-to-speech system could be evaluated with materials somewhat comparable to those used in the immediate future.

13.4.1 *Method*

13.4.1.1 *Subjects*   Forty-four additional naive undergraduate students were recruited as paid subjects. They were drawn from the same source as the subjects used in the previous studies. Some of the subjects assigned to the reading comprehension group had participated in the earlier study using the Modified Rhyme

Test. However, none of the subjects in the listening comprehension group had been in any of the prior intelligibility or word-recognition tests using synthetic speech.

13.4.1.2 *Stimuli*　Fifteen narrative passages were chosen more or less randomly from several published adult reading comprehension tests. The exact details of the passages and their original sources are provided in Table 13-1 below. An example of one of the passages is provided in Appendix G.

Table 13-1: Characteristics of the passages used to measure comprehension

Passage	Number of words	Duration (s)	Number of test questions	General topic	Source
1	212	75	6	lens buying	Coop English
2	159	56	4	measuring distance to nearby stars	Coop English
3	327	135	8	language	Iowa
4	198	75	4	retail institutions	Nelson-Denny
5	175	70	4	noise pollution	Nelson-Denny
6	204	82	4	geology	Nelson-Denny
7	206	68	4	philosophy	Nelson-Denny
8	207	80	4	radioactive dating	Nelson-Denny
9	292	117	8	history	Iowa
10	315	100	9	sea	Iowa
11	265	101	7	New Mexico	Stanford
12	322	125	6	fox hunting	Stanford
13	253	98	6	Claude Debussy	Stanford
14	267	107	7	Aluminum	Stanford
15	212	82	6	Roger Bannister	Stanford

Each passage was initially typed in orthographic form with punctuation into a text file. These files were then used as input to the text-to-speech system and as a source for preparing the typed versions of the passages used in the reading comprehension condition. All fifteen passages were recorded on audio tape at a speaking rate in excess of 180 words/minute for later playback. Two sets of response booklets were prepared, one for the listening group and one for the reading group. The booklets, which contained a varying number of multiple-choice questions keyed to each paragraph, were arranged in order according to the presentation schedule of the paragraphs on the audio tape. The booklets for subjects in the reading group also included a typed copy of the passage immediately before the appropriate set of questions. Appendix G also provides the set of questions corresponding to the passage.

13.4.1.3 *Procedure* Half of the forty-four subjects were assigned to the listening group and the other half to the reading group. Subjects assigned to the reading group were tested together in a classroom, while the subjects in the listening group were tested in small groups of five or six subjects each using the listening facilities of the previous studies. These subjects wore headphones and listened to the passages under the same conditions as the earlier subjects.

Instructions to the subjects in both groups emphasized that the purpose of the study was to evaluate how well individuals could comprehend and understand continuous synthetic speech produced by a reading machine. Subjects in the listening group were told that they would hear narrative passages about a wide variety of topics and that their task was to answer the multiple-choice questions that were keyed to the particular passages as best as they could based on the information contained in the passages they heard. Similar instructions were provided to the reading comprehension group.

As in the previous word-recognition study, the listening comprehension group was presented with test passages in a self-paced format with the experimenter present in the testing room operating the tape recorder via remote control. A given test passage was presented only once for listening, after which, subjects immediately turned their booklets to the appropriate set of test questions.

The subjects in the reading comprehension group were permitted to read each passage only once and were explicitly told that they should not go back over the passage after reading it or while answering the questions. This procedure was a departure from the typical methods used in administering standardized reading comprehension tests. Usually, the test passage is available to the subject for inspection and re-reading during the entire testing session. However, for present purposes, we felt that comparisons between reading and listening comprehension might be more closely matched by limiting exposure to one pass through the materials.

The subjects in both groups were told at the beginning of testing that the first two passages of the test and the accompanying questions were only for practice to familiarize them with the materials and nature of the test format. These two passages were not scored in the final analyses reported here.

13.4.2 *Results and discussion*

The multiple-choice questions for each of the thirteen test passages were scored separately for each subject. A composite score was then obtained by simply cumulating the individual scores for each passage and then expressing this value as a percentage of the total possible score across all of the passages.

The overall results for both reading and listening comprehension are shown in Figure 13-3 summed over all thirteen test passages. The data are also broken down in this figure by first and second half of the test.

The average percent correct was 77.2 percent for subjects in the reading comprehension group and 70.3 percent for subjects in the listening comprehension group. The 7 percent difference between these two means is small, but statistically significant by a t-test for independent groups (p < .05).

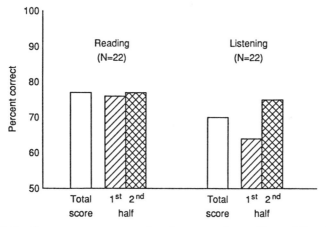

Figure 13-3: Percent correct comprehension scores for reading and listening groups

Although the reading comprehension group showed better performance overall when compared with the listening comprehension group, a breakdown of the comprehension scores for the two halves of the test showed a significant (p < .001) improvement in performance only for the subjects in the listening comprehension condition. There were no differences between first and second halves of the test for subjects in the reading comprehension group. The finding of improved performance in the second half of the test for subjects in the listening group is consistent with our earlier observations in the word-recognition tests which show that listening performance improves for synthetic speech after only a short period of exposure. When the two comprehension groups are compared on the same passages in the last half of the test, their performance is equivalent $(p > .05)$, which suggests that the overall difference between the two groups is probably due to familiarity with the output of the synthesizer and not due to any inherent difference in the basic strategies used in comprehending or understanding the content of these passages. This conclusion is strengthened even further by the fact that the thirteen passages are correlated across both testing conditions. In this case, a very high correlation $(r = +.97)$ was observed between reading and listening comprehension scores for individual passages. Passages that are difficult to comprehend when read are also difficult to comprehend when listened to, and vice versa. The time taken to complete all passages in both tests was, however, roughly the same, lasting between 45 and 50 minutes.

After the listening comprehension test was completed, we solicited additional subjective evaluations of the speech produced by the synthesizer and the nature of the comprehension test itself. Twenty of the twenty-two subjects indicated that they were able to comprehend and understand the content of the passages "well" or "very well". Only two of the subjects reported difficulty in comprehension, and even these two did not indicate that they were merely guessing, an available response alternative.

Several of the subjects reported improved ability to understand the speech as testing progressed. Others described several problems in the quality of synthesis, the location of pauses, the existence of inappropriately stressed words, and the occasional presence of very long "run-on" sentences in several passages. Finally, several other subjects suggested that each test passage should be presented twice so they could review some of the specific details and facts that were stated explicitly. For the most part, however, the subjects found listening to the speech interesting and felt that they had performed reasonably well in comprehending the passages. None of the subjects reported any major distractions in the quality of the synthetic speech that interfered with their ability to attend to or understand the content of the passages. Thus, subjects are able to adapt easily to relatively long passages of synthetic speech with little exposure or practice.

13.4.3 *Conclusions*

The results of the comprehension test indicate that naive subjects are able to comprehend synthetically produced spoken passages of narrative text output from an unrestricted text-to-speech system. Their performance is roughly comparable to subjects who have been asked to read the same passages of text and answer the same questions. As in the case of our other tests using synthetic speech, there appears to be an initial period during which subjects are simply becoming familiar with the quality of the synthesizer, the prosodic rules of the system and the style of the material. Even after only a few minutes of exposure, comprehension performance improves substantially and eventually approximates levels observed when subjects read the same passages of text.

It should also be pointed out that the comprehension performance observed in these tests was obtained with a reading rate in excess of 180 words per minute. This rate is about the rate at which people typically speak in normal conversations or when they read text aloud. The present results therefore suggest that it is not necessary to slow down the speaking rate or adjust the synthesis to obtain relatively high levels of listening comprehension for continuous text. Until the present tests were carried out, it was assumed by some investigators that synthetic speech had to be output at a much slower rate to maintain intelligibility and therefore facilitate comprehension.

Based on the results of the present comprehension test, as well as the other tests of intelligibility and word recognition that were carried out, there is good reason to believe that the basic design of the MIT text-to-speech system is valid. The system can not only produce highly intelligible synthetic speech, as shown in our earlier tests, but the quality of the synthetic speech can be understood and comprehended at reasonably high levels. While there are, no doubt, many subtle details of the system that might be improved, the results of these preliminary tests support the general conclusion that very high-quality synthetic speech can be produced automatically from unrestricted text and that such a system could be implemented in applied settings in the immediate future. After some thirty years of research, the widespread use of text-to-speech and voice response systems in computer aided instruction and as aids for the handicapped is now a realistic goal. The obstacles are no longer questions of research into the basic principles of speech production, perception, and linguistic analysis, but are simply the practical matters of implementation and economics.

13.5 General discussion and conclusions

The results of the three tests designed to evaluate intelligibility, word recognition, and listening comprehension indicated very high levels of performance for the current version of the text-to-speech system. While these tests are only preliminary, they have provided an initial benchmark against which to compare the performance of the present system with other text-to-speech systems. Moreover, the present results have provided a basis for evaluating the overall design of the system and the functioning of several of the individual components. Since a relatively large amount of text was specifically generated for this project, we were able to identify a number of errors in the operation of the system which ordinarily might not have been detected. In this last section of the chapter, we summarize briefly a few of the errors we were able to uncover during and after the evaluation. We will also point out some of the limitations of the current evaluation results and then discuss several directions for additional testing in the future.

After the test materials for the evaluation project were generated, it was possible to go back and examine the output of each module individually in order to determine whether it provided a correct analysis of the input text. Errors of various kinds in the final spoken output could originate at several different modules in the system. In addition, there could be errors resulting from transcription that we would not associate with the operation of the text-to-speech system itself.

Of all the errors observed, we discovered only one that could legitimately be classified as a transcription error. In this case, the word "harmonies" was incorrectly typed into the system as "harmonics" and was not detected in subsequent proofreading. All remaining errors could be located at one or more modules of the system. These errors consisted of incorrect parsings, pronunciations, or stress assignments. An error located at one module often affected analyses carried out by other modules. Sometimes the results of these errors were quite noticeable in the spoken output, particularly when the errors produced segmental distinctions that could be detected in pronunciation. However, in other cases, particularly where stress assignment was involved, the differences were more difficult to detect.

At the time this report was completed, we were able to locate only two errors in the operation of the first module of the system. This module (FORMAT) has a dictionary that converts abbreviations, symbols, and numbers to words for subsequent processing. One error involved the abbreviation "U.S." in which a space was incorrectly typed between "U." and "S." The rule which was applied here places an end-of-sentence period in the output if an abbreviatory period (as in "U.") is followed by one or more spaces and a capital letter (the "S"). Thus, two sentences were formed, one ending in "U." and the other beginning with "S." This error causes an incorrect pitch contour to be placed on the output, as well as inappropriate segmental durations to be assigned in later modules.

Another error involved the abbreviation "19th". In all cases, alphanumerics are spelled out completely by this module. For example, "19th" was pronounced as "one-nine-T-H" on output. In words such as "19th" or "100-yard", the alphabetic and numeric sections are separable and could be pronounced. However, in a true alphanumeric such as "103S" or "a3c", it is correct to spell out all of the symbols.

A number of errors were also detected in the module DECOMP, which is responsible for decomposing words into morphs by reference to the morph lexicon. In several cases, the wrong morphs were identified, resulting in perceptible segmental errors in the speech output. In other cases, the correct morphs were obtained, but the stress assignment of the constituent morphs was different for the morphs in isolation than for the morphs when concatenated in a polymorphemic word. We also identified several words that should have been in the lexicon since their pronunciation could not be handled by the existing spelling-to-sound rules.

Several errors in the operation of the spelling-to-sound rules were also detected. These errors resulted in the wrong pronunciation, which was quite noticeable in listening. For example, the second syllable of the word "Britain" was pronounced like the second syllable in the word "maintain".

In a number of other cases, we were able to identify problems in the operation of the parser, particularly in recognizing the correct part of speech. For example, the word "close" can be either an adjective or verb, each with a different pronunciation. Several problems were also observed with the word "affect", which can be either a noun or a verb. In each of these cases, the part of speech was incorrectly identified by the parser, resulting in the wrong choice in pronunciation on output.

Finally, there were several cases, especially with the Haskins anomalous sentences, in which the parser incorrectly assigned the verb (which could also be a noun) to the previous noun phrase. This error is not surprising since the parser has a basic preference for noun phrases anyway, when a choice is available. However, this often produced inappropriate sentence stress resulting from incorrect pitch and segmental durations. In some cases, these differences could be readily observed, whereas in others, the effects were substantially more difficult to detect even with careful and repeated listening. These observations are consistent with an earlier perceptual study of the durational rules carried out by Carlson *et al.* (1979). They found that a deletion of a phrase boundary produced only negligible effects on listeners' evaluations of the naturalness of synthetic speech.

Some of the errors described above are considered to be relatively minor and can be corrected rather easily by the simple addition of polymorphemic entries in the morph lexicon. Since this evaluation was completed, a "pre-parser" has been implemented which corrects a number of the parsing errors in which the sentential verb was included in the preceding noun phrase. However, some of the other parsing errors are not as easy to correct. Errors made by the first module and the spelling-to-sound rules are highly context-dependent, and are not easily amenable to simple change by rule. From our examination of the errors uncovered so far, all cases could be accounted for and located in some module of the system. There were no errors detected which escaped explanation at the present time, although further study is continuing.

The results of the present evaluation study have several limitations and these should be summarized here briefly for future reference. First, we did not carry out any of the control conditions for the three types of tests using natural speech. To some extent, this might be considered an important addition and extension of the current evaluation since it is the level of performance with natural speech that is frequently used as the yardstick against which to compare the quality of synthetic speech. There can be little doubt that tests with natural speech would show higher levels of performance when compared with synthetic speech. But it should be emphasized here that the levels of performance in the current study are already quite high to begin with, therefore it is not immediately obvious what would be gained from such additional tests with natural speech.

Secondly, with regard to measuring intelligibility of the segmental output, it is clear that the Modified Rhyme Test is much too easy for listeners, even naive listeners, and additional tests using an open-response set should be employed. Additional testing under varying noise conditions may also provide further information concerning the quality of the synthesis and its resistance to noise and distortion. In this regard, the analysis of the Haskins anomalous sentences should also provide a rich source of data on phonetic confusions using an open-response set. We are planning additional detailed analyses of these data.

Finally, the comprehension test used was relatively gross in its ability to distinguish between new knowledge acquired from listening to text and knowledge obtained from inferences drawn at the time of comprehension or, later, at the time of testing. Of course, this is a problem related more to several broader issues in language comprehension and understanding than to questions surrounding text-to-speech and speech synthesis-by-rule. Nevertheless, it may be possible to learn a great deal more about language comprehension and the interaction between top-down and bottom-up knowledge sources in speech perception by the advances that have been made in conceptualizing various linguistic problems within the context of a functional text-to-speech system. The success of the current system and its capabilities to process unrestricted text must be traced, at least in part, to the existence of an explicit model of the underlying linguistic structure that is common to both text and speech and to the rule systems relating the two domains.

In summary, the results of our evaluation tests designed to measure phoneme intelligibility, word recognition and comprehension of synthetic speech produced by the MIT text-to-speech system have demonstrated good to excellent performance on a wide range of materials. No major problems were uncovered in the design of the system nor were any serious errors identified in any of the component modules of the system to date. The present results, although preliminary, support the general conclusion that very high-quality synthetic speech can be produced automatically from unrestricted English text and that such a system could be implemented in an applied setting in the very near future.

14

Implementation

14.1 Conceptual organization

Throughout this book, emphasis has been placed on the representation of various data forms and rules, together with transformations between these representations. A strong effort has been made to exclude all reference to implementation concerns from these discussions. At this point, however, it is appropriate to address these issues, thus giving a view of the conceptual framework in which this research was done, as well as a perspective on economically viable implementations that can deliver the overall text-to-speech capability in real-time. With these goals in mind, we discuss first the overall conceptual organization of the MITalk system, followed by a description of the development system used as a research vehicle over the course of a dozen years, the requirements for a "performance system" suitable for practical applications, and finally, a discussion of the current system, together with examples, which serves as the basis for distribution of the MITalk system from MIT.

The overall conceptual organization of the MITalk system can be viewed on two levels. At the highest level, the system is viewed as an analysis/synthesis system. It is based on the premise that in order to transform an input textual representation (as a string of ASCII characters) to an output synthesized speech waveform, it is necessary to first analyze the text into an underlying abstract linguistic representation which can then be used as the initial basis for synthesizing the waveform. In this sense, the text and speech waveform representations are seen as two different surface representations of a common, underlying linguistic representation which unites these two surface forms. Thus, the first part of the system is oriented to transforming the input textual representation into a narrow phonetic transcription which includes the names of the constituent phonemes, stress marks, and syntactic boundaries at the syllable, morph, word, phrase, and sentence levels. It is an implicit assumption of the system that this transcription is sufficient to serve as the input for the synthesis routines which generate the timing framework, the pitch contour, and the detailed control parameters (updated at 5 msec intervals) which specify the nature of the vocal tract model, which in turn produces the final output synthetic speech waveform.

172

At a more detailed level, the analysis and synthesis phases of the MITalk system have been broken into a set of modules with well-defined interfaces at their boundaries. In this way, it is possible to break up the overall transformation process into well-specified but smaller transformations which serve to reduce the overall complexity of the system, and to provide the means for focusing on different aspects and different representations within the system. Since the system is oriented to pass information forward from module to module, using temporary data bases as well, it is possible to have well-formed boundaries and to test and evaluate each module on a module-by-module basis. This is an important consideration since quality measures can be assigned to each module, and local optimization of the modules can be expected to incrementally contribute to the overall quality of the output synthetic speech. Of course, the degree to which various refinements within the modules increase measures of intelligibility and naturalness at the output will vary substantially, but there is little need to consider the detailed way in which the results of several modules are integrated when one is working on improvements for a particular module. In this way, it has been possible to develop the individual modules of the system in parallel, while providing an overall system framework that permits separate module development. By keeping the interfaces and data base formats carefully specified, it is possible to pinpoint deficiencies in the system at various levels, and in this way to provide guidance for the allocation of research effort to the various parts of the system. In retrospect, this modular approach to the overall representation and development of the system has served very well, and continues to be the major framework in which further improvements are being made.

14.2 Development system

Given the rapid improvements in both software and hardware technology, it is not very useful to describe in detail the earlier development environments which are relevant to the 1960s and the 1970s. But it is useful to have an idea of the evolution of the computational research framework. Initially, a small single-user minicomputer was used with an analog hardware synthesizer. While some code was written in assembly language as the work evolved, particularly with the introduction of the modular organization, most of the symbolic computing was done in a variant of the BCPL language, while the phonemic synthesis was done in FORTRAN. During the 1970s, a large time-shared machine was introduced with a special purpose hardware vocal tract model (Miranker, 1978). This system was exceedingly useful since it provided the framework for several researchers to effectively collaborate and to share information in an ongoing, highly interactive way. Most recently, the entire system has been converted to run under UNIX, written mainly in PASCAL with some routines in C. This is a highly flexible system, and introduces a new overall control program which allows various subsets of the system to be effectively utilized. There is also an ability to monitor the system at several levels of detail, thus providing the user with substantial insight into the overall workings of the system. This version of the system, which is the basis for current distribution from MIT, is described in detail later in this chapter.

14.3 Performance system

The structure of the development system, even in its contemporary UNIX implementation, is not suitable for compact, real-time, and economical utilization in practical contexts. For such uses, less flexibility is required, and special purpose hardware is necessary. For example, the lexicons and rule bases can be stored in high-density memory without the necessity for utilizing electromechanical disks. A general purpose microprocessor can be utilized to provide overall system control and to provide the linguistic analysis and prosodic synthesis up to the level of the phonemic synthesis conversion to the output speech waveform. Finally, a signal processing chip can perform all of the phonemic synthesis to waveform conversion in real-time, thus meeting the overall requirements of a practical, high-performance system. Current commercial systems, many of which are based on the licensing of the MITalk system, readily provide this capability. It is important to emphasize that there are no significant hardware limitations to the real-time and economic usage of the entire span of MITalk algorithms. In the past, concerns were expressed about the size of the lexicon and the real-time signal processing requirements, but these requirements pose no difficulties for modern technology.

In the future, one can conceive of the entire MITalk system implemented on a single integrated-circuit wafer, or in a small set of chips. In this way, ASCII characters can be converted to output speech waveforms in many different environments, including highly compact terminals. While a wafer-scale system must be viewed as highly aggressive technology in the mid-1980s, there is no inherent difficulty in achieving such a system. There is no question that highly complex and capable text-to-speech systems will be available in such compact formats in the near future.

14.4 UNIX implementation

As mentioned above, the present version of the development system consists of a set of PASCAL and C programs which run in a UNIX operating system environment. There is one program per speech processing module described in previous chapters. In addition, there is a coordinator program which serves as the user-interface to the rest of the system and a "wiretap" program which translates binary program output into human-readable form.

The speech processing modules all share a common interface configuration. Each module has an input port and an output port (these are the UNIX standard input and standard output channels, respectively). Module input can come from either a disk file or from the output port of the preceding module (via a UNIX pipe). Module output can be directed to a disk file or to the input port of the next module. A group of modules connected together in sequence is called a *pipeline* in UNIX terminology.

The top level program, called MITALK, handles the creation of a speech processing pipeline. The user can call for the entire pipeline or any subsequence of the pipeline. The user specifies the names of the first and last modules in the desired pipeline and MITALK creates the pipeline processes. If the first module is FORMAT, then the user can provide input text directly from the terminal. If any other module is first, then its input must come from a previously created disk file. If the last module is COEWAV, then output can be sent to a digital-to-analog converter to be played aloud. The output from other modules can be sent to a disk file or can be translated from raw binary to human-readable form for display on the user's terminal. The program SHOW is used to perform the translation.

14.5 Using the system

Figure 14-1 demonstrates most of the features of the system. This figure contains a complete copy of a MITalk session. User-typed text is in boldface. The first line of text is the user's command to the UNIX shell to start the top-level process with the given list of parameters. Next, MITALK decodes the parameters to determine the appropriate pipeline structure. In this case, the pipeline begins with FORMAT receiving input from the user terminal (tty) and ends with SOUND1 sending output to the terminal. In addition, the contents of the pipe streams between DECOMP and PARSER, and between PARSER and SOUND1, are displayed on the terminal. Output from each module is prefixed by the module name.

```
%mitalk decomp tty parser tty sound1
MITALK: System configuration:

                        tty
                         |
                      FORMAT
                      DECOMP
                  tty<---|
                      PARSER
                  tty<---|
                      SOUND1
                         |
                        tty

    MITALK: Starting system...
    MITALK: System running
    MITALK: Please enter text: (type ^D [control-D] to
        exit)

    The old man sat in a rocker.
    ^D
     DECOMP: THE (ARTICLE) => THE
     DECOMP: OLD (ADJECTIVE, NOUN) => OLD
     DECOMP: MAN (NOUN, VERB) => MAN
     DECOMP: SAT (VERB, PAST PARTICIPLE) => SAT
     DECOMP: IN (PREPOSITION, ADVERB) => IN
     DECOMP: A (ARTICLE) => A
      PARSER: NOUN GROUP: THE OLD MAN
      PARSER: VERB GROUP: SAT
     DECOMP: ROCKER (NOUN) => ROCK+ER
     DECOMP: . (END PUNCTUATION MARK)
     DECOMP: . (END PUNCTUATION MARK)
     DECOMP: <EOF>
      PARSER: PREPOSITIONAL PHRASE: IN A ROCKER
      PARSER: UNCLASSIFIED: .
      PARSER: UNCLASSIFIED: .
      PARSER: <EOF>
       SOUND1:  DH 'AH
       SOUND1:  'OW LL DD
       SOUND1:  MM 'AE NN
       SOUND1:  SS 'AE TT
       SOUND1:  'IH NN
       SOUND1:  AX
       SOUND1:  RR 'AA KK * - ER
       SOUND1:  .
       SOUND1:  .
       SOUND1: <EOF>

    MITALK: System done
    %
```

Figure 14-1: Sample MITalk session

176

Appendix A

Part-of-speech processor

A concise description of the algorithm of the part-of-speech processor follows:

```
IF there is no decomposition
THEN assign (NOUN (NUM SING)),
            (VERB (INF TR) (PL TR)), (ADJ)
ELSEIF last morph is not a suffix
THEN IF first morph is a verb prefix
     THEN assign (VERB (INF TR) (PL TR))
     ELSEIF first morph is A
     THEN assign (ADJ), (ADV)
     ELSE assign from last morph
     END IF
ELSEIF last morph is ING
THEN assign (VERBING)
ELSEIF last morph is ED
THEN assign (VERBEN), (VERB (SING TR) (PL TR))
ELSEIF last morph is S or ES
THEN IF next morph is not a suffix
             AND first morph is a verb prefix
     THEN assign (VERB (SING TR))
     ELSE IF next morph is a verb
         THEN assign (VERB (SING TR))
         END IF
         IF next morph is a NOUN, ADJ, INTG, ER, or ING
         THEN assign (NOUN (NUM PL))
         END IF
         IF next morph is an ORD
                 AND next morph is not SECOND
         THEN assign (ORD (NUM PL))
         END IF
         IF there is no assignment
         THEN assign (NOUN (NUM PL))
         END IF
     END IF
ELSEIF last morph is ER
THEN IF next morph is an ADV
     THEN assign (ADV)
     END IF
     IF next morph is an ADJ
     THEN assign (ADJ)
     END IF
     IF next morph is a NOUN or VERB
```

```
                THEN assign (NOUN (NUM SING))
                END IF
        ELSEIF last morph is S'
        THEN assign (NOUN (POSS TR))
        ELSEIF last morph is 'S
        THEN IF next morph is a NOUN
                THEN assign (NOUN (POSS TR)),
                    copy (NOUN (CONTR TR))
                ELSEIF next morph is a PRN
                THEN copy (PRN (CONTR TR))
                        IF next morph has feature (PRNADJ TR)
                        THEN copy (PRN (CASE POSS))
                        ENDIF
                ENDIF
        ELSEIF last morph is N'T
        THEN IF next morph is NEED
                THEN assign (MOD (AUX A) (NOT TR))
                ELSEIF next morph is a BE
                THEN copy (BE (NOT TR))
                ELSEIF next morph is a HAVE
                THEN copy (HAVE (NOT TR))
                ELSEIF next morph is a MOD
                THEN copy (MOD (NOT TR))
                ENDIF
        ELSEIF last morph is 'VE
                        AND next morph is a MOD
        THEN copy (MOD (CONTR TR))
        ELSEIF last morph is 'VE, 'D, 'LL, or 'RE
        THEN IF next morph is S
                THEN assign (NOUN (NUM PL) (CONTR TR))
                ELSEIF next morph is a NOUN
                THEN copy (NOUN (CONTR TR))
                ELSEIF next morph is a PRN
                THEN copy (PRN (CONTR TR))
                ENDIF
        ELSE assign part of speech from rightmost morph
        ENDIF
```

Appendix B

Klatt symbols

Table B-1: Klatt symbols for phonetic segments

Vowels

AA	B*o*b	AE	b*a*t	AH	b*u*t	AO	b*o*ught	AW	b*ou*t
AX	*a*bout	AXR	b*ar*	AY	b*i*te	EH	b*e*t	ER	b*ir*d
EXR	b*ear*	EY	b*ai*t	IH	b*i*t	IX	impun*i*ty	IXR	b*eer*
IY	b*ee*t	OW	b*oa*t	OXR	b*oar*	OY	b*oy*	UH	b*oo*k
UW	b*oo*t	UXR	p*oor*	YU	b*eau*ty				

Sonorant Consonants

EL	bott*le*	HH	*h*at	HX	the *h*urrah	LL	*l*et	LX	bi*ll*
RR	*r*ent	RX	fi*r*e	WW	*w*et	WH	*wh*ich	YY	*y*et

Nasals

EM	keep'*em*	EN	butt*on*	MM	*m*et	NN	*n*et	NG	si*ng*

Fricatives

DH	*th*at	FF	*f*in	SS	*s*at	SH	*sh*in	TH	*th*in
VV	*v*at	ZZ	*z*oo	ZH	a*z*ure				

Plosives

BB	*b*et	DD	*d*ebt	DX	bu*tt*er	GG	*g*ore	GP	*g*ive
KK	*c*ore	KP	*k*een	PP	*p*et	TT	*t*en	TQ	a*t* Alan

Affricates

CH	*ch*in	JJ	*g*in

Pseudo-vowel

AXP Plosive release

Table B-2: Klatt symbols for nonsegmental units

Stress Symbols

' or 1	primary lexical stress	" or 2	secondary lexical stress

Word and Morpheme Boundaries

-	syllable boundary	*	morpheme boundary
C:	begin content word	F:	begin function word

Syntactic Structure

.	end of declarative utterance	)?	end of yes/no question
,	orthographic comma	)N	end of noun phrase
)P	potential breath pause	)C	end of clause

Appendix C

Context-dependent rules for PHONET

This appendix presents the context-dependent rule set used in module PHONET.

C.1 Notation

The phonetic segment to parameter conversion rules are given in a form similar to that of the lexical stress rules in Chapter 6. The following modifications are made to the rule form described in Chapter 6:

- The symbol "S" is used to represent any phonetic segment. This replaces the symbols "V" and "C" used in the previous set of rules.
- In addition to the features "+stress" and "-stress", there is a set of features used to classify phonetic segments according to general properties. These features are listed in the next section.

The general form of a rule is as follows:

$$variable \leftarrow value \:/\: pattern$$

which means: "*variable* gets set to *value* in the context of *pattern*". In addition to the $\leftarrow$ operation, there are the $\uparrow$ and $\downarrow$ operations which mean to increase or decrease (respectively) the value of *variable* by the amount *value*.

The *variable* is one of several parameters which hold state information about the current phonetic segment. For example, "Target" is a table of target values for each parameter at the end of the current segment. The rule:

$$\text{Target[avc]} \downarrow 30 \:/\: \begin{bmatrix} \text{+fricative, +voiced} \\ \underline{} \end{bmatrix} \begin{bmatrix} \text{-vowel} \\ \text{S} \end{bmatrix}$$

means that the Target value for parameter avc gets decreased by 30dB, if the current segment is a voiced fricative and the next segment is nonvocalic.

The overall structure of the program which implements these rules is as follows: The top level of the program is a loop which examines each phonetic segment from the input stream in sequence, one at a time. For each segment, the set of state variables is initialized, then the rules are applied in sequence in the order presented below. After the rules have been applied to the current segment, the information in the state variables is used to update the values of the output parameters over the current time interval (from the start time of the current segment to the end time, as previously determined by PROSOD).

The pattern in each rule is applied independently of all other rule patterns, except when it is preceded by the word "ELSE", in which case that rule is applied only if the preceding rule failed to match.

The state variables themselves are described in the following section.

C.2 State variables

Most of the state variables are one-dimensional arrays containing one value for each of the output parameters. The notation *variable[parameter]* denotes the value of variable *variable* for parameter *parameter*. If *parameter* has the form *p1, p2*, then this stands for the value of the variable for both parameters *p1* and *p2*. If *parameter* has the form *p1..p2*, then this stands for the values for parameters *p1* through *p2* inclusive.

The state variables are:

Cumdur[av..f0]

> The "current time" for each parameter for the current segment. This is the absolute time in msec at which the segment begins for each parameter, measured from the beginning of the utterance. This corresponds to t_1 in Figure 11-6.

Segdur[av..f0]

> The duration in msec of the current segment for each parameter. The ending time for parameter "x" is Cumdur[x]+Segdur[x]. This corresponds to t_2 in Figure 11-6.

Mintime[av..f0]

> This is the minimum absolute time to which "backward" smoothing of each parameter can propagate. This corresponds to t_0 in Figure 11-6.

Trantype[av..f0]

> This is the transition type from Figure 11-6.

Target[av..f0]

> The desired target values for each parameter at time Segdur+Cumdur. The dimensions of these values are dB for amplitude parameters, and Hz for frequency and bandwidth parameters.

Diptar[f1..f3]

> Diphthong target values in Hz.

Oldval[av..f0]

> This is the current value of each parameter at time Cumdur (i.e. the value at the end of the previous segment).

Nextar[av..f0]

>This is the value of Target for the next segment.

Tcf[av..f0]

>This is the duration of forward smoothing measured from Cumdur.

Tcb[av..f0]

>This is the duration of backward smoothing measured from Cumdur (limited by Mintime).

Bper[av..f0]

>This the percent of movement from locus toward target in a CV or VC transition.

Bvf[av..f0]

>This is the desired value of each parameter immediately after time Cumdur (generally derived from Bper).

Bvb[av..f0]

>This is the desired value of each parameter immediately before time Cumdur.

C.3 Phonetic segment classes

affricate   CH, JJ

alveolar   DD, DX, EN, NN, SS, TQ, TT, ZZ

aspseg   HH, HX, WH

dental   DH, TH

diphthong

>AE, AO, AW, AXR, AY, EH, EXR, EY, IH, IXR, IY, OW, OXR, OY, UH, UW, YU

f2back   IY, YU, YY

fricative   DH, FF, SS, SH, TH, VV, ZH, ZZ

front   AE, EH, EXR, EY, IH, IX, IXR, IY, YU

glottal   HH, HX, QQ, SIL

high   IH, IX, IXR, IY, UH, UW, UXR, WH, WW, YU, YY

labial   BB, EM, FF, MM, PP, VV, WW, WH

lateral	EL, LL, LX
lax	AE, AO, AX, AXP, EH IH, IX, UH
liqglide	EL, LL, LX, RR, RX, WH, WW, YY
low	AA, AE, AO, AW, AXR, AY
nasal	EM, EN, MM, NN, NG
palatal	CH, JJ, SH, YY, ZH
palvel	GP, KP
plosive	BB, CH, DD, GG, GP, JJ, KK, KP, PP, TQ, TT
retro	ER, RR, RX
rglide	AXR, EXR, IXR, OXR, UXR
round	AO, OW, OXR, OY, UH, UW, WH, WW, YU
schwa	AX, IX
sonorant	AA, AE, AH, AO, AW, AX, AXR, AY, EH, EL, EM, EN, ER, EXR, EY, HH, HX, IH, IX, IXR, IY, LL, LX, MM, NG, NN, OW, OXR, OY, RR, RX, UH, UW, UXR, WH, WW, YU, YY
stop	BB, CH, DD, DX, EM, EN, GG, GP, JJ, KK, KP, MM, NG, NN, PP, QQ, TQ, TT
syllabic	AA, AE, AH, AO, AW, AX, AXR, AY, EH, EL, EM, EN, ER, EXR, EY, IH, IX, IXR, IY, OW, OXR, OY, UH, UW, UXR, YU
velar	GG, KK, NG
voiced	AA, AE, AH, AO, AW, AX, AXR, AY, BB, DD, DH, DX, EH, EL, EM, EN, ER, EXR, EY, GG, GP, HX, IH, IX, IXR, IY, JJ, LL, LX, MM, NG, NN, OW, OXR, OY, QQ, RR, RX, TQ, UH, UW, UXR, VV, WH, WW, YU, YY, ZH, ZZ
vowel	AA, AE, AH, AO, AW, AX, AXR, AY, EH, ER, EXR, EY, IH, IX, IXR, IY, OW, OXR, OY, UH, UW, UXR, YU
wglide	AW, OW, UW, YU
yglide	AY, EY, IY, OY

C.4 Initialization

⊢—

Set manner class according to segment class:

Manner ← vowel / $\left[\begin{array}{c}+\text{vowel}\\ \underline{}\end{array}\right]$

ELSE Manner ← stop / $\left[\begin{array}{c}+\text{stop}\\ \underline{}\end{array}\right]$

ELSE Manner ← fricative / $\left[\begin{array}{c}+\text{fricative}\\ \underline{}\end{array}\right]$

ELSE Manner ← sonorant

Set amplitude, frequency, and bandwidth targets from Tables C-1 and C-2. The segments HH and HX inherit frequency targets from the next segment.

Target[fnz] ← 250 /—

Target[an] ← 0 /—

Set Tcf from Table C-3.

Buramp ← 57 /—

Aspamp ← 51 /—

Default transition type is SETSMO.
Set transition boundary value target Bper from Table C-4.

C.5 General rules

⊢—

Bper[f0] ← 75

Suppress amplitude smoothing after plosive:

Mintime[af] ← Cumdur[af] / $\left[\begin{array}{c}+\text{plosive}\\ S\end{array}\right]$—

Discontinuous transition out of unvoiced segment:

Trantype[f0, av] ← DISSMO / $\left[\begin{array}{c}-\text{voiced}\\ S\end{array}\right]$—

Mintime[f0] ← Cumdur[f0] / $\left[\begin{array}{c}-\text{voiced}\\ S\end{array}\right]$—

Do a breathy offset into a pause:

Aspdux ← 30, Oldval[avc] ↑ 6, Aspam1 ← Aspamp / $\left[\begin{array}{c}-\text{SIL}\\ S\end{array}\right]\left[\begin{array}{c}+\text{SIL}\\ \underline{}\end{array}\right]$

Table C-1: Parameter targets for nonvocalic segments

	av	avc	asp	af	a2	a3	a4	a5	a6	ab	f1	f2	f3	f4	b1	b2	b3
AXP	57	60	0	0	60	60	60	60	60	0	430	1500	2500	3300	120	60	120
BB	0	54	0	0	0	0	0	0	0	72	200	900	2100	3300	65	90	125
CH	0	0	0	0	0	60	75	70	70	0	300	1700	2400	3300	200	110	270
DD	0	54	0	0	0	0	0	50	82	0	200	1400	2700	3300	70	115	180
DH	36	54	0	60	0	0	0	0	30	54	300	1150	2700	3300	60	95	185
DX	44	60	0	0	60	60	60	60	60	0	200	1600	2700	3300	120	140	250
EL	57	57	0	0	60	60	60	60	60	0	450	800	2850	3300	65	60	80
EM	51	57	0	0	60	60	60	60	60	0	200	900	2100	3300	120	60	70
EN	51	57	0	0	60	60	60	60	60	0	200	1600	2700	3300	120	70	110
FF	0	0	31	60	0	0	0	0	0	64	400	1130	2100	3300	225	120	175
GG	0	54	0	0	70	30	30	60	10	0	250	1600	1900	3300	70	145	190
GP	0	54	0	0	30	70	60	62	62	0	200	1950	2800	3300	120	140	250
HH	0	0	60	0	60	60	60	60	60	0	450	1450	2450	3300	300	160	300
HX	44	60	57	0	60	60	60	60	60	0	450	1450	2450	3300	200	120	200
JJ	0	54	0	0	0	60	75	70	70	0	200	1700	2400	3300	50	110	270
KK	0	0	0	0	73	30	30	60	10	0	350	1600	1900	3300	280	220	250
KP	0	0	0	0	30	70	60	62	62	0	300	1950	2800	3300	150	140	250
LL	50	57	0	0	60	60	60	60	60	0	330	1050	2800	3300	50	100	280
LX	57	57	0	0	60	60	60	60	60	0	450	800	2850	3300	65	60	80
MM	51	57	0	0	60	60	60	60	60	0	480	1050	2100	3300	40	175	120
NG	51	57	0	0	60	60	60	60	60	0	480	1600	2050	3300	160	150	100
NN	51	57	0	0	60	60	60	60	60	0	480	1400	2700	3300	40	300	260
PP	0	0	0	0	0	0	0	0	0	72	300	900	2100	3300	300	190	185
QQ	0	0	0	0	60	60	60	60	60	0	400	1400	2450	3300	120	140	250
RR	50	57	0	0	60	60	60	60	60	0	330	1060	1380	3300	70	100	120
RX	57	57	0	0	60	60	60	60	60	0	460	1260	1560	3300	60	60	70
SH	0	0	31	60	0	60	75	70	70	0	400	1650	2400	3300	200	110	280
SIL	0	0	0	0	60	60	60	60	60	0	400	1400	2400	3300	120	140	250
SS	0	0	31	60	0	0	0	50	82	0	400	1400	2700	3300	200	95	220
TH	0	0	31	60	0	0	0	0	30	54	400	1150	2700	3300	225	95	200
TQ	0	0	0	0	0	0	0	50	82	0	200	1400	2700	3300	120	140	250
TT	0	0	0	0	0	0	0	50	82	0	300	1400	2700	3300	300	180	220
VV	40	54	0	60	0	0	0	0	0	64	300	1130	2100	3300	55	95	125
WH	0	57	51	0	60	60	60	60	60	0	330	600	2100	3300	150	60	60
WW	50	57	0	0	60	60	60	60	60	0	285	610	2150	3300	50	80	60
YY	50	57	0	0	60	60	60	60	60	0	240	2070	3020	3300	40	250	500
ZH	40	54	0	60	0	60	75	70	70	0	300	1650	2400	3300	220	140	250
ZZ	40	54	0	60	0	0	0	50	82	0	300	1400	2700	3300	70	85	190

Table C-2: Parameter targets for vocalic segments

	av	avc	asp	af	a2	a3	a4	a5	a6	ab	f1	f2	f3	f4	b1	b2	b3
AA	57	57	0	0	60	60	60	60	60	0	700	1220	2600	3300	130	70	160
AE	57	57	0	0	60	60	60	60	60	0	620	1660	2430	3300	70	130	300
											650	1490	2470				
AH	59	59	0	0	60	60	60	60	60	0	620	1220	2550	3300	80	50	140
AO	58	58	0	0	60	60	60	60	60	0	600	990	2570	3300	90	100	80
											630	1040	2600				
AW	57	57	0	0	60	60	60	60	60	0	640	1230	2550	3300	80	70	110
											420	940	2350				
AX	60	60	0	0	60	60	60	60	60	0	550	1260	2470	3300	80	50	140
AXR	60	60	0	0	60	60	60	60	60	0	680	1170	2380	3300	60	60	110
											520	1400	1650				
AY	58	58	0	0	60	60	60	60	60	0	660	1200	2550	3300	100	120	200
											400	1880	2500				
EH	61	61	0	0	60	60	60	60	60	0	530	1680	2500	3300	60	90	200
											620	1530	2530				
ER	62	62	0	0	60	60	60	60	60	0	470	1270	1540	3300	100	60	110
											420	1310	1540				
EXR	60	60	0	0	60	60	60	60	60	0	460	1650	2400	3300	60	80	140
											450	1500	1700				
EY	59	59	0	0	60	60	60	60	60	0	480	1720	2520	3300	70	100	200
											330	2200	2600				
IH	60	60	0	0	60	60	60	60	60	0	400	1800	2670	3300	50	100	140
											470	1600	2600				
IX	60	60	0	0	60	60	60	60	60	0	420	1680	2520	3300	50	100	140
IXR	60	60	0	0	60	60	60	60	60	0	320	1900	2900	3300	70	80	120
											420	1550	1750				
IY	60	60	0	0	60	60	60	60	60	0	310	2200	2960	3300	50	200	400
											290	2070	2980				
OW	60	60	0	0	60	60	60	60	60	0	540	1100	2300	3300	80	70	70
											450	900	2300				
OXR	60	60	0	0	60	60	60	60	60	0	550	820	2200	3300	60	60	60
											490	1300	1500				
OY	62	62	0	0	60	60	60	60	60	0	550	960	2400	3300	80	120	160
											360	1820	2450				
UH	63	63	0	0	60	60	60	60	60	0	450	1100	2350	3300	80	100	80
											500	1180	2390				
UW	64	64	0	0	60	60	60	60	60	0	350	1250	2200	3300	65	110	140
											320	900	2200				
UXR	60	60	0	0	60	60	60	60	60	0	360	800	2000	3300	60	60	80
											390	1150	1500				
YU	64	64	0	0	60	60	60	60	60	0	290	1900	2600	3300	70	160	220
											330	1200	2100				

Table C-3: Default values for duration of forward smoothing (Tcf)

av	25	avc	20	af	40	asp	20
an	40	a2p	40	a3p	40	a4p	40
a5p	40	a6p	40	ab	40	f0	120
f1	80	f2	80	f3	80	f4	80
fnz	150	b1	80	b2	80	b3	80

Table C-4: Default values for Bper

Previous manner class	Current manner class			
	vowel	stop	fricative	sonorant
vowel	50	35	50	75
stop	65	50	50	65
fricative	50	50	50	75
sonorant	25	35	25	50

Aspiration between voiced sonorant and following unvoiced consonant intrudes on the voicing:

$$\text{Aspdux} \leftarrow 10 \, / \begin{bmatrix} +\text{sonorant} \\ S \end{bmatrix} \begin{bmatrix} -\text{voiced} \\ - \end{bmatrix}$$

Start frication early if fricative follows sonorant:

$$\text{Cumdur[af]} \downarrow 20, \text{Segdur[af]} \uparrow 20 \, /$$
$$\begin{bmatrix} +\text{sonorant} \\ S \end{bmatrix} \begin{bmatrix} -\text{voiced}, +\text{fricative} \\ - \end{bmatrix}$$

$$\text{Aspam1} \downarrow 6 \, / \begin{bmatrix} +\text{sonorant} \\ S \end{bmatrix} \begin{bmatrix} -\text{voiced}, +\text{stop} \\ - \end{bmatrix}$$

If Aspdux was set above, then shift Cumdur[asp] earlier by the amount Aspdux. Force the value of asp at the new Cumdur[asp] to be Aspam1 and linearly smooth asp over the 30 msec interval preceding Cumdur[asp]. (See Figure C-1.)

F0 transitions into and out of voiceless segments are discontinuous:

Trantype[av] ← SMODIS / $\begin{bmatrix} \text{-voiced} \\ \underline{\quad} \end{bmatrix}$

Trantype[f0] ← DISCON / $\begin{bmatrix} \text{-voiced} \\ S \end{bmatrix}\begin{bmatrix} \text{-voiced} \\ \underline{\quad} \end{bmatrix}$

Trantype[f0] ← SMODIS / $\begin{bmatrix} \text{+voiced} \\ S \end{bmatrix}\begin{bmatrix} \text{-voiced} \\ \underline{\quad} \end{bmatrix}$

Tcf[f1..b3] ← Tcobst[X] / $\begin{bmatrix} \text{+stop} \\ X \end{bmatrix}\begin{bmatrix} \text{-stop} \\ \underline{\quad} \end{bmatrix}$

Trantype[av,avc] ← DISCON,

Trantype[af..b3] ← DISSMO / $\begin{bmatrix} \text{+stop, +nasal} \\ S \end{bmatrix}\begin{bmatrix} \text{-stop, +voiced} \\ \underline{\quad} \end{bmatrix}$

ELSE Trantype[av..ab,avc] ← DISSMO,
Trantype[f1..b3] ← SETSMO

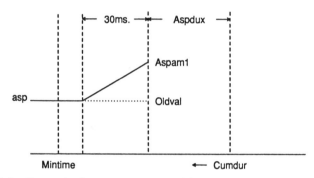

Figure C-1: Pre-aspiration parameter smoothing

C.6 Sonorant rules

$/\begin{bmatrix} \text{+sonor} \\ \underline{\quad} \end{bmatrix}$

Lower f4 if lips rounded:

Target[f4] ↓ 100 / $\begin{bmatrix} \text{+round} \\ \underline{\quad} \end{bmatrix}$

F4 higher in retro and lateral segments:

Target[f4] ↑ 300 / $\left\{ \begin{bmatrix} \text{+retro} \\ \underline{\quad} \end{bmatrix} / \begin{bmatrix} \text{+lateral} \\ \underline{\quad} \end{bmatrix} \right\}$

Transitions shorter out of liquids and glides:

$$\text{Tcf[f1..b3]} \leftarrow 110 \,/\, \begin{bmatrix} +\underset{S}{YY} \end{bmatrix} \begin{bmatrix} +\text{round} \\ - \end{bmatrix}$$

$$\text{ELSE Tcf[f1..b2]} \leftarrow 75 \,/\, \begin{bmatrix} +\underset{S}{\text{liqgli}} \end{bmatrix} -$$

$$\text{Tcf[f3]} \leftarrow 90 \,/\, \begin{bmatrix} +\underset{S}{\text{liqgli}}, +\text{retro} \end{bmatrix} -$$

W and Y-glides act like sonorants:

$$\text{Bper[f1..f3]} \leftarrow 35 \,/\, \left\{ \begin{bmatrix} +\underset{S}{\text{wglide}} \end{bmatrix} \,/\, \begin{bmatrix} -\underset{S}{\text{yglide}} \end{bmatrix} \right\} -$$

Increase transition between back vowels and palatalized consonants:

$$\text{Tcf[f2]} \uparrow 50 \,/\, \begin{bmatrix} +\underset{S}{\text{palatal}} \end{bmatrix} \begin{bmatrix} +\text{round} \\ - \end{bmatrix}$$

C.6.1 *Aspiration of an unvoiced fricative or plosive intrudes on the sonorant*

$$/ \begin{bmatrix} -\text{voiced, -glotstop, -SIL, -HH} \\ S \end{bmatrix} -$$

Assume a stressed, word-initial voiceless plosive:

Aspdur $\leftarrow$ 40

Apsam1 $\leftarrow$ Aspamp

Reduce aspiration if the preceding obstruent is unstressed:

$$\text{Aspdur} \leftarrow 20, \text{Aspam1} \downarrow 3 \,/\, \begin{bmatrix} -\underset{S}{\text{stress}} \end{bmatrix} -$$

Lengthen aspiration in plosive-obstruent clusters:

$$\text{Aspdur} \leftarrow 55 \,/\, \begin{bmatrix} -\underset{S}{\text{labial}} \end{bmatrix} \begin{bmatrix} -\text{vowel, -lateral} \\ - \end{bmatrix}$$

$$\text{ELSE Aspdur} \leftarrow 50 \,/\, \begin{bmatrix} -\text{vowel} \\ - \end{bmatrix}$$

Little aspiration if preceding segment voiced and current syllable unstressed:

$$\text{Aspdur} \downarrow 10 \,/\, \begin{bmatrix} +\underset{S}{\text{voiced}} \end{bmatrix} S \begin{bmatrix} -\text{stress} \\ - \end{bmatrix}$$

Large aspiration into silence:

$$\text{Aspdur} \leftarrow 70 \,/\, \begin{bmatrix} +\text{AXP} \\ - \end{bmatrix}$$

Aspiration starts during plosive burst:

Cumdur[asp,av,b1] ↑ Burdur[X] - 5,

Aspdur ↑ Burdur[X] - 5 / $\left[\begin{array}{c} +\text{plosive} \\ X \end{array}\right]$—

Aspiration duration is longer if fricative followed by a sonorant consonant:

Aspdur ← 10 / $\left[\begin{array}{c} +\text{fricative} \\ S \end{array}\right]\left[\begin{array}{c} +\text{vowel} \\ — \end{array}\right]$

Aspdur ← Segdur[asp]/2 / $\left[\begin{array}{c} +\text{fricative} \\ S \end{array}\right]\left[\begin{array}{c} -\text{vowel} \\ — \end{array}\right]$

Draw aspiration segment:

Aspdur ← min(Aspdur, Segdur[asp], segdur[av])

Aspam1 ↑ 9 / $\left[\begin{array}{c} +\text{alveolar} \\ S \end{array}\right]\left[\begin{array}{c} +\text{retro} \\ — \end{array}\right]$

If Aspdur is now nonzero, then draw an aspiration segment with duration Aspdur starting at time Cumdur[asp] where the values of asp, av, avc, and b1 are Aspam1, 0, 0, and 150, respectively. Shift Cumdur forward by Aspdur for these four parameters. If the previous segment is a fricative, then smooth asp backward over the 30 msec interval before Cumdur[asp].

C.6.2 *Nonnasal sonorants*

/ $\left[\begin{array}{c} -\text{vowel} \\ — \end{array}\right]$

F2 and f3 coarticulate with next vowel targets in RR and LL:

Target[av] ↓ 3 / $\left[\begin{array}{c} +\text{LL} \\ — \end{array}\right]$

Target[f2] ← .9*Target[f2] + .1*TARGET[f2, X] /
$\left[\begin{array}{c} +\text{LL} \\ — \end{array}\right]\left[\begin{array}{c} +\text{sonorant, -nasal} \\ X \end{array}\right]$

Coart(75), Target[f3] ← Target[f2]+250 / $\left[\begin{array}{c} +\text{RR} \\ — \end{array}\right]$

Target[f2] ← .75*Target[f2] + .25*TARGET[f2, X] /
$\left[\begin{array}{c} +\text{RR} \\ — \end{array}\right]\left[\begin{array}{c} +\text{sonorant, -nasal} \\ X \end{array}\right]$

Coarticulate with schwa if next segment is nonsonorant or nasal:

$$\text{Target[f2]} \leftarrow .9*\text{Target[f2]} + .1*1450 /$$
$$\begin{bmatrix} +\text{LL} \\ — \end{bmatrix} \left\{ \begin{bmatrix} -\text{sonorant} \\ X \end{bmatrix} / \begin{bmatrix} +\text{nasal} \\ X \end{bmatrix} \right\}$$

$$\text{Target[f2]} \leftarrow .75*\text{Target[f2]} + .25*\text{TARGET[f2, X]} /$$
$$\begin{bmatrix} +\text{RR} \\ — \end{bmatrix} \left\{ \begin{bmatrix} -\text{sonorant} \\ X \end{bmatrix} / \begin{bmatrix} +\text{nasal} \\ X \end{bmatrix} \right\}$$

Transitions shorter into liquids and glides:

$$\text{Bper[f1..f3]} \leftarrow 90 / \begin{bmatrix} -\text{nasal, +sonor} \\ S \end{bmatrix} \begin{bmatrix} +\text{lateral} \\ — \end{bmatrix}$$

Transitions between retro and lateral are short:

$$\text{Tcf[f1..b3]} \leftarrow 90 / \begin{bmatrix} -\text{liqgli} \\ — \end{bmatrix}$$
$$\text{ELSE Tcf[f1..b3]} \leftarrow 50 / \begin{bmatrix} +\text{liqgli} \\ S \end{bmatrix} —$$
$$\text{ELSE Tcf[f1..b3]} \leftarrow 70$$

$$\text{Tcf[f3]} \leftarrow 90 / \begin{bmatrix} +\text{retro} \\ — \end{bmatrix}$$

C.7 Vowels

$$/ \begin{bmatrix} +\text{vowel} \\ — \end{bmatrix}$$

Heavy forward coarticulation of schwa:

$$\text{Target[f2]} \leftarrow \text{avg(Target[f2], TARGET[f2, X]) /}$$
$$\begin{bmatrix} +\text{sonor, -nasal} \\ X \end{bmatrix} S \begin{bmatrix} +\text{AXP} \\ — \end{bmatrix}$$

No schwa offglide before velar consonant:

$$\text{Diptar[f2]} \leftarrow \text{Target[f2]} / \begin{bmatrix} +\text{front, +lax} \\ — \end{bmatrix} \begin{bmatrix} +\text{velar} \\ S \end{bmatrix}$$

Velarization of front vowels if followed by +lateral:

$$\text{Diptar[f2]} \downarrow 300 / \left\{ \begin{bmatrix} +\text{front} \\ — \end{bmatrix} / \begin{bmatrix} +\text{yglide} \\ — \end{bmatrix} \right\} \begin{bmatrix} +\text{lateral} \\ S \end{bmatrix}$$

$$\text{Diptar[f2]} \downarrow 300 /$$
$$\left\{ \begin{bmatrix} +\text{front, -diphthong} \\ — \end{bmatrix} / \begin{bmatrix} +\text{yglide, -diphthong} \\ — \end{bmatrix} \right\} \begin{bmatrix} +\text{lateral} \\ S \end{bmatrix}$$

YU fronted if alveolar plosive follows:

$$\text{Diptar[f2]} \uparrow 200 \; / \begin{bmatrix} +\text{YU} \\ \underline{} \end{bmatrix} \begin{bmatrix} +\text{alveolar, +plosive} \\ \text{S} \end{bmatrix}$$

F2 time constant longer in +F2back, +round transition:

$$\text{Tcf[f2]} \uparrow 50 \; / \begin{bmatrix} +\text{f2back} \\ \text{S} \end{bmatrix} \begin{bmatrix} +\text{round} \\ \underline{} \end{bmatrix}$$

Y-glide not as dramatic before alveolar consonant:

$$\text{Diptar[f2]} \downarrow 150 \; / \begin{bmatrix} +\text{yglide} \\ \underline{} \end{bmatrix} \begin{bmatrix} +\text{alveolar} \\ \text{S} \end{bmatrix}$$

Formant centralized in a short nonretro vowel: Shift Target[f1..f3] and Diptar[f1..f3] towards 490,1450,2500 Hz by an amount which varies as a dying exponential with time constant 60 msec in the duration of the segment.

Schwa takes on formant targets of adjacent segments:

$$\text{Target[f3]} \leftarrow \text{average(Oldval[f3], Target[f3], Nextar[f3])}/ \begin{bmatrix} +\text{schwa} \\ \underline{} \end{bmatrix}$$

Back cavity resonances assume target quickly:

$$\text{Tcf[f2]} \downarrow 20 \; / \begin{bmatrix} +\text{f2back} \\ \underline{} \end{bmatrix}$$

C.7.1 *Diphthong rules*

$$/ \begin{bmatrix} +\text{diphthong} \\ \underline{} \end{bmatrix}$$

Set Tcdiph and Tdmid from Table C-5.

$$\text{Tcenter[f1..f3]} \leftarrow \text{Tdmid} * \text{Segdur[f1]}$$

$$\text{Tcdips[f1..f3]} \leftarrow \text{Tcdiph} * .5 * (1 + \text{Segdur[f1]} / 45)$$

Earlier diphthongization after HH in tense vowels:

$$\text{Tcenter[f1..f3]} \leftarrow \text{Tcenter[f1..f2]} * .67 \; / \begin{bmatrix} +\text{HH} \\ \text{S} \end{bmatrix} \begin{bmatrix} +\text{lax} \\ \underline{} \end{bmatrix}$$

$$\text{Bvalf[f1..f3]} \leftarrow \text{average(Target[f1..f3], Diptar[f1..f3])}$$

$$\text{Bvalf[f1]} \uparrow 70 \; / \begin{bmatrix} +\text{OY} \\ \underline{} \end{bmatrix}$$

$$\text{Bvalf[f2]} \uparrow 200 \; / \left\{ \begin{bmatrix} +\text{AY} \\ \underline{} \end{bmatrix} \; / \; \begin{bmatrix} +\text{OY} \\ \underline{} \end{bmatrix} \right\}$$

$$\text{Bvalf[f3]} \downarrow 200 \; / \left\{ \begin{bmatrix} +\text{AY} \\ \underline{} \end{bmatrix} \; / \; \begin{bmatrix} +\text{OY} \\ \underline{} \end{bmatrix} \right\}$$

$$\text{Tcenter[f3]} \leftarrow \text{Tcenter[f3]} * .3 / \begin{bmatrix} +\text{YU} \\ \underline{} \end{bmatrix}$$

$$\text{Tcenter[f3]} \leftarrow \text{Tcenter[f3]} * .6 / \left\{ \begin{bmatrix} +\text{EXR} \\ \underline{} \end{bmatrix} / \begin{bmatrix} +\text{IXR} \\ \underline{} \end{bmatrix} \right\}$$

$$\text{Bvalb[f1..f3]} \leftarrow \text{Bvalf[f1..f3]}$$

Temporarily replace Target[f1..f3] with Diptar[f1..f3] and move Cumdur[f1..f3] to Cumdur[f1..f3] + Tcenter[f1..f3], then draw a transition (see Figure C-2).

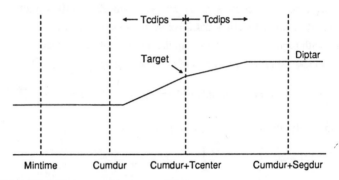

Figure C-2: Diphthong transition smoothing

Table C-5: Diphthong transition parameters

	Tcdiph	Tdmid		Tcdiph	Tdmid		Tcdiph	Tdmid
AA	0	80	AE	100	75	AH	0	0
AO	110	80	AW	120	70	AXR	125	40
AY	100	55	EH	60	70	ER	180	50
EXR	100	50	EY	140	55	IH	90	65
IXR	100	50	IY	200	45	OW	150	50
OXR	110	60	OY	150	60	UH	90	65
UW	140	55	UXR	150	50	YU	100	45

C.8 Obstruents

$$/ \begin{bmatrix} -\text{sonor}, +\text{nasal} \\ \underline{} \end{bmatrix}$$

194

C.8.1 *Fricatives and plosives*

$$/\left\{ \begin{bmatrix} +\text{plosive} \\ — \end{bmatrix} / \begin{bmatrix} +\text{fricative} \\ — \end{bmatrix} \right\}$$

Devoice if not followed by vowel:

$$\text{Target[avc]} \downarrow 30 / \begin{bmatrix} +\text{voiced} \\ — \end{bmatrix} \begin{bmatrix} -\text{vowel} \\ S \end{bmatrix}$$

$$\text{Target[f4]} \downarrow 150 / \begin{bmatrix} +\text{palatal} \\ — \end{bmatrix}$$

$$\text{Target[a2p..a6p]} \leftarrow 0,67,60,65,65 /$$
$$\begin{bmatrix} +\text{alveolar}, +\text{plosive} \\ — \end{bmatrix} \begin{bmatrix} -\text{alveolar}, +\text{retro} \\ S \end{bmatrix}$$

$$\text{Target[a2p..a6p]} \leftarrow 0,52,60,70,73 /$$
$$\begin{bmatrix} +\text{alveolar}, +\text{plosive} \\ — \end{bmatrix} \begin{bmatrix} -\text{alveolar}, -\text{retro} \\ S \end{bmatrix}$$

$$\text{BurAmp} \downarrow 5 / \begin{bmatrix} +\text{velar} \\ — \end{bmatrix} \begin{bmatrix} -\text{vowel} \\ S \end{bmatrix}$$

No voicebar in voiced plosive if preceded by obstruent:

$$\text{Target[avc]} \leftarrow 0 /$$
$$\left\{ \begin{bmatrix} -\text{voiced} \\ S \end{bmatrix} / \begin{bmatrix} -\text{sonor} \\ S \end{bmatrix} \right\} \begin{bmatrix} +\text{voiced}, +\text{plosive} \\ — \end{bmatrix}$$

C.8.2 *Fricatives only*

$$/\begin{bmatrix} +\text{fricative} \\ — \end{bmatrix}$$

$$\text{Target[af]} \downarrow 4 / \text{—SIL}$$

Short fricatives don't reach target, so increase target:

$$\text{Target[af]} \uparrow \text{IF Segdur[af]} < 80 \text{ THEN}$$
$$(80 - \text{Segdur[af]})*\text{deltat}/7 / \begin{bmatrix} -\text{fric}, -\text{stop} \\ S \end{bmatrix} — \begin{bmatrix} +\text{vowel} \\ S \end{bmatrix}$$

Stronger voicing between vowels:

$$\text{Target[avc]} \leftarrow 60 / \begin{bmatrix} +\text{vowel} \\ S \end{bmatrix} \begin{bmatrix} +\text{voiced} \\ — \end{bmatrix} \begin{bmatrix} +\text{vowel} \\ S \end{bmatrix}$$

Palatal fricative rounding before rounded vowel:

$$\text{Target[f2]} \downarrow 50, \text{Target[f3]} \downarrow 200 \text{ /}$$
$$\begin{bmatrix} +\text{palatal} \\ - \end{bmatrix} \begin{bmatrix} +\text{vowel, +round} \\ S \end{bmatrix}$$

C.8.3 *Stops*

$$/ \begin{bmatrix} +\text{stop} \\ - \end{bmatrix}$$

Transition into stop is partially discontinuous (except f0):

$$\text{Trantype[av..f1]} \leftarrow \text{SMODIS, Trantype[f2..b3]} \leftarrow \text{SETSMO},$$
$$\text{Trantype[avc]} \leftarrow \text{SMODIS} / \begin{bmatrix} -\text{stop} \\ S \end{bmatrix} -$$

$$\text{Tcf[f2..b3]} \leftarrow 10, \text{Tcf[f1]} \leftarrow 15 / \begin{bmatrix} +\text{high} \\ S \end{bmatrix} -$$

$$\text{Tcf[f2..b3]} \leftarrow \text{Tcobst[---], Tcf[f1]} \leftarrow \text{average(Tcobst[---], 20) /}$$
$$\begin{bmatrix} -\text{high} \\ S \end{bmatrix} -$$

Table C-6: Duration of forward smoothing for obstruents (Tcobst)

BB	60	CH	100	DD	80	DH	80
EL	80	EM	60	EN	80	FF	60
GG	100	GP	100	HH	80	HX	80
KK	100	KP	100	MM	60	NG	100
NN	80	PP	80	QQ	80	SH	100
SIL	80	SS	80	TH	80	TQ	80
TT	80	VV	60	ZH	100	ZZ	80

C.8.3.1 *Insert burst at expense of closure duration*

$$/ \begin{bmatrix} +\text{plosive, -gltstop} \\ - \end{bmatrix} \begin{bmatrix} -\text{stop, -SIL} \\ S \end{bmatrix}$$

Set Burdur from Table C-7.

$$\text{Burdur} \uparrow 10 / \begin{bmatrix} +\text{TT} \\ - \end{bmatrix} \begin{bmatrix} +\text{retro} \\ S \end{bmatrix}$$

Burdur ← Segdur[af] IF Burdur > Segdur[af]

Burdur ← 5 IF Burdur = 0

Decrease the value of af by 20 dB at Cumdur[af] and smooth this value backward 30 msec.

Draw an af segment with value zero and duration Segdur[af]-Burdur beginning at Cumdur[af]. Shift Cumdur[af] and Segdur[af] accordingly. (Segdur[af] will now equal Burdur.)

$$\text{Buramp} \uparrow 6 \, / \, \begin{bmatrix} \text{-voiced} \\ \text{—} \end{bmatrix}$$

$$\text{Buramp} \downarrow 6 \, / \, \begin{bmatrix} \text{+nasal} \\ \text{S} \end{bmatrix} \begin{bmatrix} \text{-stress} \\ \text{—} \end{bmatrix}$$

$$\text{Buramp} \downarrow 3 \, / \, \begin{bmatrix} \text{-nasal} \\ \text{S} \end{bmatrix} \begin{bmatrix} \text{-stress} \\ \text{—} \end{bmatrix}$$

$$\text{Buramp} \downarrow 3 \, / \, \text{—} \left\{ \begin{bmatrix} \text{+AXP} \\ \text{S} \end{bmatrix} \, / \, \begin{bmatrix} \text{+fricative} \\ \text{S} \end{bmatrix} \right\}$$

Target[af] ← Buramp

Trantype[af] ← DISCON

Target[fnz] ← 450, Bper[fnz] ← 100,

  Trantype[af..b3] ← SMODIS, Trantype[av] ← DISCON /
$$\begin{bmatrix} \text{+nasal} \\ \text{—} \end{bmatrix}$$

Trantype[av, avc] ← DISSMO / $\begin{bmatrix} \text{-voiced} \\ \text{S} \end{bmatrix} \begin{bmatrix} \text{+nasal} \\ \text{—} \end{bmatrix}$

Table C-7: Default plosive burst duration

BB	5	CH	15	DD	10	DX	10
GG	20	GP	20	JJ	10	KK	25
KP	25	MM	0	NG	0	NN	0
PP	5	TQ	15	TT	15		

C.8.4 *Nasals*

$$/ \begin{bmatrix} \text{+nasal} \\ \text{—} \end{bmatrix}$$

  Target[fnz] ← 450

  Trantype[af..b3] ← SMODIS

$$\text{Bper[fnz]} \leftarrow 100$$

$$\text{Trantype[av]} \leftarrow \text{DISCON}$$

$$\text{Trantype[avc, av]} \leftarrow \text{DISSMO} / \begin{bmatrix} \text{-voiced} \\ \text{S} \end{bmatrix}-$$

C.9 Adjustments

$/-$

(swap current and previous segments if Manner[current] > Manner[previous])

$$\text{Bper[f2]} \leftarrow 75, \text{Bper[f3]} \leftarrow 75 / \begin{bmatrix} \text{+retro} \\ - \end{bmatrix}$$

SH and ZH highly constrain boundary unless stop is adjacent:

$$\text{Bper[f2]} \leftarrow 20, \text{Tcf[f2]} \uparrow 30 / \begin{bmatrix} \text{+palatal, -sonor} \\ \text{S} \end{bmatrix}-$$

C.9.1 *Boundary values for stops*

$$/ \begin{bmatrix} \text{+stop} \\ \text{S} \end{bmatrix} \begin{bmatrix} \text{-stop} \\ - \end{bmatrix}$$

$$\text{Bper[f2]} \leftarrow 50$$

$$\text{Bper[f2]} \leftarrow 0$$

$$\text{Bper[f3]} \leftarrow 0$$

$$\text{Bper[fnz]} \leftarrow \text{IF Mancur - Manlas} > 1 \text{ THEN } 100 \text{ ELSE } 0,$$
$$\text{Tcf[fnz]} \leftarrow 150, \text{Bper[f1]} \leftarrow 0 / \begin{bmatrix} \text{+nasal} \\ \text{S} \end{bmatrix}-$$

$$\text{Bper[f2]} \leftarrow 65, \text{Bper[f3]} \leftarrow 20 / \begin{bmatrix} \text{+labial} \\ \text{S} \end{bmatrix} \begin{bmatrix} \text{-glottal, +front} \\ - \end{bmatrix}$$

$$\text{Bper[f2]} \leftarrow 20, \text{Bper[f3]} \leftarrow 70 / \begin{bmatrix} \text{+labial} \\ \text{S} \end{bmatrix} \begin{bmatrix} \text{-glottal, -front} \\ - \end{bmatrix}$$

$$\text{Oldval[f3]} \leftarrow 1750, \text{Bper[f3]} \leftarrow 20 / \begin{bmatrix} \text{+labial} \\ \text{S} \end{bmatrix} \begin{bmatrix} \text{-glottal, +retro} \\ - \end{bmatrix}$$

$$\text{Oldval[f2]} \leftarrow 1050 / \begin{bmatrix} \text{+alveolar} \\ \text{S} \end{bmatrix} \begin{bmatrix} \text{+lateral} \\ - \end{bmatrix}$$

$$\text{Oldval[f2]} \leftarrow 1400 / \begin{bmatrix} \text{+NN} \\ \text{S} \end{bmatrix} \begin{bmatrix} \text{-lateral} \\ - \end{bmatrix}$$

$$\text{Oldval[f2]} \leftarrow 1600 / \begin{bmatrix} \text{+alveolar, -NN} \\ \text{S} \end{bmatrix} \begin{bmatrix} \text{-lateral} \\ \text{---} \end{bmatrix}$$

$$\text{Oldval[f3]} \leftarrow 2300 / \begin{bmatrix} \text{+alveolar} \\ \text{S} \end{bmatrix} \begin{bmatrix} \text{+retro} \\ \text{---} \end{bmatrix}$$

$$\text{Oldval[f3]} \leftarrow 2620 / \begin{bmatrix} \text{+alveolar} \\ \text{S} \end{bmatrix} \begin{bmatrix} \text{-retro} \\ \text{---} \end{bmatrix}$$

Add f1 and f2 vowel targets to compute f2 locus for velar (f1 reflects lip-rounding and f2 reflects fronting components of systematic shift in locus):

$$\text{Oldval[f2]} \leftarrow \text{Target[f2]} + (\text{Target[f1]} - 300)*2 / \begin{bmatrix} \text{+velar} \\ \text{S} \end{bmatrix}\text{---}$$

$$\text{Oldval[f3]} \leftarrow \text{Oldval[f2]} + 800 / \begin{bmatrix} \text{+velar} \\ \text{S} \end{bmatrix} \begin{bmatrix} \text{+labial} \\ \text{---} \end{bmatrix}$$

$$\text{Oldval[f3]} \leftarrow \text{Oldval[f2]} + 400 / \begin{bmatrix} \text{+velar} \\ \text{S} \end{bmatrix} \begin{bmatrix} \text{-labial} \\ \text{---} \end{bmatrix}$$

$$\text{Oldval[f2,f3]} \leftarrow \text{KP-target[f2,f4]} / \left\{ \begin{bmatrix} \text{+front} \\ \text{---} \end{bmatrix} / \begin{bmatrix} \text{+AA} \\ \text{---} \end{bmatrix} \right\}$$

f2 lower in NG:

$$\text{Oldval[f2,f3]} \leftarrow (\text{Oldval[f2,f3]} + \text{Target[f2,f3]})/2 / \begin{bmatrix} \text{+NG} \\ \text{S} \end{bmatrix}\text{---}$$

Fronted articulation of KK, GG, and NG adjacent to IY and IH:

$$\text{Oldval[f2]} \uparrow 250, \text{Oldval[f3]} \uparrow 50 / \left\{ \begin{bmatrix} \text{+IY} \\ \text{---} \end{bmatrix} / \begin{bmatrix} \text{+IH} \\ \text{---} \end{bmatrix} \right\}$$

(end of manner class reversal)

C.9.2 *All segments*

$$\vdash$$

$$\text{Oldval[f2, f3, f4]} \leftarrow 1200, 2050, 2500, \text{Bper[f4]} \leftarrow 0, \text{Tcf[f4]} \leftarrow 30 /$$
$$\begin{bmatrix} \text{+alveolar, +stop} \\ \text{S} \end{bmatrix} \begin{bmatrix} \text{+WW} \\ \text{---} \end{bmatrix}$$

$$\text{Target[f2, f3]} \leftarrow 1850, 2200, \text{Target[f4]} \uparrow \text{f4} /$$
$$\left\{ \begin{bmatrix} \text{+rglide} \\ \text{S} \end{bmatrix} / \begin{bmatrix} \text{+retro} \\ \text{S} \end{bmatrix} \right\} \begin{bmatrix} \text{+alveolar} \\ \text{---} \end{bmatrix}$$

$$\text{Target[f2, f3]} \leftarrow 1700, 1900 /$$
$$\left\{ \begin{bmatrix} \text{+rglide} \\ \text{S} \end{bmatrix} / \begin{bmatrix} \text{+retro} \\ \text{S} \end{bmatrix} \right\} \begin{bmatrix} \text{+velar} \\ \text{---} \end{bmatrix}$$

$$\text{Oldval[f2, f3]} \leftarrow 1100, 1500 \,/\, \begin{bmatrix} +\text{velar} \\ S \end{bmatrix} \begin{bmatrix} +\text{retro} \\ - \end{bmatrix}$$

$$\text{Oldval[f3]} \leftarrow 2100 \,/\, \begin{bmatrix} +\text{alveolar} \\ S \end{bmatrix} \begin{bmatrix} +\text{retro} \\ - \end{bmatrix}$$

$$\text{Oldval[f3]} \leftarrow 1700 \,/\, \begin{bmatrix} +\text{labial} \\ S \end{bmatrix} \begin{bmatrix} +\text{retro} \\ - \end{bmatrix}$$

$$\text{Target[f2, f3]} \leftarrow 900, 2000 \,/\, \begin{bmatrix} +\text{wglide} \\ S \end{bmatrix} \begin{bmatrix} +\text{velar} \\ - \end{bmatrix}$$

ELSE Target[f2] $\leftarrow$ 1900

$$\text{Oldval[f2]} \leftarrow 1850 \,/\, \begin{bmatrix} +\text{alveolar, +stop} \\ S \end{bmatrix} \begin{bmatrix} +\text{f2back} \\ - \end{bmatrix}$$

C.10 Modifications

$\longleftarrow$

Target[f1..f3] $\leftarrow$

average(Target[f1..f3], Oldval[f1..f3], Nextar[f1..f3]) $/\, \begin{bmatrix} +\text{DX} \\ - \end{bmatrix}$

f2 transitions involving f2back segments are shorter:

$$\text{Tcf[f2]} \downarrow 20 \,/\, \begin{bmatrix} +\text{f2back} \\ S \end{bmatrix} \longleftarrow$$

Minimum formant separation is 200 Hz: raise Target[f2..f4] such that separation is at least 200Hz.

Set boundary values and Tcb:

Tcb[av..f0] $\leftarrow$ Tcf[av..f0]

Bvalf[av..f0] $\leftarrow$ (Bper[av..f0] * Target[av..f0]
       + (100 - Bper[av..f0]) * Oldval[av..f0]) / 100

Discontinuous formant jump in a lateral release:

$$\text{Bvalf[f1,f2]} \uparrow 50, \text{Bvalb[f1,f2]} \downarrow 50 \,/\, \begin{bmatrix} +\text{lateral} \\ S \end{bmatrix} \longleftarrow$$

DISSMO in diphthongs are changed to SMOOTH, so change boundary instead:

$$\text{Bvalb[f1..f3]} \leftarrow \text{Oldval[f1..f3]} \,/\, \begin{bmatrix} +\text{nasal} \\ S \end{bmatrix} \begin{bmatrix} +\text{diphthong} \\ - \end{bmatrix}$$

Special treatment for amplitude parameters:

Bvalf[av..ab,avc] ← average(Target[av..ab,avc], Oldval[av..ab,avc])

Vowel amplitude offset more gradual:

$$\text{Tcb[av]} \leftarrow 30 \; / \begin{bmatrix} +\text{vowel} \\ S \end{bmatrix} -$$

Voicing offset in stop or fricative more gradual, in onset too:

$$\text{Bvalb[av]} \downarrow 6, \text{Bvalf[av]} \leftarrow \text{Bvalb[av]} / \begin{bmatrix} +\text{voiced} \\ S \end{bmatrix} \begin{bmatrix} -\text{voiced, -sonor} \\ - \end{bmatrix}$$

$$\text{Bvalb[av]} \downarrow 4, \text{Bvalf[av]} \leftarrow \text{Bvalb[av]} /$$
$$\left\{ \begin{bmatrix} +\text{voiced, +stop} \\ S \end{bmatrix} / \begin{bmatrix} +\text{voiced, +fric} \\ S \end{bmatrix} \right\} \begin{bmatrix} +\text{sonor, +nasal} \\ - \end{bmatrix}$$

Glottal segments (including SIL) have no inherent "articulatory" targets:

Bvalb[a2p..b3] ← Target[a2p..b3],

Bvalf[a2p..b3] ← Target[a2p..b3],

$$\text{Oldval[a2p..b3]} \leftarrow \text{Target[a2p..b3]} / \begin{bmatrix} +\text{glottal} \\ S \end{bmatrix} -$$

Stops have abrupt offset:

$$\text{Bvalf[af]} \leftarrow \text{Target[af]} / \begin{bmatrix} +\text{plosive} \\ S \end{bmatrix} -$$

Draw all parameter tracks.

Appendix D

Sample test trials from the Modified Rhyme Test

1.	a) bad	b) back	c) ban	d) bass	e) bat	f) bath
2.	a) beam	b) bead	c) beach	d) beat	e) beak	f) bean
3.	a) bus	b) but	c) bug	d) buff	e) bun	f) buck
4.	a) case	b) cave	c) cape	d) cane	e) cake	f) came
5.	a) cuff	b) cut	c) cuss	d) cub	e) cup	f) cud
6.	a) dip	b) din	c) dill	d) dig	e) dim	f) did
7.	a) dub	b) dun	c) dung	d) dug	e) duck	f) dud
8.	a) fizz	b) fin	c) fill	d) fig	e) fib	f) fit
9.	a) hear	b) heath	c) heal	d) heave	e) heat	f) heap
10.	a) kid	b) kit	c) kill	d) kin	e) king	f) kick
11.	a) lace	b) lame	c) lane	d) lay	e) lake	f) late
12.	a) man	b) math	c) mad	d) mat	e) mass	f) map
13.	a) pace	b) pane	c) pave	d) page	e) pay	f) pale
14.	a) path	b) pat	c) pack	d) pad	e) pass	f) pan
15.	a) peas	b) peak	c) peal	d) peace	e) peach	f) peat
16.	a) pip	b) pick	c) pin	d) pill	e) pit	f) pig
17.	a) puff	b) pus	c) pub	d) pun	e) puck	f) pup
18.	a) rate	b) race	c) ray	d) raze	e) rave	f) rake
19.	a) safe	b) sake	c) same	d) sane	e) save	f) sale
20.	a) sat	b) sag	c) sack	d) sap	e) sass	f) sad
21.	a) seed	b) seek	c) seen	d) seep	e) seem	f) seethe
22.	a) sill	b) sick	c) sing	d) sit	e) sin	f) sip
23.	a) sup	b) sud	c) sun	d) sum	e) sub	f) sung
24.	a) tap	b) tang	c) tam	d) tan	e) tab	f) tack
25.	a) tease	b) tear	c) teak	d) teal	e) team	f) teach

Appendix E

Sample test materials from the Harvard Psychoacoustic Sentences

1. The birch canoe slid on the smooth planks
2. Glue the sheet to the dark blue background
3. It's easy to tell the depth of a well
4. These days a chicken leg is a rare dish
5. Rice is often served in round bowls
6. The juice of lemons makes fine punch
7. The box was thrown beside the parked truck
8. The hogs were fed chopped corn and garbage
9. Four hours of steady work faced us
10. A large size in stockings is hard to sell
11. The boy was there when the sun rose
12. A rod is used to catch pink salmon
13. The source of the huge river is the clear spring
14. Kick the ball straight and follow through
15. Help the woman get back to her feet
16. A pot of tea helps to pass the evening
17. Smoky fires lack flame and heat
18. The soft cushion broke the man's fall
19. The salt breeze came across from the sea
20. The girl at the booth sold fifty bonds
21. The small pup gnawed a hole in the sock
22. The fish twisted and turned on the bent hook
23. Press the pants and sew a button on the vest
24. The swan dive was far short of perfect
25. The beauty of the view stunned the young boy

Appendix F

Sample test materials from the Haskins Anomalous Sentences

---

1. The wrong shot led the farm
2. The black top ran the spring
3. The great car met the milk
4. The old corn cost the blood
5. The short arm sent the cow
6. The low walk read the hat
7. The rich paint said the land
8. The big bank felt the bag
9. The sick seat grew the chain
10. The salt dog caused the show
11. The last fire tried the nose
12. The young voice saw the rose
13. The gold rain led the wing
14. The chance sun laid the year
15. The white bow had the bed
16. The near stone thought the ear
17. The end home held the press
18. The deep head cut the cent
19. The next wind sold the room
20. The full leg shut the shore
21. The safe meat caught the shade
22. The fine lip tired the earth
23. The plain can lost the men
24. The dead hand armed the bird
25. The fast point laid the word

Appendix G

Sample passage used to test listening comprehension

The lens buyer must approach the problem of purchasing a lens of large aperture with caution. The first question to consider is whether the work one intends doing will actually require the extreme speed afforded by such a lens. Despite the glowing advertising claims, no extremely rapid lens is capable of giving, even when stopped down to its best aperture, the sharpness of definition which may be obtained with a well-corrected (and much lower-priced) lens of smaller maximum aperture. It is very doubtful if there exists a lens with maximum aperture in excess of F 4.5 which will give really sharp definition, whether wide open or at any smaller opening; the deficiencies of the large-apertured lens, if it is a fairly good one, will not be noticed in small contact prints; but in pictures enlarged to any considerable extent, they will be evident (or examination of the print with the low magnification of a reading glass will make them evident). With modern, extremely rapid films and with synchronized flash available for the amateur who can afford to go in for the type of photography that requires this kind of equipment, the occasions are indeed rare when a lens faster than F 4.5 is really needed.

G.1 Test questions for the comprehension passage

1. The main thought of this passage is that
   1. good photographic work requires the use of a fast lens
   2. lenses of small aperture provide less sharpness than lenses of large aperture
   3. lenses of small aperture are to be preferred for most photographic work
   4. modern photographic equipment requires the use of lenses of large aperture
2. We may infer that some advertisements for photographic lenses tend to recommend the purchase of
   1. large-aperture lenses
   2. small-aperture lenses
   3. the most appropriate lenses
   4. F 4.5 lenses

3. As the aperture of a lens is increased, the
   1. price tends to decrease
   2. speed of the lens tends to decrease
   3. sharpness of its focus tends to decrease
   4. speed of the lens tends to remain constant

4. The writer's attitude toward the advertising materials which are mentioned is one of
   1. indifference
   2. disbelief
   3. acceptance
   4. enthusiasm

5. The writer's main purpose is to
   1. encourage the use of synchronized flash
   2. discourage the use of synchronized flash
   3. encourage the use of rapid films
   4. discourage the purchase of fast lenses

6. To obtain pictures of maximum sharpness, the writer strongly recommends the use of
   1. lenses of large aperture
   2. lenses of small aperture
   3. lower priced films
   4. contact prints

References

Anonymous 1960. Cooperative English Tests: Reading Comprehension, Form 1B. Princeton, New Jersey: Educational Testing Service.

Anonymous 1972. Iowa Silent Reading Tests, Level 3, Form E. New York: Harcourt Brace Jovanovich.

Anonymous 1972. Stanford Test of Academic Skills: Reading, College Level II-A. New York: Harcourt Brace Jovanovich.

Anonymous 1973. The Nelson-Denny Reading Test, Form D. Boston: Houghton-Mifflin.

Akers, G. and M. Lennig 1985. Intonation in text-to-speech synthesis: Evaluation of algorithms. *Journal of the Acoustical Society of America* 77: 2157-65.

Allen, J. 1968. A Study of the Specification of Prosodic Features of Speech From a Grammatical Analysis of Printed Text. PhD thesis, Massachusetts Institute of Technology, Cambridge, Massachusetts.

Allen, J. 1973. Reading Machines for the Blind: The Technical Problems and the Methods Adopted for Their Solution. *IEEE Transactions on Audio and Electroacoustics* AU-21: 259-64.

Allen, J. 1976. Synthesis of Speech from Unrestricted Text. *Proceedings of the IEEE* 64: 422-33.

Allen, J. 1977. A Modular Audio Response System for Computer Output. *Proceedings of the International Conference on Acoustics, Speech, and Signal Processing*, 579-81. New York: IEEE. IEEE Catalog No. 77CH1197-3 ASSP.

Allen, J., S. Hunnicutt, R. Carlson, and B. Granstrom 1979. MITalk-79: The MIT Text-to-Speech System. *Speech Communication Papers Presented at the 97th Meeting of the Acoustical Society of America*. New York: Acoustical Society of America.

Bolinger, D. 1972. Accent is Predictable if You Are a Mind-Reader. *Language* 48: 633-44.

Buron, R.H. 1968. Generation of a 1000-Word Vocabulary for a Pulse-Excited Vocoder Operating as an Audio Response Unit. *IEEE Transactions on Audio and Electroacoustics* AU-16: 21-5.

Caldwell, J. 1979. Flexible, High-Performance Speech Synthesizer Using Custom NMOS Circuitry. *Journal of the Acoustical Society of America* 64, Supplement 1: S72. (Abstract).

Carlson, R., B. Granstrom, and K. Larsson 1976. Evaluation of a Text-to-Speech System as a Reading Machine for the Blind. In Speech Transmission Laboratory Quarterly Progress and Status Report 2-3/1976, 9-13. Royal Institute of Technology, Stockholm.

Carlson, R., B. Granstrom, and D.H. Klatt 1979. Some Notes on the Perception of Temporal Patterns in Speech. In B. Lindblom and S. Ohman (eds.), *Frontiers of Speech Communication Research,* New York: Academic Press.

Carlson, R. and B. Granstrom 1973. Word Accent, Emphatic Stress, and Syntax in a Synthesis-by-Rule Scheme for Swedish. In Speech Transmission Laboratory Quarterly Progress and Status Report 2-3/1973, 31-6. Royal Institute of Technology, Stockholm.

References

Carlson, R. and B. Granstrom 1976. A Text-to-Speech System Based Entirely on Rules. *Proceedings of the International Conference on Acoustics, Speech, and Signal Processing,* 686-8. New York: IEEE. IEEE Catalog No. 76-CH-1067-8 ASSP.

Chapman, W.D. 1971. Techniques for Computer Voice Response. *IEEE International Conference Record,* 98-9. New York: IEEE.

Coker, C.H. 1967. Synthesis by Rule from Articulatory Parameters. Paper presented at the 1967 Conference on Speech Communication and Processing. L.G. Hanscom Field, Bedford, Massachusetts: Air Force Cambridge Research Laboratories, Office of Aerospace Research, United States Air Force.

Coker, C.H. 1976. A Model of Articulatory Dynamics and Control. *Proceedings of the IEEE* 64: 452-9.

Coker, C.H., N. Umeda, and C.P. Browman 1973. Automatic Synthesis from Ordinary English Text. *IEEE Transactions on Audio and Electroacoustics* AU-21: 293-397.

Cooper, F.S. 1963. Speech from Stored Data. *IEEE Convention Record, part 7,* 137-49. New York: IEEE.

Cooper, F.S., A.M. Liberman, and J.M. Borst 1951. The Interconversion of Audible and Visible Patterns as a Basis for Research in the Perception of Speech. *Proceedings of the National Academy of Science* 37: 318-25.

Cooper, W.A., J.M. Paccia, and S.G. Lapointe 1978. Hierarchical Coding in Speech Timing. *Cognitive Psychology* 10: 154-77.

Denes, P.B. 1979. Automatic Voice Answerback Using Text-to-Speech Conversion by Rule. *Journal of the Acoustical Society of America* 64, Supplement 1: S162. (Abstract).

Dixon, R.N. and H.D. Maxey 1968. Terminal Analog Synthesis of Continuous Speech Using the Diphone Method of Segment Assembly. *IEEE Transactions on Audio and Electroacoustics* AU-16: 40-50.

Dudley, H.W. 1939. The Vocoder. *Bell Laboratories Record* 17: 122-6.

Dudley, H., R.R. Riesz, and S.A. Watkins 1939. A Synthetic Speaker. *Journal of the Franklin Institute* 227: 739-64.

Dunn, H.K. and S.D. White 1940. Statistical Measurements on Conversational Speech. *Journal of the Acoustical Society of America* 11: 278-88.

Egan, J.P. 1948. Articulation Testing Methods. *Laryngoscope* 58: 955-91.

Epstein, R. 1965. A Transistorized Formant-Type Synthesizer. In Status Report on Speech Research SR-1, part 7. Haskins Laboratories, New Haven, Connecticut.

Estes, S.E., H.R. Kirby, H.D. Maxey, and R.M. Walker 1964. Speech Synthesis from Stored Data. *I.B.M. Journal of Research and Development* 8: 2-12.

Fairbanks, G. 1958. Test of Phonemic Differentiation: The Rhyme Test. *Journal of the Acoustical Society of America* 30: 596-600.

Fant, C.G.M. 1956. On the Predictability of Formant Levels and Spectrum Envelopes from Formant Frequencies. In *For Roman Jakobson,* The Hague: Mouton.

Fant, C.G.M. 1959. *Acoustic Analysis and Synthesis of Speech with Applications to Swedish.* Ericsson Technics 1.

Fant, C.G.M. 1960. *Acoustic Theory of Speech Production.* The Hague:Mouton.

Fant, G. and J. Martony 1962. Speech Synthesis. In Speech Transmission Laboratory Quarterly Progress and Status Report 18-24/1962. Royal Institute of Technology, Stockholm.

Flanagan, J.L. 1957. Note on the Design of Terminal Analog Speech Synthesizers. *Journal of the Acoustical Society of America* 29: 306-10.

Flanagan, J.L. 1958. Some Properties of the Glottal Sound Source. *Journal of Speech and Hearing Research* 1: 99-116.

Flanagan, J.L. 1972. Voices of Men and Machines. *Journal of the Acoustical Society of America* 51: 1375-87.

Flanagan, J.L., C.H. Coker, and C.M. Bird 1962. Computer Simulation of a Formant Vocoder Synthesizer. *Journal of the Acoustical Society of America* 35: 2003. (Abstract).

Flanagan, J.L., C.H. Coker, L.R. Rabiner, R.W. Schafer, and N. Umeda 1970. Synthetic Voices for Computers. *IEEE Spectrum* 7: 22-45.

Flanagan, J.L., K. Ishizaka, and K.L. Shipley 1975. Synthesis of Speech from a Dynamic Model of the Vocal Cords and Vocal Tract. *Bell System Technical Journal* 54: 485-506.

Flanagan, J.L. and K. Ishizaka 1976. Automatic Generation of Voiceless Excitation in a Vocal Cord-Vocal Tract Speech Synthesizer. *IEEE Transactions on Acoustics, Speech, and Signal Processing* 24: 163-70.

Flanagan, J.L. and L.R. Rabiner 1973. *Speech Synthesis.* Stroudsberg, Pennsylvania:Dowden, Hutchinson and Ross.

French, N.R. and J.C. Steinberg 1947. Factors Governing the Intelligibility of Speech Sounds. *Journal of the Acoustical Society of America* 19: 90-119.

Fujimura, O. 1961. Analysis of Nasalized Vowels. In Research Laboratory of Electronics Quarterly Progress Report 62, 191-2. Massachusetts Institute of Technology, Cambridge, Massachusetts.

Fujimura, O. 1962. Analysis of Nasal Consonants. *Journal of the Acoustical Society of America* 34: 1865-75.

Fujimura, O. and J. Lindqvist 1971. Sweep-Tone Measurements of Vocal Tract Characteristics. *Journal of the Acoustical Society of America* 49: 541-58.

Fujimura, O. and J. Lovins 1978. Syllables as Concatenative Phonetic Elements. In A. Bell and J.B. Cooper (eds.), *Syllables and Segments,* New York: North-Holland.

Gagnon, R.T. 1978. Votrax Real Time Hardware for Phoneme Synthesis of Speech. *Proceedings of the International Conference on Acoustics, Speech, and Signal Processing,* 175-8. New York: IEEE.

Gaitenby, J. 1965. The Elastic Word. In Status Report on Speech Research SR-2, 1-12. Haskins Laboratories, New Haven, Connecticut.

Gauffin, J. and J. Sundberg 1974. An Attempt to Predict the Masking Effect of Vowel Spectra. In Speech Transmission Laboratory Quarterly Progress and Status Report 4/1974, 57-62. Royal Institute of Technology, Stockholm.

Gold, B. and L.R. Rabiner 1968. Analysis of Digital and Analog Formant Synthesizers. *IEEE Transactions on Audio and Electroacoustics* AU-16: 81-94.

Goldman-Eisler, F. 1968. *Psycholinguistics: Experiments in Spontaneous Speech.* New York:Academic Press.

Haggard, M.P. and I.G. Mattingly 1968. A Simple Program for Synthesizing British English. *IEEE Transactions on Audio and Electroacoustics* AU-16: 95-9.

Halle, M. and S. J. Keyser 1971. *English stress: Its form, its growth, and its role in verse.* New York:Harper and Row.

Holmes, J.N. 1961. *Research on Speech Synthesis.* Report JU 11.4. Joint Speech Research Unit, British Post Office, Eastcote, England.

References

Holmes, J.N. 1973. The Influence of the Glottal Waveform on the Naturalness of Speech from a Parallel Formant Synthesizer. *IEEE Transactions on Audio and Electroacoustics* AU-21: 298-305.

Holmes, J., I. Mattingly, and J. Shearme 1964. Speech Synthesis by Rule. *Language and Speech* 7: 127-43.

Homsby, T.G. 1972. Voice Response Systems. *Modern Data* November: 46-50.

House, A.S., C.E. Williams, M.H.L. Hecker, and K.D. Kryter 1965. Articulation-Testing Methods: Consonantal Differentiation with a Closed-Response Set. *Journal of the Acoustical Society of America* 37: 158-66.

House, A.S. and G. Fairbanks 1953. The Influence of Consonantal Environment Upon the Secondary Acoustical Characteristics of Vowels. *Journal of the Acoustical Society of America* 25: 105-13.

Hunnicutt, S. 1976a. A New Morph Lexicon for English. *Proceedings of the Sixth International Conference on Computational Linguistics.* Ottawa, Canada: Association for Computational Linguistics.

Hunnicutt, S. 1976b. Phonological Rules for a Text-to-Speech System. *American Journal of Computational Linguistics* Microfiche 57: 1-72.

Ingeman, F. 1978. Speech Synthesis by Rule Using the FOVE Program. In Status Report on Speech Research SR-54, 165-73. Haskins Laboratories, New Haven, Connecticut.

Jayant, N.S. 1974. Digital Coding of Speech Waveforms: PCM, DPCM, and DM Quantizers. *Proceedings of the IEEE* 62: 611-32.

Kaiser, J.F. 1966. Digital Filters. In F.F. Kuo and J.F. Kaiser (eds.), *System Analysis by Digital Computer,* New York: Wiley.

Klatt, D.H. 1970. Synthesis of Stop Consonants in Initial Position. *Journal of the Acoustical Society of America* 47: 93. (Abstract).

Klatt, D.H. 1972. Acoustic Theory of Terminal Analog Speech Synthesis. *Proceedings of the 1972 International Conference on Speech Communication and Processing,* 131-5. New York: IEEE. IEEE Catalog Number 72 CHO 596-7 AE.

Klatt, D.H. 1973. Interaction between Two Factors that Influence Vowel Duration. *Journal of the Acoustical Society of America* 54: 1102-4.

Klatt, D.H. 1974. Review of Speech Synthesis. *Journal of the Acoustical Society of America* 55: 900. J.L. Flanagan and L.R. Rabiner (eds.).

Klatt, D.H. 1975. Vowel Lengthening is Syntactically Determined in a Connected Discourse. *Journal of Phonetics* 3: 129-40.

Klatt, D.H. 1976a. Structure of a Phonological Rule Component for a Synthesis-by-Rule Program. *IEEE Transactions on Acoustics, Speech, and Signal Processing* ASSP-24: 391-8.

Klatt, D.H. 1976b. The Linguistic Uses of Segmental Duration in English: Acoustic and Perceptual Evidence. *Journal of the Acoustical Society of America* 59: 1208-21.

Klatt, D.H. 1976c. A Speech Synthesis-by-Rule Program for Response Generation and for Word Verification. In W.A. Woods (ed.), Speech Understanding Systems Final Report 3438, Volume 2, 40-57. Bolt, Beranek and Newman Incorporated, Cambridge, Massachusetts.

Klatt, D.H. 1979a. Synthesis by Rule of Consonant-Vowel Syllables. In *Speech Communication Group Working Papers,* Cambridge, Massachusetts: Massachusetts Institute of Technology.

Klatt, D.H. 1979b. Synthesis by Rule of Segmental Durations in English Sentences. In B. Lindblom and S. Ohman (eds.), *Frontiers of Speech Communication Research,* New York: Academic Press.

Klatt, D.H. 1980. Software for a Cascade/Parallel Formant Synthesizer. *Journal of the Acoustical Society of America* 67: 971-95.

Klatt, D.H., C. Cook, and W.A. Woods 1975. *PCOMPILER -- A Language for Stating Phonological and Phonetic Rules.* Report 3080. Bolt, Beranek and Newman Incorporated, Cambridge, Massachusetts.

Kryter, K.D. 1962. Methods for the Calculation and Use of the Articulation Index. *Journal of the Acoustical Society of America* 34: 1689-97.

Kucera, H. and W.N. Francis 1967. *Computational Analysis of Present-Day American English.* Providence, Rhode Island:Brown University Press.

Kurzweil, R. 1976. The Kurzweil Reading Machine: A Technical Overview. In M.R. Redden and W. Schwandt (eds.), *Science, Technology and the Handicapped,* Report 76-R-11, 3-11. American Association for the Advancement of Science.

Lawrence, W. 1953. The Synthesis of Speech from Signals Which Have a Low Information Rate. In W. Jackson (ed.), *Communication Theory,* London: Butterworth's Scientific Publications.

Lehiste, I. 1977. Isochrony Reconsidered. *Journal of Phonetics* 5: 253-63.

Lehiste, I., J.P. Olive, and L.A. Streeter 1976. The Role of Duration in Disambiguating Syntactically Ambiguous Sentences. *Journal of the Acoustical Society of America* 60: 1199-202.

Lehiste, I. 1975a. Some Factors Affecting the Duration of Syllabic Nuclei in English. In G. Drachman (ed.), *Proceedings of the First Salzburg Conference on Linguistics,* Verlag Gunter Narr.

Lehiste, I. 1975b. The Phonetic Structure of Paragraphs. In A. Cohen and S. Nooteboom (eds.), *Structure and Process in Speech Perception,* Heidelberg: Springer-Verlag.

Liberman, M.Y. 1977. Further Work on Duration Modeling in Reiterant Speech. *Journal of the Acoustical Society of America* 62, Supplement 1: S48. (Abstract).

Liberman, M.Y. 1979. Phonemic Transcription, Stress, and Segment Durations for Spelled Proper Names. *Journal of the Acoustical Society of America* 64, Supplement 1: S163. (Abstract).

Liberman, A., F. Ingeman, L. Lisker, P. Delattre, and F. Cooper 1959. Minimal Rules for Synthesizing Speech. *Journal of the Acoustical Society of America* 31: 1490-9.

Liljencrants, J. 1968. The OVE-III Speech Synthesizer. *IEEE Transactions on Audio and Electroacoustics* AU-16: 137-40.

Liljencrants, J. 1969. Speech Synthesizer Control by Smoothed Step Functions. In Speech Transmission Laboratory Quarterly Progress and Status Report 4, 43-50. Royal Institute of Technology, Stockholm.

Lindblom, B. and K. Rapp 1973. *Some Temporal Regularities of Spoken Swedish.* Publication 21. Institute of Linguistics, University of Stockholm, Stockholm.

Lovins, J.B. and O. Fujimura 1976. Synthesis of English Monosyllables by Demisyllable Concatenation. *Journal of the Acoustical Society of America* 60, Supplement 1: S75. (Abstract).

Macchi, M. and G. Nigro 1977. Syllable Affixes in Speech Synthesis. *Journal of the Acoustical Society of America* 61, Supplement 1: S67. (Abstract).

References

Maeda, S. 1974. A Characterization of Fundamental Frequency Contours of Speech. In Research Laboratory of Electronics Quarterly Progress Report 114, 193-211. Massachusetts Institute of Technology, Cambridge, Massachusetts.

Makhoul, J. 1975. Spectral Linear Prediction: Properties and Applications. *IEEE Transactions on Acoustics, Speech, and Signal Processing* ASSP-23: 283-96.

Markel, J.D. and A.H. Gray 1976. *Linear Prediction of Speech.* New York:Springer-Verlag.

Marslen-Wilson, W.D. and A. Welsh 1978. Processing Interactions and Lexical Access During Word Recognition in Continuous Speech. *Cognitive Psychology* 10: 29-63.

Mattingly, I. 1966. Synthesis by Rule of Prosodic Features. *Language and Speech* 9: 1-13.

Mattingly, I. 1968a. Synthesis-by-Rule of General American English. In Supplement to Status Report on Speech Research. Haskins Laboratories, New Haven, Connecticut.

Mattingly, I. 1968b. Experimental Methods for Speech Synthesis by Rule. *IEEE Transactions on Audio and Electroacoustics* AU-16: 198-202.

Miller, G.A., G. Heise, and W. Lichten 1951. The Intelligibility of Speech as a Function of the Context of the Test Materials. *Journal of Experimental Psychology* 41: 329-35.

Miller, G.A. and S. Isard 1963. Some Perceptual Consequences of Linguistic Rules. *Journal of Verbal Learning and Verbal Behavior* 2: 217-28.

Miranker, G.S. 1978. A Digital Signal Processor for Real Time Generation of Speech Waveforms. *Proceedings of the Fifth Annual Symposium on Computer Architecture.* New York: IEEE.

Morris, L.R. 1979. A Fast Fortran Implementation of the NRL Algorithm for Automatic Translation of English Text to Votrax Parameters. *Proceedings of the International Conference on Acoustics, Speech, and Signal Processing*, 907-13. New York: IEEE.

Nakata, K. and T. Mitsuoka 1965. Phonemic Transformation and Control Aspects of Synthesis of Connected Speech. *Journal of the Radio Research Laboratories* 12: 171-86. Tokyo.

Nye, P., J. Hankins, T. Rand, I. Mattingly, and F. Cooper 1973. A Plan for the Field Evaluation of an Automated Reading System for the Blind. *IEEE Transactions on Audio and Electroacoustics* AU-21: 265-8.

Nye, P.W., F. Ingeman, and L. Donald 1975. Synthetic Speech Comprehension: A Comparison of Listener Performances with and Preferences Among Different Speech Forms. In Status Report on Speech Research SR-41, 117-26. Haskins Laboratories, New Haven, Connecticut.

Nye, P.W. and J. Gaitenby 1973. Consonant Intelligibility in Synthetic Speech and in a Natural Speech Control (Modified Rhyme Test Results). In Status Report on Speech Research SR-33, 77-91. Haskins Laboratories, New Haven, Connecticut.

Nye, P.W. and J. Gaitenby 1974. The Intelligibility of Synthetic Monosyllable Words in Short, Syntactically Normal Sentences. In Status Report on Speech Research SR-37/38, 169-90. Haskins Laboratories, New Haven, Connecticut.

O'Shaughnessy, D. 1976. Modelling Fundamental Frequency, and its Relationship to Syntax, Semantics, and Phonetics. PhD thesis, Massachusetts Institute of Technology, Cambridge, Massachusetts.

O'Shaughnessy, D. 1977. Fundamental frequency by Rule for a Text-to-Speech System. *Proceedings of the International Conference on Acoustics, Speech, and Signal Processing*, 571-4. New York: IEEE.

Olive, J.P. 1974. Speech Synthesis by Rule. In G. Fant (ed.), *Speech communication: Volume 2*, New York: Halsted Press.

Olive, J.P. 1977. Rule synthesis of speech from Diadic Units. *Proceedings of the International Conference on Acoustics, Speech, and Signal Processing*, 568-70. New York: IEEE. IEEE Catalog No. 77CH1197-3 ASSP.

Olive, J.P. 1979. Speech Synthesis from Phonemic Transcription. *Journal of the Acoustical Society of America* 64, Supplement 1: S163. (Abstract).

Olive, J.P. and L.H. Nakatani 1974. Rule Synthesis of Speech by Word Concatenation: A First Step. *Journal of the Acoustical Society of America* 55: 660-6.

Olive, J.P. and N. Spickenagle 1976. Speech Resynthesis from Phoneme-Related Parameters. *Journal of the Acoustical Society of America* 59: 993-6.

Oller, D.K. 1973. The Effect of Position in Utterance on Speech Segment Duration in English. *Journal of the Acoustical Society of America* 54: 1235-47.

Peterson, G., W. Wang, and E. Sivertsen 1958. Segmentation Techniques in Speech Synthesis. *Journal of the Acoustical Society of America* 30: 739-42.

Peterson, G.E. and I. Lehiste 1960. Duration of Syllabic Nuclei in English. *Journal of the Acoustical Society of America* 32: 693-703.

Pierrehumbert, J. 1979. Intonation Synthesis Based on Metrical Grids. Paper presented at the 97th Meeting of the Acoustical Society of America. New York: The Acoustical Society of America. ASA Preprint.

Pisoni, D.B. 1978. Speech Perception. In W.K. Estes (ed.), *Handbook of Learning and Cognitive Processes (Volume 6)*, Hillsdale, New Jersey: Lawrence Erlbaum Associates.

Rabiner, L.R. 1968a. Speech Synthesis by Rule: An Acoustic Domain Approach. *Bell System Technical Journal* 47: 17-38.

Rabiner, L.R. 1968b. Digital-Formant Synthesizer for Speech-Synthesis Studies. *Journal of the Acoustical Society of America* 43: 822-8.

Rabiner, L.R., R.W. Schafer, and J.L. Flanagan 1971. Computer Synthesis of Speech by Concatenation of Formant-Coded Words. *Bell System Technical Journal* 50: 1541-58.

Rabiner, L.R., L.B. Jackson, R.W. Schafer, and C.H. Coker 1971a. A Hardware Realization of a Digital Formant Speech Synthesizer. *IEEE Transactions on Communication Technology* COM-19: 1016-70.

Rabiner, L.R., and R.W. Schafer 1976. Digital Techniques for Computer Voice Response: Implementations and Applications. *Proceedings of the IEEE* 64: 416-33.

Rosen, G. 1958. A Dynamic Analog Speech Synthesizer. *Journal of the Acoustical Society of America* 34: 201-9.

Rothenberg, M., R. Carlson, B. Granstrom, and J. Gauffin 1974. A Three-Parameter Voice Source for Speech Synthesis. In G. Fant (ed.), *Speech Communication*, Uppsala, Sweden: Almqvist and Wikell.

Schwartz, R. *et al.* 1979. Diphone Synthesis for Phonemic Vocoding. *Proceedings of the International Conference on Acoustics, Speech, and Signal Processing*, 891-4. New York: IEEE.

Scott, R.J., D.M. Glace, and I.G. Mattingly 1966. A Computer-Controlled On-Line Speech Synthesizer System. *1966 IEEE International Communications Conference, Digest of Technical Papers,* 104-5. New York: IEEE.

Stevens, K.N. 1956. Synthesis of Speech by Electrical Analog Devices. *Journal of the Audio Engineering Society* 4: 2-8.

Stevens, K.N. 1971. Airflow and Turbulence Noise for Fricative and Stop Consonants: Static Considerations. *Journal of the Acoustical Society of America* 50: 1180-92.

Stevens, K.N. 1972. The Quantal Nature of Speech: Evidence from Articulatory-Acoustic Data. In E.E. David and P.B. Denes (eds.), *Human Communication: A Unified View,* New York: McGraw-Hill.

Stevens, K.N., S. Kasowski, and G. Fant 1953. An Electrical Analog of the Vocal Tract. *Journal of the Acoustical Society of America* 25: 734-42.

Stevens, K.N., R.P. Bastide, and C.P. Smith 1955. Electrical Synthesizer of Continuous Speech. *Journal of the Acoustical Society of America* 27: 207. (Abstract).

Stevens, K.N. and D.H. Klatt 1974. Current Models of Sound Sources for Speech. In B.D. Wyke (ed.), *Ventilatory and Phonatory Control Systems: An International Symposium,* London: Oxford University Press.

Tomlinson, R.S. 1966. SPASS - An Improved Terminal Analog Speech Synthesizer. In Research Laboratory of Electronics Quarterly Progress Report 80, 198-205. Massachusetts Institute of Technology, Cambridge, Massachusetts.

Umeda, N. 1975. Vowel Duration in American English. *Journal of the Acoustical Society of America* 58: 434-45.

Umeda, N. 1976. Linguistic Rules for Text-to-Speech Synthesis. *Proceedings of the IEEE* 64: 443-51.

Umeda, N. 1977. Consonant Duration in American English. *Journal of the Acoustical Society of America* 61: 846-58.

Wang, W. and G.E. Peterson 1958. Segment Inventory for Speech Synthesis. *Journal of the Acoustical Society of America* 30: 743-6.

Wiggins, R. 1979. The TMC 0280 Speech Synthesizer. *Journal of the Acoustical Society of America* 64, Supplement 1: S72. (Abstract).

Woods, W. 1970. Transition Network Grammars for Natural Language Analysis. *Communications of the ACM* 13: 591-606.

Woods, W. *et al.* 1976. *The BBN-HWIM Speech Understanding System Final Report.* Report 3438, Volume V. Bolt, Beranek and Newman, Cambridge, Massachusetts. 47-58.

Young, S.J. and F. Fallside 1979. Speech Synthesis from Concept: A Method for Speech Output from Information Systems. *Journal of the Acoustical Society of America* 66: 685-95.

Index